PSYCHOTHERAPEUTIC APPROACHES
TO THE RESISTANT CHILD

PSYCHOTHERAPEUTIC APPROACHES TO THE RESISTANT CHILD

Richard A. Gardner, M.D.

Assistant Clinical Professor
of
Child Psychiatry
Columbia University
College of Physicians & Surgeons

Faculty
William A. White
Psychoanalytic Institute

Jason Aronson, Inc.   New York

To Children:

> whose infectious *joie de vivre* elates us,
>
> whose ingenuousness refreshes us,
>
> whose guilelessness embarrasses
>   and teaches us,
>
> whose undiscriminating love flatters us,
>
> whose optimism gives us hope,
>
> and who, as our progeny, provide us with our
>   most meaningful link to immortality.

Richard A. Gardner

OTHER BOOKS BY RICHARD A. GARDNER:

The Child's Book about Brain Injury;
The Boys and Girls Book about Divorce;
Therapeutic Communication with Children: The Mutual
Storytelling Technique;
MBD: The Family Book about Minimal Brain Dysfunction;
Understanding Children;
Dr. Gardner's Stories about the Real World;
Dr. Gardner's Fairy Tales for Today's Children

ACKNOWLEDGMENTS

If not for resistant children this book would never have been written. It was from the frustration I experienced in trying to engage them in what I considered meaningful psychotherapeutic endeavors that I developed many of the techniques and therapeutic approaches described herein. To their parents as well, I am grateful. They taught me much about the ways in which they can contribute to a child's resistances in treatment and stimulated me thereby to devise methods to circumvent and avoid the development of these antitherapeutic attitudes. In addition, they have granted me permission to use the clinical material (appropriately disguised) that is a vital part of this work.

I am deeply indebted to my secretary, Mrs. Linda Gould, who dedicated herself to the typing of this manuscript in its various renditions and graciously and patiently undertook the formidable task of transcribing verbatim material from the audio- and videotape recorders.

I appreciate the permission granted to me by the editors to quote from the following previously published work of mine:

The private practice of child psychiatry. In *Career Directions: Careers in Child Psychiatry*, ed. J. Schimel, Vol. 2, No. 2, pp. 35-42. Hanover, New Jersey: Sandoz Pharmaceuticals, 1971.

The mutual storytelling technique in the treatment of anger inhibition problems. *International Journal of Child Psychotherapy*, 1(1):34-64, 1972.

Little Hans—the most famous boy in the child psychotherapy literature. *International Journal of Child Psychotherapy*, 1(4): 24-50, 1972.

The role of seduction in child psychotherapy. *International Journal of Child Psychotherapy*, 2(2):135-137, 1973.

Psychotherapy of the psychogenic problems secondary to minimal brain dysfunction. *International Journal of Child Psychotherapy*, 2(2):224-256, 1973.

Understanding Children. New York: Jason Aronson, Inc., 1973.

I am indebted to Dr. Jason Aronson, who has always shown the deepest appreciation for my work. He early recognized the importance of a book such as this and was supportive and cooperative at every step in its publication. I appreciate also the dedicated efforts of Mildred Troup and Warren Paul in editing and producing the manuscript. I am especially indebted to Dr. Anna Gourevitch who, as my supervisor during my training at the William A. White Psychoanalytic Institute, imbued in me the appreciation that the basic human elements in the psychotherapeutic process are far more important than insights — a philosophy that pervades this book.

My wife Lee, as a child psychiatrist, was one of the first to try out many of the methods described in this book and provided me with valuable advice and recommendations. In addition, as a uniquely devoted mother she has taught me firsthand many things about dealing with children that were successfully applied in my work with the children described herein.

CONTENTS

INTRODUCTION

Every child therapist has been confronted with a patient who is unreceptive to involving himself in the various activities available in the typical child therapist's office. We all appreciate that only a small fraction of children are going to sit with us and talk directly about their difficulties in an attempt to delve into the psychodynamic roots that underlie their problems and to utilize the insights so gained toward their alleviation. (We have enough trouble getting adults to do this — professions of the patient's motivation to do so notwithstanding.) Furthermore, most children will not even talk at length about their problems at a more superficial level. More are willing to talk about other things; but often the therapist then feels that the issues being focused upon by the child are so remote from the resenting complaints that he may question the therapeutic efficacy of such discussions.

Involving the child in play has proved effective in facilitating the child's revealing his underlying psychodynamics. Play is one of the child's natural modes of communication and the fantasies that are often verbalized while involved in play can provide important information about the psychological processes that are at the roots of the child's problems. However, play can be used in the service of resistance. Every therapist has had the experience of the child's endlessly arranging the furniture in the playhouse without ever verbalizing his thoughts. Although the configurations of the furniture and other associated activities may provide some information, the amount is so miniscule that it is most often of little therapeutic value. Or the child may involve himself in age-appropriate stereotyped games. The boy who plays "war" or "cowboys and Indians" may be letting off a little hostility, and the girl who plays "house" may be gratifying her maternal needs and entrenching maternal identifications; but these activities do not usually lend themselves to meaningful therapeutic interchanges and experiences. Similarly, I consider building models and playing checkers with a child to have the same low level of therapeutic efficacy. I am not claiming that these activities have *no* therapeutic value (in fact, I have written an article [1969c] describing some of the therapeutic uses of the game of checkers); rather, I believe that they have a low level of therapeutic efficiency and they quickly reach a point of ever-diminishing therapeutic returns.

For the purposes of this book I refer to these children as *resistant*. I am not using the term in the strictly psychoanalytic sense in which it refers to the various defense mechanisms that the patient may utilize in order to protect himself from painful self-awareness. Rather, I use it in the broader sense to refer to all children who resist involvement in the therapeutic situation, i.e., children who are uncooperative, inhibited, frightened, shy, withdrawn, etc. However, the techniques described herein can be quite useful in helping children work through the kinds of resistances referred to when one uses the term psychoanalytically.

It was from the recognition of these limitations of some of the traditional approaches and the frustrations I experienced in utilizing them that I have devoted myself in recent years to the development of methods that might more predictably involve such children in meaningful therapeutic endeavors. In my book *Therapeutic Communication with Children* (1971a) I described *The Mutual Storytelling Technique*, one method I have found useful in engaging such children. Here I present, as well, a number of other methods that I have more recently found useful in working with such children. My purpose is to enable the reader to utilize these techniques himself. Accordingly, in addition to theoretical material I have provided clinical case vignettes (most often verbatim) so that the reader can learn more intimately the kinds of interchanges I have with the child when I use the methods I describe. I have not only included material from successful cases but from unsuccessful ones as well. Our literature is replete with case descriptions of successful cases; there is little on the failures. I know of no articles in which the therapist devotes himself to discussing the reasons why he has fouled up a particular case. In this book I have described a few such situations.

I make no claims that the problem of engaging these children is even close to being solved. There are many types of resistant children who still cannot be drawn into treatment with the methods I describe here. However, my experience has been that these techniques can successfully reach many in that heretofore "unreachable" group. My hope is that this book will enable the reader to enjoy similar experiences as well.

PSYCHOTHERAPEUTIC APPROACHES
TO THE RESISTANT CHILD

Chapter One
The Therapist's Personality

The therapist's personality, probably more than anything else that I will discuss in this book, is the ultimate determinant as to whether he will be able to engage the resistant child. The personality qualities that contribute to one therapist's being successful in his work with children and another's failing are vital to understand and yet we know little about them. There is a paucity of articles in the psychiatric and psychological literature describing this crucial entity. Yet we cannot continue to neglect what may very well be the most important focus for our investigations. Many believe that the reason why therapists of different persuasions can report successes is not that the techniques utilized are so valuable or that one technique is better than another, but that subtle personality characteristics of the therapist have been the crucial elements in bringing about the described improvements. Accordingly, we are ill-equipped to evaluate and compare the efficacy of various therapeutic techniques if we remain ignorant of the personality characteristics of the therapists who have been using them.

Language Limitations

In this chapter I will attempt to delineate some of these qualities. I recognize that in attempting to do so I am handicapped not only by our ignorance of the processes but by the limitations of our language, which does not have specific words for many of the characteristics I will attempt to delineate. Our English language, the richest on earth, with almost five hundred thousand words, is still inadequate to define certain phenomena accurately. For example, my dictionary defines *déjà vu* as "the illusion of having previously experienced something actually being experienced for the first time." It informs me, as well, that in French *déjà vu* means "already seen." Most of us have had, at some time or other, a *déjà vu* experience. And we know how insufficient that definition is. There are other qualities in the experience that make the words *already seen* banal to the point of being misleading. The dictionary says nothing of the *uncanniness* of the experience, the altered state of consciousness, the futile quest for the time and place of the alleged original experience, and the frustration in not being able to pinpoint it. Even my description of these other elements in the phenomenon does not accurately convey what it is actually like to a person who never had the experience. It does not enable him *really* to know what I am talking about. My term *uncanny* is in itself too vague, too inaccurate, to truly convey the feelings.

Our language is replete with words that only purport to describe the phenonema they are labeling. When people use such words, we get fooled into thinking that they are talking about the same thing. Take the word *orgasm*, for example. In interviewing a woman suspected of frigidity, a therapist generally does not rely on a yes or no answer to the question of whether she has ever achieved orgasm. He goes by the *quality* of her response — by whether the affirmative answer communicates: "I know exactly what you're talking about." If she says, "I think so," or "Maybe," then the therapist knows that she hasn't. There are many other examples of such words: *beautiful, schizophrenia, cool, rapport,* and *love.*

I recognize that the qualities that I will attempt to describe are not those that a therapist can easily acquire. Either he has them or he hasn't. With some, the recognition of their absence may be a step toward their acquisition. With others, the therapist may have to accept his deficiency. However, this need not mean that he discontinue child therapy. No therapist can possibly have all the qualities that he should ideally possess if he is to be effective. However, if he has few, if any of them, then, the likelihood that he will work successfully with children is, in my opinion, small.

Liking Children

The first, and possibly most important quality, is that of genuinely liking children. I cannot imagine someone's involving himself meaningfully and effectively in the field of child therapy without basically liking children. I am not suggesting that he need like children *all the time*; in fact, I would be distrustful of anyone who claimed that he did. (Children inevitably cause us periods of resentment and exasperation.) Rather, most of his therapeutic experiences with them should be benevolent and moderately enjoyable.

Self-projection

The therapist must have the capacity to project himself into the child's situation, to see the world through the child's eyes — and probably to feel the way the child feels. We know little of this phenomenon. Why is it easy for some and for others impossible? Piaget's panoramas (in which the child is asked to determine which card shows the view that the little model man in the center of the panorama sees as his position is changed) could give us information about this quality. Some would easily be able to see the view of the model, and others would have trouble. But this is only part of the phenomenon. It describes only a *visual-mechanical* aspect of the projective process. The *human* elements are far more complex. We use such terms as *sympathy* and *empathy* in our feeble attempt to describe this quality, but we still have much to learn about it — its mechanics, its psychodynamics, and the factors that play a role in its development. Does an accurate memory of one's own childhood play a role in this capacity? I think so, but as far as I know this has not been tested. And, indeed, it might be hard to evaluate accurately. *Egocentricism* (another one of those umbrella terms) may inhibit this quality. But we still have to define how. The therapist who lacks this capacity to a significant degree is ill-equipped to help his patient. If he cannot *see* the world through his patient's eyes (not necessarily agree with the patient, however) then he is handicapped in helping him.

Memory of One's Own Childhood

The ability to remember one's own childhood experiences deserves further emphasis. There are people who will say with all honesty that they cannot remember a thing about their lives before the age of eight, or ten, or even twelve. The person who is so repressed regarding memories of his childhood experiences is not likely to be an effective child therapist. One has to recall how it was when he was the age of his child patient if he is to optimally appreciate the child's situation. The adult therapist has to be able to put himself in the position of his patient if he is to be successful. But he need not project himself back in time. The child therapist's task is therefore a more difficult one in this regard.

Excitation

I introduce discussion of the next quality anecdotally. When I was a freshman medical student, an instructor once commented to a small group of us, "You fellows are still in the 'gee whiz' phase of medicine." To which I replied, "I hope I never get out of that phase." (I would like to think I haven't.)Many gifted child therapists carry this quality with them throughout life. One such person was D. W. Winnicott who exhibited many of the qualities I describe in this chapter. To say he was enthusiastic and interested in what he was doing when he was with child patients is an understatement. There was a certain "wow" quality (I cannot describe it any better, but that's close to it) to him which he shared with his child patients. This was not loudly stated; he did not seem the kind of man who would loudly say, "Wow!" Rather it came through in the tonal qualities of his voice. There were intonations of excitement and of slight breathlessness — all subtle, but nevertheless there. These qualities, of course, are exhibited by all but the most sick children, and Donald Winnicott retained them to the end of his life. They must have contributed to his patients' thinking, at some level, "He's one of us, even though he's a grown-up. He gets excited about the same kinds of things we get excited about."

How this quality contributes to therapeutic change is speculative. But I shall speculate. With such a person, the child cannot help but feel better about himself. Here is an adult who enjoys being with him — and this cannot but raise the child's self-esteem. Since most, if not all, psychogenic symptoms are formed, at least in part, to adapt to or bolster a low self-esteem, this esteem-enhancing experience with Dr. Winnicott was salutary. Having someone share his pleasure enhances the child's pleasure — and healthy pleasure is one of the universal antidotes to psychogenic pathology.

The Inner Warmth Response

The next quality of Donald Winnicott's that I wish to describe is also best introduced anecdotally — this with an incident that occurred during my residency training. I was seeing a little boy of four who had what I can best describe as an *infectious personality* (another one of those vague terms). When I would walk down the hall with him from the waiting room to my office, adults who passed us would look at him and smile. There was a *cuteness* (another one of those words) about him which engendered a heartwarming feeling in adults. I cannot say exactly what it was about the child that produced this response. I know it had something to do with his smile, his seriousness, and his little-man-trying-to-act-big quality as he strutted down the hall. Once, in the midst of a session with him, a schizophrenic woman mistakently came to my office earlier than the appointed time. She opened the door, saw that I was still with the boy, and with a stony facial expression closed the door. I was struck by the fact that she did not smile. Although rivalrous feelings with another patient and disappointment that she could not see me exactly when she wanted may have contributed to her reaction, I believe that she was incapable of the "inner warmth" response that other adults almost invariably had to this child. (I even thought half-seriously that with this episode I might have come upon a good test for schizophrenia).

Donald Winnicott had this "warm inner glow" response. Those who have had it know exactly what I am talking about. Those who have not may never appreciate what I am saying. We use the term *heartwarming* to describe the phenomenon. It does feel as if it comes from the chest, but this may be socially induced. We are taught that love comes from the heart, yet to the best of our knowledge the brain and often the genitalia seem to have something to do with it as well. There must be physiological correlates to the experience that can be measured: changes in blood pressure, cardiac rate, and biochemical reactions. These have yet to be identified. When with a person who enjoys such a response to him, the child cannot but feel: "He likes me. I am likable. I give him pleasure. I am worthwhile." And such responses contribute to the child's improvement.

Childlike Personality Characteristics

M. Masud R. Khan (1972) describes Dr. Winnicott as having had: "A childlike clownish spontaneity [that] imbued his movements." All of us retain some childlike, even childish (the pejorative term), qualities. Some of these are probably necessary to preserve our sanity. When someone retains, as an adult, too many childhood characteristics, we call him "immature," "fixated at infantile levels of development," or "regressed." Where does one draw the line? Where does the normal, healthy degree end and the neurotic begin? Dr. Winnicott had, without question, more than the average degree of childlike qualities. Since they were obviously so constructively used, one cannot label them neurotic. The effective child therapist has, in my opinion, more such childhood residua than his adult counterpart, and these can serve him well in his work. They enable him to unself-consciously (or less self-consciously) play on the floor with his patients. They contribute to the pleasure of his work. They are a dangerous asset, however, in that the therapist may go too far in this regard when he does play therapy and accomplish more *play* than *therapy*. Where one ends and the other begins is still a relatively unexplored area.

"On the Same Wavelength"

An analogy from the physical sciences may be of help in describing my next point. When a vibrating tuning fork is placed next to a nonvibrating fork of the same intrinsic frequency of vibration, the second will begin to vibrate along with the first. We know that there are people with whom we "vibrate" and there are others with whom we do not. We say, "I can really talk to him; he understands me," or "There are times when we don't even have to say certain things; we just know what one another is thinking," or "We think alike; we're on the same track." Many young people today even use the term *vibrate* to describe this phenomenon. Donald Winnicott vibrated with children. He was on the same wavelength as most of them. And this, I am sure, contributed to this therapeutic efficacy. But what is this phenomenon? We know so little about it. Why do we experience it with some people and not with others? Does some form of extrasensory perception have something to do with it? It is another important element in the therapeutic process that is yet to be understood.

A Strong Parental Instinct

Then there are the so-called instincts. We speak in psychiatry and psychoanalysis about maternal instincts, but far less about paternal instincts. Dr. Winnicott, most would agree, exhibited toward his patients what appeared to be a strong paternal instinct. Mr. Khan (1972), refers to him as "a caring and concerned mother." What is this instinct? Why do some exhibit it more than others? Is this merely biological variation? Or can environmental factors significantly influence its expression? And how does this play a role in the child therapist's work with his patients? The term *paternal instinct* is only a rubric, subsumed under which are a host of qualities and personality characteristics. Feeding, protecting, touching, cleaning, loving, guiding, and enjoying are only some of these elements. Mr. Khan refers to Donald Winnicotts's generosity to his regressed patients and at times his exaggerated need in this regard. He refers to Mrs. Winnicott's reference to her husband's "illusions of munificence." How therapeutic was Dr. Winnicott's tendency to give? When was it excessive? And by what criteria? The therapist has to be giving to some degree if he is to help his patient. But how far should he go? Where do we draw the line? There is still much we have to learn in this area. The reader interested in further comments of mine regarding qualities in D. W. Winnicott that I consider operative in his therapeutic successes should refer to my article on him (1972d) and my review of two of his books (1973f). And the reader who is interested in reading about the work of Edgar Baldock, another man who I consider to possess similar qualities, may wish to refer to his article on the therapeutic relationship (1974).

Frustration Tolerance

There are certain frustrations that the child therapist must be willing to tolerate that his adult counterpart need not contend with. One such potential problem is the child's parents. They often feel threatened by the whole process. Having a child in therapy may be considered proof of the parents' failure, and many defenses may be utilized to avoid coming to terms with this notion. Many parents come not because they have seen the problem themselves (it has often been denied for months to years), but because some outside agency (most often the school) has suggested psychiatric consultation. These parents often hope to hear that nothing is wrong and that the referrer was in error. Once the child is in therapy, their ambivalence may manifest itself through forgotten appointments, lateness, cancellations with meager excuses, witholding payment of bills, failure to follow through with recommendations, hostility toward the therapist, and other gambits. Sudden withdrawal of the child from treatment is common. At any given time I have to keep three people involved: a child who would prefer to be playing with friends; a mother whose life is hectic enough caring for the house and other children without having to bring the patient to me; and a father who could find much better ways to spend his money. If, at any point, any one of these three develops significant psychological resistances, the others are dragged down and the project fails. Some therapists get fed up and gradually confine themselves to adult work.

However, the above frustrations may be more than counterbalanced by certain gratifications that the adult therapist may not so frequently enjoy. The satisfactions of therapeutic success are more easy to come by in child work than in adult therapy. The child's problems are generally of shorter duration than the adult's and may be less deeply imbedded in his psyche. In addition, more change can be effected in his environment. The adult who comes for treatment is usually deeply entrenched in his life situation: his marriage and his career. Changes in these areas are not readily effected. The deleterious influences to which the child is exposed can be altered more readily — parental attitudes modified; misconceptions rectified; management advice provided; and schools, clubs, and camps recommended.

Flexibility and Creativity

The child psychiatrist must be capable of utilizing a greater number of therapeutic techniques than those of adult therapists, and must be flexible enough to alter these at a moment's notice. He is often requested to make specific recommendations for immediate action. The parents who ask what to do about a child's fire setting cannot be told that no immediate or specific suggestions can be given and that the child must work this through in his therapeutic sessions. The therapist must be able to say: "On the basis of what I know thus far, I suggest we try this. If it doesn't work out there are other alternatives. As I learn more, I hope to be in a better position to advise you." He must, therefore, be comfortable when providing tentative advice. If the child therapist has had adult analytic training he may be faced with a conflict. His adult training emphasizes the importance of a very passive role, whereas in child work such passivity can be antitherapeutic and even, at times, dangerous. Accordingly, such a therapist must be able to switch readily between the two orientations. At times the two types of training may tend to contaminate one another. The analytic training may result in the therapist's being too passive in his work with children; and the child therapy training causes the therapist to be too active in his work with adults. I would not, however, recommend that the child therapist avoid psychoanalytic training in order to

escape these problems. The enrichment that psychoanalytic training can provide the child therapist far
outweighs its disadvantages (which, for most, are not
difficult to avoid).

The Therapist as Parent

The question is sometimes raised as to whether it is
necessary for the child therapist to have had children of his
own. It is certainly possible to be an effective and
accomplished psychotherapist without having had such
experiences, although I believe that the lack may compromise one's therapeutic abilities. The child, when seen in
an office setting, is in an artificial situation. The childless
therapist has not had the experience of living and growing
with children in their natural setting; of fathering and
mothering; of worrying and scolding; of changing their
diapers; of seeing them through physical illness; of
handling their fights with siblings and peers; and of
involving himself in the thousands of other activities that
enrich one's knowledge and appreciation of children. The
childless therapist, no doubt, gains many of these experiences vicariously through his patients. He may, indeed,
be able to involve himself with his patients to a greater
degree than the therapist who has children of his own.
These considerations notwithstanding, I believe that
having one's own children enhances one's efficacy as a
child therapist.

Boredom

If the therapist lacks enthusiasm and interest in his
work the patient will sense these feelings and will respond
similarly. I cannot imagine effective therapy being done in
such an atmosphere. I am not suggesting that the therapist
should *never* be bored during the session (I myself at times
get bored); we can't possibly be on a "high" all the time.
Rather, I am suggesting that when the therapist does

occasionally find himself bored he try to look into the reasons why and attempt to rectify the situation — both for his own sake and that of his patient. The therapist does well to avoid involving himself in therapeutic activities that he basically does not like. To do so inevitably produces resentment which will be picked up by the child. A child cannot, in my opinion, possibly gain anything therapeutic at a time when his therapist is in such a state of mind. Some of the games and therapeutic activities I will be describing in this book have served to reduce such antitherapeutic reactions in me, and my hope is that they will serve the reader similarly.

I wish to emphasize that we cannot be all things to all people; that the personality characteristics we possess will inevitably attract some and alienate others. There have been many patients with whom, in spite of my best efforts, I have been unable to relate to in a way that I would consider therapeutically beneficial. My practice in such cases has been to inform the child and his parents my feeling that things are not working out, and I suggest that we all together try to find out what the difficulties are and try to rectify them. At times we have been able to improve things, and at other times referral to another therapist or total discontinuation of treatment at that time has been necessary.

Comfort with Therapeutic Failure

Lastly, it is important that the therapist be comfortable with therapeutic failure. If he thinks that it behooves him to alleviate the difficulties of all those who come to him, he will suffer significant frustration and a deep sense of failure. The child often presents a total life of exposure (even though only three to four years) to the deleterious influences that have contributed to his difficulties. His parents generally have been living with their problems for many years as well. But things do not stop there. Not only may the pathological processes have been transmitted down countless generations, but social and cultural processes have usually contributed as well. It is, therefore, grandoise of the therapist to consider himself capable of rectifying all these pathological influences and he is assuming unrealistic obligations if he considers it his responsibility to do so. The best attitude the therapist can take is that he will commit himself to the therapeutic process and try his best to do what he can. If he can say to himself, with regard to the unsuccessful case, that he has tried his best and possibly learned a few things that will serve him in good stead in the future, he should be able to accept the failure without undue guilt and self-recrimination.

Chapter Two
The Therapist-Patient
Relationship

Possessing certain qualities requisite to doing effective work with children is of little value if these qualities are not utilized in building a good relationship with the child. A good therapist-patient relationship is crucial to successful therapy. It is the focal point around which the various therapeutic experiences occur and I cannot imagine therapy's being successful if the relationship is not a good one.

A meaningful relationship with other human beings is vital to survival. Provide a newborn infant with food, clothing, and shelter but deprive it of the tender loving care of a mother (or her substitute) and the child will lose his appetite, become unresponsive to his environment, and may actually waste away and die. Others similarly deprived may survive infancy but may develop such severe withdrawal from others that they become effectively nonfunctioning individuals, living in their own mental worlds, and gaining whatever little gratification they can from their fantasies. The deprivation need not be overt (such as physical abandonment) but can result from psychological rejection in the form of parental withdrawal, hostility, uninvolvement, or other kinds of deleterious interaction with the child. In short, it is only through meaningful and gratifying involvement with others that we develop into human beings; without such exposure we may survive, but we cannot then be called truly human.

Meaningful relationships with others are the stuff of life. More than anything else they enrich us; without them we become shells — mere imitations of living individuals. From the moment we are born until the time of our death we need others — necessary times for solitude notwithstanding. The child in treatment has generally suffered some difficulties in his ability to form and gain gratifications from his involvement with others. Hopefully, therapy will help him to be able to do so. But I cannot imagine its being successful in this regard if a meaningful relationship hasn't been accomplished between the therapist and his patient.

Factors in the Therapeutic Relationship

Time Alone Together. I can conceive of an experiment in which all patients coming to a mental health clinic were divided into three groups which were matched for age, sex, socioeconomic status, and diagnosis. Children in the first group would receive the full course of treatment indicated for their particular problems. Children in the second group would come to the clinic with a parent at a frequency that would be indicated for the treatment of their problems. However, instead of receiving therapy, the parent and child would merely sign in and then immediately return home. No therapy would be given. Those in the third group would not come to the clinic at all and receive no therapy at home either. Then, at the end of a prescribed period (such as two years) all three groups of children would be reevaluated with particular emphasis on whether there had been any improvement in the presenting problems. I believe that those children in the first group would exhibit the most improvement; those in the second group some improvement as well (but less than those in the first group), and those in the third group, least of all. I suspect that the second group would *not* be halfway between the other two with regard to the degree of improvement, but closer to the first group than the third. In addition, if one studied the second group in detail to determine if there was any relationship between the distance traveled to the clinic and the amount of clinical improvement, I believe a positive correlation would be found. In other words, the longer the child had to travel to get to the clinic the greater would be his improvement. Furthermore, I would guess that the same would hold true for those in the first group as well..

We have not given proper attention to the therapeutic effects of the parent's (usually the mother's) time alone with the child as they travel to and from the therapist. Often, it may be the only time the child and mother may be able to be alone together. At home, the child must vie with his siblings for his mother's time and attention; when traveling to the therapist, she is his captive. Often the mother may bring books and games along in order to entertain the child. Sometimes they may talk together in depth, and such discussions can be extremely therapeutic. Most children's symptoms are, in part, the result of some degree of deprivation of parental affection. Spending time alone with a parent while engaged in pleasurable activities is the most specific therapy for such deprivation. Similarly, enjoyable time spent by the child with the therapist can also be therapeutic. Accordingly, even if all the child does is play games (and unfortunately this is all that does happen in some children's therapy), he can derive some therapeutic benefit. This is one of the reasons, I believe, that practitioners of a wide variety of therapeutic techniques can each claim that his methods produce clinical improvement. Hopefully, his play therapy will involve more therapy than that which can be derived from play. It is the purpose of this book to provide the therapist with some methods of enhancing this likelihood.

The Therapist's Affection for the Patient. The therapist's affection for the child can serve to compensate for some of the deprivations the patient may have experienced in his relationships with others. However, as I will discuss in greater detail in Chapter Four, there are significant limitations in the degree to which the therapist can do this. Nevertheless, such affection can be ego-enhancing to the child and therefore therapeutic. In a way, it is easier for the therapist to provide the child with unadulterated affection than his parents and others may be able to give. The situation is so structured that he need not have to do much of the "dirty work." He doesn't have to get the child off to school, to the doctor in emergencies, get him to sleep, care for him in the middle of the night, etc. He, like the grandparents, can enjoy the child at his best — when few demands and restrictions are placed on him — and so there is less chance that there will be conflicts, power struggles, and other difficulties.

I am not suggesting that the therapist should like the child all the time. It is unrealistic to expect anyone to like anyone else more than a significant percentage of the time. The child will at times do things that will irritate the therapist, bore him, and alienate him in a variety of ways. Hopefully, the therapist will use his negative reactions in constructive and therapeutic ways. I do not agree with those who hold that the therapist should have "unconditional positive regard" for his patients. Those who claim they do are not, I believe, in touch with the inevitable frustrations and irritations we experience in our relationships with all human beings — patients included. The patient who is told that his therapist "accepts him" (a condescending remark if there ever was one) regardless of what he says and does will distrust the therapist (and justifiably so). He will recognize the duplicity inherent in such an attitude and this must be antitherapeutic. Accordingly, the optimum experience the child can have with regard to the therapist's affection for him is that he sees the therapist as someone who likes him most of the time and that when he does things that alienate the therapist, the latter uses his negative reactions in the service of helping the child.

Intimately associated with the affection the therapist has for the child is the feeling of pleasure that the therapist experiences with the child. The child's appreciation, at some level, that he is capable of providing another individual with pleasure on a continual (but not necessarily uninterrupted) basis is gratifying and ego-enhancing. And this is yet another element in the therapist-patient relationship that can be therapeutic.

The Therapist's Protection of the Child. As I will discuss in detail in Chapter Four, the therapist's seeing himself primarily as the protector of the child against the indignities he suffers at the hands of the parents is divisive for the family and thereby antitherapeutic. However, if he takes the position of being impartially willing to side with healthy forces — regardless of who exhibits them — he may avoid the schismatic effect on the family of his consistently siding with the child. In the context of such impartiality he can still serve to protect the child from irrational and inappropriate attitudes and reactions he may be exposed to. In such situations the child may feel quite helpless; having someone whom his parents respect (and this must be worked at, as I will discuss in Chapter Four) and who can bring about a reduction and even elimination of his deleterious exposures is most salutary. It reduces tension and anxiety, takes a heavy burden off the child, and removes elements that may be significantly contributory to the child's symptomology.

Ideally, the therapist's position should be one of providing information and advice to both parents and child. Hopefully, the parents will wish to take his recommendations. If not, he should listen with receptivity to their disagreements. If modification is justified he should be comfortable doing so. If he remains unconvinced that his suggestions should be altered, his position with them should be: "Well, this is what I think would be in the best interests of your child. Perhaps one of us may change his opinion in the future." He should not be seen by the child as the manipulator of the parents, but as someone who provides advice and information for them. If he is seen as the manipulator and if the child sees his parents as being unduly dependent on the therapist — as people who hang on his every word and put them into action immediately — this situation can compromise the child-parent relationship. In addition, such a situation must produce some discomfort with the therapist because he is jeopardizing the respect the child has for his parents.

The Resolution of the Transference Neurosis. Of the innumerable patterns of human interaction each person tends to select a few favorites. From earliest childhood (primarily as the result of our interaction with our parents) we develop a constellation of patterns of relating to others that are unique. As we grow older these patterns become strengthened and we tend to utilize them in preference to others that may be either absent from our repertoire or have lower priority for utilization. Some of these patterns of interaction are healthy and enhance our effectiveness in life. Others are maladaptive and often cause us significant difficulty, both personally and in our interaction with others. These patterns are strongly repetitive — almost reflexly so. Accordingly, in new situations we tend to use the old patterns even though we may suffer significantly because of our injudicious reactions.

Using psychoanalytic terminology, we tend to *transfer* onto others reactions that we had toward our parents in infancy and childhood. We tend to interact with others in a manner similar to the way we interacted with our parents. When these modes of interaction are neurotic and they exhibit themselves in the therapeutic relationship they are termed *transference neuroses*. Specifically, the patient tries to involve the therapist in the same neurotic patterns in which he was involved with his parents and in which he tries to involve others as well. Those who comply with his request (because of their own neurotic needs) maintain their relationship with the patient (he may call such individuals his "friends"); those who do not comply with the neurotic request avoid or sever ties (and may be regarded as "unfriendly"). When the analyst refuses to involve himself in the neurotic pattern, the patient will generally react with resentment, anxiety, or other unpleasant thoughts and emotions. At such a point he may leave therapy and consider the therapist uncaring, unloving, disinterested, hostile, etc. Or, he may choose to try to gain insight into what is going on and attempt to change the neurotic pattern. Such working-through is referred to as the *resolution of the transference neurosis* and is an important step in the alleviation of the patient's difficulties. Hopefully, once the pathological pattern of interaction is alleviated in the patient's relationship with the therapist, he will exhibit his healthier modes of interaction in his relationships with others as well.

Although child analysts differ regarding whether a child can exhibit what can justifiably be termed a transference neurosis (see M. Klein [1932] and A. Freud [1965]), I believe that most children will do so *if* they get involved with the therapist. In other words the deeper the child's relationship with the therapist the greater the likelihood he will exhibit his neurotic patterns of interaction to him and the greater the chance he will try to involve the therapist in them. For example, the little girl who uses coyness and seductivity to get her way with adults may try to involve the therapist similarly. In response to his failure to react with the expected "affection," she may become angry, consider him mean and unfriendly, and refuse to return. However, if such a child can be engaged (and it is the purpose of this book to help the therapist accomplish this) she may be helped to appreciate that there are more effective and predictably gratifying ways of relating to others. Similarly, the therapist who does not give in to a child's temper tantrums, or allow himself to be bribed, or coax the pouting child, is helping the child resolve his transference neurosis.

If a good relationship is not established, the child will

be less willing to tolerate the frustrations attendant to the therapist's refusal to comply with the neurotic requests. And the child will thereby be less likely to gain this important therapeutic benefit that can be derived from the relationship.

The Transference Cure. When a patient, very early in treatment, exhibits a sudden and dramatic alleviation (and even cure) of his presenting symptoms, he is described by psychoanalysts as having exhibited a *transference cure*. Specifically, because the patient hasn't delved into the unconscious roots of the neurosis and worked out the basic problems that underlie it (something that generally takes a long time to do), the therapeutic change is usually considered specious. When this occurs extremely early in therapy (such as after the first or second session), it is understood to reflect the patient's resistance to entering into treatment:

> *Patient:* You are, without doubt, the most brilliant doctor I've ever met. Since I saw you last time, I'm one hundred percent better. I'm feeling so good that I'm wondering whether I need any more treatment.
>
> *Therapist:* But all I did was ask you some questions about your problems and get some background history.
>
> *Patient:* Oh, it was much more than that, doctor. There was something about the way you asked me those questions — I don't know what it was — that made me feel so much better.

When the "cure" occurs a little later in treatment, it often relates to an attempt on the part of the patient to get the therapist to like or even love him. After all, if the primary goal of the therapist is to cure the patient then it is reasonable to assume that the therapist will love someone who helps him quickly achieve this goal. Of course, both of the aforementioned factors may be operating simultaneously, and others as well. Rarely is there a simple explanation for anything that occurs in psychoanalytic treatment — or any other kind of psychotherapy as well.

These specious kinds of cure are well known to most psychotherapists. Because they are generally manifestations of a pathological pattern, the term *transference cure* is generally spoken of with a certain amount of derision. This, I believe, is unfortunate because there is a useful, and often unappreciated, element in the transference cure. All patients, I believe, change partly in the attempt to ingratiate themselves to the therapist. From the very first encounter the patient has with the therapist he wants to be liked. (This doesn't differ in any way from all other first encounters with nontherapists.) The anxiety the patient experiences in the first session is, in part, a manifestation of his fear that he will be considered loathesome and unworthy because of the things he will reveal to the therapist. As the relationship intensifies, there is usually an even greater need to be liked by the therapist. The patient has invested much time and (often) money in the project, and his reliance on the therapist to help him with his difficulties is great.

I believe that *one* element that plays a role in a patient's exhibiting therapeutic change is the desire to get the therapist to like him. Others are certainly operative. But this factor is, I believe, an important one in the early phases of alleviation of a symptom. The patient knows that when he tells the therapist that improvement has occurred, the therapist cannot but feel good about himself for his contribution to the success. (Some therapists, in accordance with their theoretical position, deny having any such gratification. I don't believe them.) If the patient has it within his power to make the therapist feel good, then it follows that the therapist will like the patient. After all, we generally like most those who have the good sense to provide us with the gratifications we seek. Hopefully, the new mode of adaptation will become more deeply entrenched as the patient gains greater insights into the causes of his symptoms and as he has the experience that the newer way is the more judicious and gratifying. Hopefully, he will then maintain the healthier adaptation because he himself, through knowledge and experience, will have the inner conviction that it is the preferable alternative. Hopefully, he will then no longer need to maintain it in order to please the therapist (whom he will probably never see again anyway after the treatment is over — psychological ties, fond memories, gratitude, and other positive feelings notwithstanding).

The younger the patient the greater the likelihood he will change his behavior in order to please the therapist. Children are constantly concerning themselves with the approbations of parents, teachers, and other authorities. They are constantly being told about whether what they do and say is "good" or "bad," "right" or "wrong." And the therapist is just another authority from whom they usually wish to gain acceptance. It behooves the child therapist to make use of this phenomenon. It can significantly enhance the efficacy of his treatment. He does well to praise the child (often profusely) for his newly gained healthier modes of behavior. Hopefully, he will help the child reach the point where he engages in the healthier adaptations, both from the inner conviction and the experience that his life is much more gratifying when he does so.

The Corrective Emotional Experience. In the process of working through or resolving the transference neurosis a particularly effective therapeutic phenomenon that may occur is the corrective emotional experience (Alexander, French, et al., 1946; Alexander, 1950). Essentially, the patient has a living experience (often associated with a significant upheaval of emotional reaction) that alters significantly a previous pattern. For example, a girl whose father has been significantly punitive may generalize and expect similar treatment from all men, including her male therapist. For the therapist to tell such a child that he will treat her differently will not generally be very effective because intellectual processes only are involved in the communication. However, if the child has the living experience, over an extended period of time, that the therapist indeed does not react punitively then her view of men may indeed change. Her fearful reactions lessen and relaxation and trust gradually replace them. It is this combination of insight, feeling, and experience that brings about some of the most meaningful changes that can occur in psychotherapy.

When a child cheats during a game I may say: "You know, it's no fun for me to play this game when you cheat. If you do that again I'm going to stop playing and we'll do something else." To simply discuss why the patient cheats may have some value. However, if this discussion takes place in a setting in which the patient experiences some frustration over the alienation his symptom causes, the conversation is more likely to be therapeutically meaningful. In such a discussion we might talk about whether this might be one of the reasons why children don't like to play with him, or about the futility of this way of trying to compensate for feelings of inadequacy, or about other aspects of the problem which may be of psychological significance. But, without the emotional reactions attendant to the threat of alienating the therapist and/or interrupting an enjoyable experience, such discussions are not likely to be very effective.

Identification with the Therapist. Just as the child imitates his parents and acquires many of their traits (both adaptive and maladaptive), he will tend to identify with the therapist if the relationship is a good one. Hopefully, the personality qualities that the child acquires in this way will serve him in good stead. There are those who believe that what I am saying is risky business — that such a process is dangerous and antitherapeutic. They would hold that the therapist must do everything possible to make himself like a blank screen upon which the patient's fantasies can be projected. Some believe that the therapist should encourage the child's realizing his "true self." Central to such a theory is that there exists such an entity — that each individual has within himself a personality pattern that is blocked from free expression and that such blockage is central to psychopathological behavior. They hold that an important aspect of treatment involves helping the individual freely express these hidden personality characteristics.

Although I certainly agree that many people who are in treatment are repressed and need to be helped to express themselves (although there are many who need some repression more than anything else), I believe most people usually need to express some specific pent-up thoughts or feelings. I am somewhat dubious about the concept of a whole personality being hidden inside, knocking for release. Rather, I believe that certain aspects of our personality may be genetically determined (such as certain temperamental patterns as activity level, assertiveness, passivity, and curiosity); but most are environmentally determined (and even the genetic ones are subject to significant environmental modification). I see core *potentials* not core personalities. Most of our character traits, I believe, are derived from the environment — more specifically from what we learn from those in the world around us and what we acquire by imitation of significant individuals in our lives. The therapist becomes another in the series of individuals whom the child may copy, emulate, and identify with. Even the kind of therapist described above, who tries to provide his patient with a neutral atmosphere to facilitate his "self-actualization" sends many subtle cues that encourage the patient to proceed in specific directions. In addition, the therapist still has a personality, and no matter how much he may try to suppress it, much is still revealed — much that the patient can identify with.

As mentioned, it is obviously preferable that the qualities of the therapist that the patient does identify with will serve him well. For example, a child's father may have operated in accordance with the principle that admitting any deficiencies to his children will lessen their respect for him. The child, then, may take on this similar maladaptive pattern and find himself having trouble with his classwork because he cannot tolerate admitting errors. If his therapist, however, is the kind of person who can, without discomfort, admit errors when they naturally arise (to do so in a contrived situation is not only therapeutically worthless but may be antitherapeutic because it is basically dishonest), and the patient comes to see that this is a desirable and effective pattern, he may take on the quality himself. The child may have acquired the pattern of lying (in both subtle and overt ways) as a significant part of his interactional repertoire. Observing the therapist to be one who is consistently honest and experiencing, as well, that such honesty makes the therapist's life simpler, enables him to enjoy the esteem of others, and has numerous other benefits, may result in the child's attempting to acquire this valuable asset himself.

Therapists traditionally encourage their patients to express their pent-up thoughts and feelings in appreciation that such expression, properly directed and utilized (not often the case [Gardner, 1968b, 1971c]), can be therapeutic. However, many therapists attempt to do this in a setting where they do little if any such expression themselves. They thereby serve as poor models for their patients and so impede the process they are attempting to achieve. The therapist who expresses himself in situations where such expression is appropriate and in the best interests of the patient (and, as mentioned, without artificiality) has a much better chance of getting his patient to do so as the latter identifies with him. The therapist who asserts himself and does not let himself be taken advantage of serves as a good model for the patient who is inhibited in these areas. And it is only in the context of a good patient-therapist relationship that such salutary identifications can occur.

The Therapist as Educator. We learn best from those we respect and admire. The disliked, hated, or disrespected teacher will teach his students little of educational value (although he may teach them something about having to tolerate a despised person in certain situations). If the therapist is basically respected, there is much that he can teach his patients that can be of therapeutic value. The therapist helps the patient alter distortions. For example, all of us carry with us into adult life distorted concepts of the world that we blindly accept. Adherence to these dicta may cause us many difficulties and yet they may never be questioned. It is one of the purposes of treatment to help a patient examine (sometimes for the first time in his life) these premises that guide his behavior. Some of the more common ones that adult (and often child) therapists must deal with are: "No one is to be trusted," "Sex is bad," "Fun is sinful," "I must do everything to avoid criticism because all negative comments about me must be correct," "I must do everything possible to avoid anyone's getting angry at me," and "If there's a choice between another person's being inconvenienced and my being so, rather it be me." Some common dicta of childhood (which may continue throughout life) are: "Mother and father are always right," "Nice boys and girls never have hateful thoughts toward their parents," "Thoughts can harm, that is, wishing that something bad will happen to someone can make it happen," "If my mother and/or father doesn't love me very much, I can't be very good and no one can ever love me," "One fault makes you totally worthless," "There are perfect people who never make mistakes and never do anything wrong or bad," and "An unacceptable thought is as bad as an unacceptable act."

I agree with those who hold that emotions follow cognition and that many feelings of guilt, fear, anger, etc. can be alleviated if notions such as the aforementioned are corrected. Albert Ellis (1963) holds that the correction of such cognitive distortions are the basic issues to be focused upon in psychotherapy and has coined the term *Rational-Emotive Psychotherapy* for this type of therapeutic approach. I am in agreement with Ellis that emphasis on this element is important in practically everyone's treatment, regardless of age. However, I believe that things are more complex and that many other factors contribute to symptom formation. (Although Ellis admits to other facts, he considers them far less important than cognitive distortions in producing psychopathology.)

From the earliest days of psychoanalysis Freud (1895) considered reducing the patient's guilt to be one of the analyst's most important tasks. With less guilt, there is less repression and hence symptoms are less likely to persist.

Although his subsequent experience convinced him that things were far more complex (some have yet to read his later work), the concept is certainly still valid if one considers it to be one of the possible contributing factors in *some* patients' difficulties. Partly by virtue of the therapist's position of authority and his experience in matters of things such as guilt, the patient becomes convinced that his urges are very common, if not universal, and that the difference between him and others is not so much that he has the particular thoughts and feelings but that he feels so guilty over them. In essence the analyst communicates to the patient: "You're still acceptable to me, even though you have those ideas." (Condescending elements in the communication notwithstanding, the message is often helpful.)

In my work with the child who needs some loosening up of his superego I will make such comments as: "Most children I know would get very angry when something like that happens. I guess you must have been pretty mad also," "I can't believe that somewhere, someplace, you weren't a little bit angry when that happened," "So what's so terrible about *wanting* to do that? You know wanting is not the same as doing."

Many children I see, however, do not need any loosening up of their consciences. They have what Adelaide Johnson (1949, 1959) called "super-ego lacunae," that is, like Swiss cheese they seem to have holes in the part of the brain where the superego is (I speak figuratively, of course). Again, as part of the therapy of such children cognitive changes have to be made. Some comments that I may make in the service of this goal: "That's terrible. She really must have felt bad after you ripped up her new kite," and "I really don't think you could have felt very good about yourself getting 100% on that test after copying most of the answers from the children around you."

Most neurotic symptoms are developed, in part, in an attempt to enhance and compensate for feelings of low self-worth. However, they are misguided solutions and usually result in the individual's feeling even worse about himself than before—temporary ego-enhancement notwithstanding. The child who feels unpopular may attempt to gain respect and admiration by boasting about various exploits, travels, etc. However, the fear of exposure and possible guilt he may feel generally result in his feeling even worse about himself than before. And if (as is often the case) others learn of his duplicity, his social position is further worsened. As part of the therapy of such symptoms the therapist does well to inform the child of the injudiciousness of his mode of compensation. For example: "I know you think that clowning around in class gets the kids to like you. And I know you think that their laughing at your proves this. However, I believe that although you're good for laughs, they really don't like you in other ways. They still don't seem to invite you to parties nor do they seem to want to see you after school," "I know you think you're quite a big shot when you beat up those little kids. But deep down inside, you know that there's nothing so great about it and that must make you feel kind of bad about yourself," "You think the kids think you're hot stuff when you go around beating up lots of kids. Some of them may; but others, I am sure, don't like you at all. They feel sorry for the children you're hitting and I'm sure you've noticed how they stay away from you." Although these comments can be very bitter medicine to swallow, they are accepted if the patient has a good relationship with the therapist. In addition, as mentioned, the therapist's attitude is more important than the content in determining whether his comments will alienate a patient. When benevolently communicated in the context of a firm relationship the most painful confrontations may be accepted.

All patients, regardless of their age, have to be helped in treatment to gain a clearer view of their parents. As children, we tend to operate on the principle: "If it's good enough for them, it's good enough for me." We tend to incorporate most if not all of their traits — healthy and unhealthy. We swallow the whole bag, without separating the good from the bad. Therapy, in part, involves making (often very belatedly) these vital discriminations. And the child therapist has the opportunity to provide this at a time when it can do the most good, at a time before the deleterious results of such indiscriminating incorporation and acceptance have had a chance to become deeply entrenched. The child has to be helped to see that his parents, like all other human beings (including the therapist), are not perfect. We all have our deficits. Helping the child become clear regarding which personality traits of his parents are assets and which are liabilities can be very useful. And the therapist is in a unique position to provide such information. (This, of course, may require some advance work with the parents; but if the relationship with them is a good one [and I will discuss in Chapter Four the ways that may help bring this about], their cooperation can often be relied upon.)

The phobic child of a phobic mother can be told: "You know that your mother has many fears that she herself realizes are not real. She knows that there's nothing to be afraid of in elevators or crowded places, but she just can't help herself. She'd prefer not to have these fears and that's why she's seeing a psychiatrist." Ideally, it can be helpful to get the mother herself to verbalize to the child comments such as these. (The reader interested in a detailed account of such parental divulgences in the therapy of a phobic child may wish to refer to Chapter 16 of my text *Therapeutic Communication with Children* [1971a].) The child of divorce can be told: "Your father can be counted upon to give your mother the money she needs to take care of herself and the children. However, as you know, he's not very reliable when it comes to showing up for appointments on visiting days. This doesn't mean that he doesn't love you at all. It does mean that he has less love for you than a father has who does show up all the time. This doesn't mean that you are unlovable or that no one else can love you more. You still have many people who like being with you and you can spend time with them when your father doesn't show up."

I introduce my next point anecdotally. A number of years ago Listerine mouthwash was advertised with the slogan "Your best friend won't tell you." In the typical pitch a young girl cannot understand why dates persistently reject her even though she is bright, pretty, etc. Finally, she realizes that *bad breath* is driving them away! Happily, she chances on Listerine, washes her mouth with it, and the boys come flocking. I believe that the therapist should be better than one's best friend. He should be able to tell his patient things that even his best friend will hesitate to reveal. And if his motivation is benevolent and his timing judicious he should be able to do so with only occasional difficulty or hesitation.

To put it another way. Robert Burns (1786) once wrote:

'O wad some Pow'r the giftie [small gift] gie [give] us
To see oursels as others see us!'

It is the therapist's job to help his patient see himself as others see him. And this is one of the significant benefits that all patients, regardless of age, can derive from treatment. He should be able to gain, as well, what Harry Stack Sullivan (1953) called "consensual validation" of his views of the world. For example, a child can be told: "You think that the kids really like you when they play with you after you give them candy. If you think about it, I think you'll agree that they don't play with you *unless* you give them candy. I suspect you're doing things that turn them off." And if the patient agrees: "I wonder what those things might be?"

Another can be told: "You always seem to want your way when you're here in the office. You always seem to want to do only those things you want. You never seem to care about what your mother or father or I would like to do or talk about. If you act this way with friends, perhaps that's why they don't want to play with you." Another example: "You say you're sorry in the hope that a person will no longer be bothered or angry about what you've done. Although the person may *say* that he accepts your apology and that he's not angry, *deep down inside he really still is*. Even though you've told your father that you're sorry that you broke the television set, I think he's still angry that it's cost him all that money to fix it." (I often suggest that children who utilize this common manipulative device [invariably taught by parents] read my story "Say You're Sorry" in my book of psychologically oriented children's stories, *Dr. Gardner's Stories about the Real World* [1972a].)

Part of the confrontational process involves helping the child gain a more accurate picture of his assets and liabilities (both inborn and acquired). The child with an organic coordination deficit should be discouraged from intensive involvement in competitive sports (although special training and exercises preparing for minimal to moderate involvement may be indicated). In the earliest years the child's view of himself is acquired from what Harry Stack Sullivan called "reflected appraisals" (Mullahy, 1970). In essence, the child comes to view himself in accordance with information about him provided by significant figures in his life, especially his parents. The four-year-old runs into the house crying, "Mommy, the kids all call me stupid. Mother replies, "You're not stupid. You're very smart." The child leaves the house reassured. As he grows older the child generally gathers information from others (teachers, neighbors, peers, etc.) that may modify and expand this information — which becomes his criteria for judging his self-worth. Hopefully, his data will be accurate and it is one of the therapist's jobs to help correct any distortions that may have arisen.

Lastly, it is part of the therapeutic educational process to introduce to the child alternative modes of adaptation to those neurotic and self-defeating ones that he may be utilizing. These options may never have occurred to the child, nor may he ever have been introduced to them. For example, in his family, denial of or flight from awareness of one's deficiencies may have been the only reactions. Such a child must be helped to appreciate the value of dealing directly with one's deficits and he must be encouraged to try this alternative to see for himself its advantages.

In the following clinical examples I will demonstrate

what I consider to have been both good and bad therapeutic relationships that I have had with patients. In each case I will try to identify those factors that contributed to the kind of relationship that evolved.

Clinical Examples

"Can I call you Dick?" When eight-year-old George's divorced mother called to make his first appointment, she told me that he was not attending to his studies and that he was fighting so excessively with peers that he had no friends. Her former husband was living in South America and although he often wrote George letters professing his intense love for him and promising future visits, the latter rarely materialized. Accordingly, George's life was fraught with frustration and disillusionment.

At the time of their first visit, when I entered the waiting room to greet George and his mother, he told me that his name was George, but that his friends called him Jojo. I asked him which name he preferred I use with him and he answered, "Jojo. What do your friends call you?" "Dick," I replied. "Can I call you Dick?" he asked. "Of course," I answered. It was clear that George was craving a close, friendly relationship. To have insisted that he call me "Dr. Gardner" or to have inquired as to the reasons why he wished to call me by my first name would have squelched him at this vital point and lessened the possibility of our forming a good relationship. (It is of interest that about three months later George began calling me Dr. Gardner. I think that he was basically uncomfortable with this "egalitarianism" and was able to give up the contrived symbol of friendliness when we had the real thing going for us.)

"I made this present for you, Dick." Following the interchange in which we decided what names we would use with one another, George presented me with a clay figurine that he had made for me in school. "I made this present for you, Dick," he said. I admired the piece of work, told him how proud he must be to have made such a thing, and thanked him warmly for the gift. Although there was a pathetic quality in George's intense craving for me to like him (even to the point where one has to consider there may have been a bribing element in the gift), there was also a warmth and optimism communicated as he gave me the present. To have hesitated to take the gift and/or to have conducted a psychoanalytic inquiry into his motivations would have compromised our already budding relationship, for such an inquiry would have robbed us of the warm feelings being engendered in both of us. But worse, it would have been inhumane. I am not suggesting that one never question a gift given by a patient. Rather, I am only saying that for this patient, at this time, such a reaction would definitely have been antitherapeutic.

"You shrinks are all the same... same stupid couch ... same stupid diplomas ..." Henry, a fourteen-year-old boy, was referred for treatment because of delinquent behavior. His defiance of authority was ubiquitous. His father was an extremely rigid and punitive person who made Henry feel quite impotent. From ages ten to twelve he had worked with another therapist without too much success. Unfortunately, this therapist had died a year previously.

When he entered his first session he smugly looked around and said, "You shrinks are all the same . . . same stupid couch . . . same stupid diplomas on the walls . . . same damn pictures of your family on the desk." I understood Henry to be trying to lessen his anxiety in this new situation. By finding similarities between my office and that of his previous therapist he was reducing his feelings of strangeness. In addition, he was trying to identify me with his former therapist in order that I could better serve as his replacement. The hostile veneer was also anxiety-alleviating; acting like a tough guy is a typical teenage defense against fear. Although anger displaced from his father onto me was also contributing to Henry's hostility, I felt that the anxiety-alleviating factor was the most important at that time. To have delved into the hostility at that point would have missed the aforementioned important issues and would have robbed the patient of his defenses at a time when he was very much in need of them. Appreciating his need for reassurance that his therapist and I did indeed have many similarities, I replied, "Yes, we psychiatrists often have much in common." These comments made Henry less tense and less hostile.

An Attempt on the Therapist's Life. In spite of a promising beginning, I cannot say that Henry and I had a very good relationship during the subsequent months. This was primarily due to the fact that I could not identify well with him when he engaged in antisocial behavior — especially when it took on dangerous proportions. I was, however, making some headway when the father angrily stated in a joint session that he was fed up with Henry's long hair and that he wanted him to cut it shorter. (This occurred in the mid to late 1960's when the long hair vogue [and its antisocial value] had reached a peak.) I tried to dissuade the father from putting pressure on Henry and tried to explain to him that it was one of the most innocuous forms of rebellion ever invented and he should be happy that Henry was resorting more to it and less to the more destructive and violent forms. The father was deaf to my advice. Following the session he took Henry to a barber shop. There he and a barber held Henry down while another barber gave him a very short haircut. Following this, Henry completely refused to attend school. (During the course of therapy he had gotten to the point of attending most of the time.) In subsequent sessions it became apparent that Henry considered himself to have been castrated by his father and his rage was enormous.

About two weeks after this incident Henry came to my office with a teenage friend and asked if the latter could wait for him in the waiting room. The session was not particularly eventful. During my session with the patient who followed, she thought she smelled smoke. I didn't smell anything and neither of us thought it was necessary to investigate. At the end, when we walked out into the waiting room, I was horrified to see that attempts had been made to set my waiting room on fire. Fortunately, the curtains were made of fire-resistant material and so did not completely ignite. The bathroom toilet tissue and paper hand towels had all burned, but fortunately the flames did not spread to the walls. Had the waiting room caught on fire, my only exit would have been out the thirteenth-story window.

I summoned Henry and his family back for a session at the end of my day. When I asked Henry about the incident, he admitted that he and his friend were responsible. When I asked him if he appreciated that I might have been killed, he smugly replied, "Doc, you gotta die sometime." I concluded that this was not a time for analytic inquiry. Since I was discharging Henry from treatment, such inquiry would have served little, if any, purpose. Besides, I was not particularly interested in spending time helping Henry to gain insight into such things as his act being a reflection of rage felt toward his father being displaced onto me. I was just interested in getting rid of him as quickly and efficiently as possible. I called his parents in, told them about the fire incident, explained that I could not effectively treat anyone who had tried to kill me, and refused their request that I recommend them to someone else — explaining that I had too much concern for my respected colleagues to refer someone such as Henry to them. Although I recognized that this rejection might help Henry appreciate that there could be untoward repercussions to his dangerous behavior, this was not my motivation in discharging him. My intent was not to provide him with any kind of therapeutic "corrective emotional experience"; rather, I just wanted to get rid of him.

Before they left I suggested the parents give me the name of Henry's friend, so I could call his parents and inform them about what their son had done. I called the boy's father, a lawyer, whose immediate response was, "Can you prove it?" I replied, "You and your son deserve one another." And I hung up. A more blatant example of a parent's sanctioning a son's antisocial behavior (so often the case) would be hard to find.

Rebuking the Patient. Harry entered treatment at the age of fourteen because of poor school performance, in spite of extremely high intelligence, and profound shyness. Both of his parents were professional scientists and highly unemotional and intellectualized. Their pressures on Harry to perform well in the academic area were formidable. Harry's poor school performance was, in part, a rebellion against his parents' coercions. In addition, they had a condescending attitude toward practically everyone and little meaningful involvement with anyone outside their family. Harry's shyness and uninvolvement with others was a reflection of his parents' attitudes. The family was Catholic, very religious, and puritanical in their attitudes about profanity, sex, and pleasurable activities.

After about a year of therapy, Harry joined his parochial school's computer club, where he immediately became recognized as the most knowledgeable and enthusiastic member. The activity well suited him because of his very high intelligence and his interest in activities that did not involve emotional expression. A few months after joining he began to report in session his club's new project: computerized matching of boys in his school with the girls of a nearby Catholic school. All students in both schools were to fill out a questionnaire describing various basic physical characteristics, interests, personality preferences in members of the opposite sex, etc. All these data were to be fed into a computer and every boy and girl would be matched to three others. A large dance was to be held, everyone was to be assigned a number, and at prescribed times each student would dance with the partner assigned by the computer.

For weeks Harry excitedly spoke of the details of this project. I was most pleased about it not only because of his enthusiasm (a rare quality for Harry to express) but because it would provide Harry with the opportunity to involve himself with girls in a way that would produce less anxiety than some of the more traditional methods of boy-girl meeting. When the week came for the students to fill out their questionnaires, Harry spoke animatedly about the large number of questionnaires being received and how happy he was that everything pointed to the program's being a success. In the context of this discussion I casually asked Harry what answers he had written on his questionnaire. Harry replied, "Oh, I'm not putting in any questionnaire. My job is to organize the whole thing and make sure that everything works well with the computer." I was astonished. For weeks we had spoken about this activity and not once did I ever consider the possibility that Harry himself would not enter. The session took place the day before the deadline for the submission of the questionnaires. There was little time to work things out, to help Harry assuage his anxieties, and to help Harry appreciate what he was doing.

Speaking more as a frustrated father than as a therapist, I told Harry that I was flabbergasted that he wasn't submitting his own questionnaire. I told him that he was making a grave error, that everybody gets nervous in such situations, and that one has to push through his anxieties if he is to enjoy the rewards of a new situation. I spoke quickly and somewhat heatedly — ending with the warning that if he came back to the next session without having submitted his questionnaire I would not only be very disappointed in him but very irritated with him as well.

One could argue that my approach was extremely antitherapeutic. I was coercing this boy; I was pushing him into an anxiety-provoking situation; I would be producing unnecessary guilt and self-loathing if he did not comply with my request; and I was jeopardizing the therapeutic relationship by such coercive and antitherapeutic tactics. I agree completely with these criticisms and I was completely aware of these dangers as I spoke to Harry. My hope was that this risk would be more than counterbalanced by Harry's appreciation, at some level, that my frustration, anger, and coercion came from a deep sense of concern; that only an uninvolved therapist could sit calmly by and allow him to pass by this wonderful opportunity. (I am reminded at this point of a psychiatric ward nurse who once reported to me overhearing a conversation among three children. The first said, "My mother's a bitch." The second, "My father's always hitting me." And the third, "My father never even hits me!" Obviously the third's situation was the worst. Having a father who never even bothers to discipline and even punish is a severe deprivation indeed.) I hoped also that the general strength of our relationship was such that he not only would comply but that he would appreciate that I was being basically benevolent.

Harry did submit his questionnaire. On the night of the dance he "could not find" one of the girls with whom he was matched and the second "didn't show up." However, he did spend some time with the third. But because he didn't know how to dance (and forgot my suggestion that he ask her to teach him a few steps), they talked awhile and then went their separate ways. I was not surprised that no great romance developed from this first encounter with a female. One cannot expect a patient to overcome lifelong inhibitions in one evening. However, the ice was broken. Had I not reacted as I had, I believe that Harry would not have taken this step and I would have therefore been somewhat remiss in my obligation to him. I saw no evidence that Harry's relationship with me had in any way suffered because of my coercion; in fact, I believe that it strengthened. However, this improvement could not have taken place if the coercion had not occurred at a time after a good relationship had already formed. To have used such an approach very early in treatment might very well have destroyed, or seriously compromised, our relationship.

The "Amotivational Syndrome." It is sometimes said that the patient who has been a failure in most areas of his life is likely to be a failure in therapy as well. Unfortunately, this has been my experience. I cannot say that I have had much success salvaging patients who present with massive difficulties in most areas of functioning. My best successes have been with those who have proved themselves capable of succeeding in at least some areas of functioning. One group of such difficult patients

are those who present with the parents' complaint that
they just aren't interested in anything — a total
"amotivational syndrome." They sit in school and couldn't
care less. They forget homework assignments, hand in
sloppy work, daydream in class, and are generally tuned
out. These are not psychotic children nor are they
significantly depressed or unhappy. They just plod along.
They have little, if any, interest in playing with friends.
They do not seem to be in much pain and can be quite
content to spend all their free time watching television.
Usually they are of average intelligence (but on occasion
may be a little higher or lower). Many are "shlubbey" or
"nebische" kids.

In the therapy sessions they act similarly. They just sit
there — having little to talk about. There is no spontaneity,
no dreams to be recalled, nothing of interest to report to the
therapist. They will often passively go along with playing
games, but their lack of interest becomes infectious and the
therapist soon finds himself yawning. I have had the
feeling at times when working with such children that I
have been "turning myself inside out" or "standing on my
head" to draw them out — but to no avail. They may even
tell stories, but their stories are often short, stereotyped,
and not particularly revealing of significant psychodynamic material. One gets the feeling that they are
telling the story, drawing the picture, playing the game,
etc., in order to comply with the therapist's request as fast
as possible. It is as if their main message to parents,
teachers, and the therapist is: "Just leave me alone. I'm
perfectly content with myself the way I am. I'm getting
food, clothing, and shelter from my parents; what else
should anyone want in life?" But even this "statement" is
made in such a way that both patient and therapist find
themselves on the verge of falling asleep as it is being said.
Although I have been able, in most of these cases, to
delineate those factors which I believe have contributed to
the formation of this type of personality disturbance, I have
been uniformly unsuccessful in helping such children.

The Passive-Aggressive Child. The aforementioned children are not passive-aggressive, that is, they are not particularly angry nor using obstructionism as a way of expressing their hostility. The passive-aggressive represent another category of children who are extremely difficult to engage. They are basically very angry children who express their anger by thwarting those around them. They seem to operate in accordance with the principle: "What he wants me to do is the very thing I will not do." The request becomes the cue for not doing. It provides the child with his weapon. It tells him exactly what particular kind of refusal will be most effective at that particular time. Home life provides a continuous opportunity for such negativistic expression: they dawdle in practically everything, they forget to do what's expected of them, they won't eat or eat very slowly or messily. Everything quickly turns into a power struggle. In school also, where things are expected of them, they do not comply. They exasperate the teacher who finds them fighting her at every point — always silently and passively. And it is no surprise that they react similarly in the session with the theapist. He asks the child to talk; so the child has nothing to say. The therapist asks the child to play games; the reply: "not interested," "can't think of a story," "I don't like to draw," etc.

The therapist who is willing to spend weeks, months, and perhaps even years sitting silently and not falling into the child's trap of reaching out and then being thwarted may be providing such a child with a therapeutically beneficial experience. I, however, like myself too much to endure such boredom for the sake of a patient. In fact, the resentment I would feel in such sessions could not but be antitherapeutic. In addition, my experience has been that the child who is willing to sit silently as a gratification of passive-aggressive needs knows that the therapy is costing his parents money and so the therapist's participation in such sessions makes him an ally in the child's acting-out — an obviously antitherapeutic situation. I have sometimes tried to work with such children in family sessions. I take the tack: "We are talking here about you and it behooves you to participate in this discussion because we'll be making decisions that concern you." I try to draw the child into the discussion to get his opinion — especially when it may behoove him to talk in order to argue against a decision's being made that may make him uncomfortable. Again, I cannot say that this approach has been particularly successful either.

The Hostile Parent. The parent who is actively antagonistic to the therapist and who still brings the child (for a variety of neurotic reasons) impedes and even prevents formation of a working therapist-patient relationship. Torn between the two, the child usually sides with the one who is most important: the parent. A good example of such interference occurred with Carol, a nine-and-a-half-year-old girl with stuttering, insomnia, and poor peer relationships, who was placed in just such a difficult bind quite early in treatment. Her mother, a very angry woman, became increasingly hostile toward me and tried to get the patient to side with her against me. She would interrogate the patient after each session in an attempt to point out what she considered to be my defects. On one occasion, after two months of treatment, the following dialogue — related by the patient and confirmed by the mother — took place:

> *Mother* (in a tone of biting sarcasm): So what did you and Dr. Gardner talk about today?
> *Patient:* We talked about a nightmare I had. I dreamed monsters were chasing me.
> *Mother:* And what did *he* think about *that*?
> *Patient:* He thought I had a lot of anger in me that I was scared to let out.
> *Mother:* I think he's full of shit!

Following similar reports by the patient, I arranged an interview with the parents. I told them that the likelihood of therapy succeeding was small as long as the mother continued to try to undermine Carol's relationship with me. My invitation to the mother to air her complaints to me directly, in the hope that at least some of the difficulties might be resolved, was greeted with a barrage of invective.

Attempts to help her gain insight into her reactions were futile. She did agree, however, to consult with another therapist regarding treatment for herself. It was also decided that if, after another month, there was still no appreciable difference in the mother's attitude, treatment would be discontinued.

One month later the mother, although in treatment, was as hostile as ever toward me, and it was agreed that there was no point to my working further with the child, who had been in treatment for three months. The parents also decided not to seek treatment elsewhere for the child at that time.

Office Souvenirs. One day, Bernard, during his sixth month of treatment, saw a clock in my wastepaper basket. When he asked if he could have it I told him yes, but informed him that it was broken and that was why I had thrown it away. Two years later, during our last session, his mother said to me: "Doctor, do you remember that clock from the wastepaper basket you once let Bernard have?" Since it had never been mentioned again, I had a little difficulty recalling it, but the patient soon refreshed my memory by describing the incident in which I had given it to him. "Well," she continued, "I don't know whether you know it or not but he sleeps with that broken clock under his pillow every night."

The Cassette Tape Recorder. One girl asked if she could bring her own cassette tape recorder and tape her sessions — especially the stories we tell — so she could bring them home and listen to them. I readily agreed, and it was from this request that I ultimately suggested that all patients do so because it provides such a good opportunity for reiteration of the therapeutic messages and in many cases an entrenchment of the relationship with me.

Sole Brothers. Michael, whose divorced father rarely visited, when he sat opposite me often put his feet up on the ottoman between us — in obvious imitation of me. At times, he would place the soles of his feet against the soles of mine and we would continue talking in this way. This was never discussed. To have done so would have robbed the experience of some of its beauty and import. There are certain times in therapy when talking about something robs it of therapeutic benefit — and this is one such example.

"Hey, Benjy, look over there. That's Dr. Gardner. He's my psychiatrist!" Joel lived in the same town as I and belonged to the same community swim club. One day, as I was walking at the edge of the pool, he yelled from the other side of the pool to a boy in the water, about halfway between us: "Hey, Benjy, look over there (pointing to me). That's Dr. Gardner. He's my psychiatrist!" Although the boy's mother (who was standing next to him) cringed beyond description, he beamed with pride as many in the pool looked at me as I waved to Joel. About one year after the completion of his treatment Joel, then age ten, came up to me at the pool one day and said: "Dr. Gardner, I know you're off duty. But I had this dream last night that bothers me. Would you help me analyze it? I don't have much money; but I can pay you fifty cents." I told him that there was no charge for postgraduate dream analyses and we sat down together and discussed the dream.

Sally came to the session the day after Christmas and wanted to take my picture with her new camera so that she could show all her friends what I looked like. Helen, age twelve, came to her second session with a notebook entitled: "Secret Things to Tell Dr. Gardner." And Susan's younger sister is reported to have told her mother, "I wish that I had a problem so that I could go and see Dr. Gardner too."

As is obvious, forming a good relationship with the child has more benefits than just helping the child's therapy. It can be extremely gratifying for the therapist in its own right. My hope is that the methods described in this book will be useful to the reader in helping him form such satisfying and enriching relationships himself.

Chapter Three
The Role of Seduction

Generally, at some point during the introductory
lecture of one of my courses on child psychotherapy, I ask
the students if they are familiar with two main forms of
reasoning: *inductive* and *deductive*. They usually are. I
then tell them that in doing child psychotherapy one must
utilize a third form of reasoning: *seductive* reasoning.

The child (and to a lesser extent, the adult) does not
come to therapy motivated to gain insight into the
psychodynamic processes which underlie his problems. In
fact, he generally does not consider himself to have
difficulties. It is his parents, teachers, and other powerful
authority figures who have decided that he has them. But
even those children who recognize that they do, do not
clearly appreciate how the things we want them to do with
us in our offices are going to bring about an alleviation of
their troubles.(We ourselves have difficulty clearly understanding the relationship between our therapeutic
approaches and the changes we hope to effect with them.)
Therefore, the child therapist does well to avoid too much
emphasis on trying to derive a statement from the child

about the exact nature of his difficulties and on extracting avowals of the child's desire to alleviate them. Even when he does get such testimonials of insight and intent to change, he should not take them too seriously; more often than not they are professed to ingratiate the therapist and to comply with parental requests. One should be thankful that the child is coming and hope that, at some level, he does so because he wants to lessen his difficulties.

Fun

If the child isn't coming primarily to alleviate his problems, why else is he there? The word that answers that question better than any other is *fun*. I believe that the therapist who does not provide a significant amount of fun for his child patient (I refer only to the prepubertal child in this discussion; much of what I say here is *not* applicable to the adolescent) is not likely to keep the child in therapy for very long; or, if the child does continue to come, little will be accomplished. Children are extremely hedonistic; they are not particularly renowned for their willingness to suffer discomforts in the present in the hope of enjoying future rewards. (Adults are not particularly famous in this department either, but many of us do acquire the capacity.) In addition, the therapist is often competing for his patient's time with the child's friends and enjoyable afterschool recreational activities. It behooves the therapist, then, to make his sessions as enjoyable as possible. This does not mean that he should reduce himself to the level of the clown or function as a playgound director. (The observer should not be able to ask: "To do this, he had to become a doctor?") Rather, he must weave the therapy into the play and other enjoyable experiences he provides the child. He must make the therapy an intrinsic part of the enjoyable experience. The therapy and pleasurable experience must be the warp and woof of the same fabric. He must so sweeten the medicine that there is little, if any, evidence of its sour taste. If he uses play therapy, it should be both *play* and *therapy*. All too often it is only *play* rationalized as therapy. It is this necessity to combine art and science that is the child therapist's greatest challenge, but it can also provide him with his greatest gratifications.

I refer to these factors that attract the child into involving himself in the therapeutic activities as the *seductive* elements in child therapy. They not only serve to keep the child coming but, in addition, enrich the therapy and make it far more likely that the child will find his experiences with the therapist meaningful. If we liken pure intellectual insight to the words of a play on the printed page, then the true therapeutic experience would be analogous to actually being a participant and playing one of the parts. Obviously, a play is far more meaningful when one acts one of the parts than when one merely reads the script. Other analogies come to mind: the difference between seeing the blueprints of a building and actually viewing and walking through the edifice, or between reading a musical score and actually listening to the music played by an orchestra, or between hearing about a sexual act and actually engaging in it oneself. To provide our patients with insight alone is to give them a relatively sterile experience compared with the deeper impact we possibly can offer them. Frieda Fromm-Reichmann put it well when she said, "The patient doesn't need an insight. He needs an experience."

Many forms of therapy attempt to provide the child with such enriching experiences. This is particularly true of the various forms of play therapy. When storytelling is a part of such therapy (whether the stories be told by the child and/or the therapist) one can gain the benefit of allegorical communication — so universally enjoyable to the child. Dramatization of one's therapeutic messages is a most efficacious way of communicating them, especially with younger children. This requires of the therapist the ability to be somewhat of a "ham" himself as well as some degree of comfort with involving himself in floor play, animal noises, various forms of childlike physical activity, etc. If the therapist is comfortable enough to allow himself such regressive behavior, he can provide the child with highly valuable therapeutic exposures.

The ability to introduce these elements into the child's therapeutic situation requires the acquisition of talents far above those required of the adult therapist — who need only devote his life to the overwhelming task of acquiring competence in helping his patients gain insight and providing them with the array of other traditional therapeutic experiences.

Candy and Other Foods

There are therapists who claim that having candy and other foods available is very helpful in establishing a good relationship with the child — especially since food is so often a symbol of love. I believe that it is important that the therapist appreciate that he can provide the child with some affection (that may even be very deep), but the parents of his patients — whatever their problems, whatever their deficiencies, and whatever deprivations the child may have suffered because of them — are generally more loving of the child than he. They are the ones who are providing the child with food, clothing, and shelter. They are the ones who continually devote themselves to him. Generally, at least one of them is ever available to protect, guide, educate, nurse, discipline, and involve himself in whatever else may be necessary to the child's welfare. They are the ones who suffer all the discomforts and sacrifices attendant to his upbringing — their gratifications from the process notwithstanding. Their bringing their child to therapy — involving as it does sacrifices of time and money — is in itself another manifestation of their love. The therapist is getting, therefore, a selected population. Those who have little, if any, affection for their children are not bothering, not suffering the discomforts of bringing the child to treatment. It is the parents who are changing the diapers in the middle of the night, sitting up with the sick child, worrying about his being scapegoated, etc. The therapist doesn't have these obligations. It is easier for him, therefore, to exhibit affection; but it is naive of him to think that he can provide a degree of love anywhere close to that which most of the parents of his patients are providing.

At best the therapist can provide the child with some affection in compensation for some of the privations he may have suffered. This, if it is in any way to be meaningful, must evolve from an ever-deepening relationship. At best, candy can play an insignificant role in bringing about such a relationship. The therapist must appreciate that food is a *symbol* for love; it is not a *replacement* for love. It is not the real thing. There are therapists who are somewhat deficient in providing that degree of affection optimum in the therapeutic situation and who may try to compensate for their deficiencies in this regard by providing food. Such therapists may be entrenching a common parental problem in which the parent uses food to compensate for his deficiencies in providing genuine affection.

Accordingly, I feel that the important thing is that a good relationship be established with the child. If this exists then the need to provide substitutes or symbols will not be there. I myself do have lollipops available for their minor seductive value and that's all. I do not provide other foods. I would not say that providing more food is necessarily therapeutically contraindicated; rather, I believe that it doesn't help significantly and that there is a danger that it can be used, as described, in an antitherapeutic way. In short, I think that there are more disadvantages than advantages to using food as a method of engaging the child in entrenching the therapeutic relationship.

Taking the Child's Side in His Conflict with His Parents

There are therapists who believe that taking the child's side against parents or other authority figures is a good way of engaging the child in treatment and entrenching the therapeutic relationship. One of the earliest and most well-known proponents of this approach was August Aichhorn, a Viennese schoolmaster who tried to apply Freudian psychoanalytic techniques to the treatment of delinquent boys. In his classic *Wayward Youth* (1925) he describes the difficulties that arose in such boys' treatment because they were very defiant of authority and tended to see him as another such authority against whom to rebel. He found however, that if he looked at the world from their vantage point and identified with them in their antisocial attitudes, he could form a relationship with them. In words, but not in act, he expressed sympathy for their antisocial behavior. He would become a psychological ally in order to win their confidence. Once such a relationship was established he would gradually shift his position and attempt to bring about a stronger superego in the youngsters. His hope was that their desire to maintain their relationship with him would motivate them to follow along with him as he encouraged and became a model for pro-social behavior.

There is an obvious duplicity involved in such an approach and I myself would not be comfortable utilizing it. I think that most youngsters would sense the therapist's artificiality and would thereby lose respect for him — and this could not but be antitherapeutic. Most therapists today would not utilize this approach.

There are therapists, however, who consider themselves to be the protectors of the child against the indignities he suffers at the hands of the parents. Such a position has a divisive effect on the family. It puts the child in between the therapist and the parents in a tug-of-war — and this cannot but be antitherapeutic. To a lesser degree there are therapists who feel that they should try to take the child's position whenever possible and tend to side with him in order to engage him in treatment and entrench the relationship. I think this is an error. I think that the child should come to see the therapist as impartial, as being ready to criticize him when he feels the child is criticizable, and equally ready to criticize the parents when he considers them to be in error. Ideally, both parties, both parents and child, should come to see the therapist as truly impartial, as attempting to be as objective as possible, and not favoring anyone. They should come to see him as siding with healthy behavior, regardless of who exhibits it; and siding against unhealthy behavior, regardless of who manifests it. Generally, the criticisms tend to balance out and no one tends to feel that the therapist is prejudiced against him. In such an atmosphere both the child and parents will generally come to respect the therapist. Whereas, when the therapist attempts to favor the child, he will alienate the parents and lose the respect of the child, who will sense his duplicity — a situation that is most antitherapeutic.

Child Talk

There are those (both therapists and nontherapists) who tend to use "baby talk" with children in the obvious attempt to ingratiate themselves to them. Although infants may like this sort of thing, the average child of five to six and above gets turned off by it. He wants to believe that he is more mature than he actually is; therefore, communicating with him with babyish intonations and language is alienating.

Generally, the therapist does well to speak to the child as he would to an adult — with the important exception that he avoids using words that he suspects the child will not understand. Such an approach can in itself be therapeutic. Speaking to the child in this manner helps enhance his self-esteem, (as mentioned, enhancing self-esteem is one of the universal antidotes to most, if not all, forms of psychogenic pathology.) It makes him feel bigger and more mature. Avoiding the use of words he will not understand protects him from the ego-debasing experience of his being talked to with words he cannot comprehend. Such exposure may result in his thinking: "How stupid I am. I cannot understand what he is saying."

To avoid using words that the child cannot understand

and to speak at his level, I have found certain words and expressions particularly useful. They are terms that the child is generally familiar with and they not only enhance communication but improve the therapist-patient relationship. When referring to the child's psychological difficulties I usually prefer to use words such as *worries, troubles,* or *problems.* One does better to use the word *scared* rather than *afraid* and *mad* rather than *angry.* Other useful words are: *mean* (rather than *cruel*), *brave* ("That was very brave of you"), *silly* (instead of *foolish*), *dirty trick, grown-up* (instead of *adult*), *kind* ("That was a very kind thing to do"), *big* (rather than *large*), *make believe, manners* ("That was very bad manners"), *mistake* ("That was a big mistake"), *pick on, polite* ("That wasn't very polite"), *proud* ("That must have made you very proud"), *student* (rather than *pupil*), *scold, scary, really* ("He smiled but he was really very sad inside"), *share, smart, tease, teenager* (the incarnation of all the desirable traits the child may aspire to acquire), *treat, trick, cry* (not *weep*), and *whisper.* When referring to other children's behavior or to a figure in a story (who may symbolically represent the patient), I have found useful such words as : *brat, spoiled brat, dumb, bully, crybaby, stupid, bad* (rather than *naughty*), *stingy, teacher's pet, temper tantrum, selfish, sissy, stupid, sore loser,* and *scaredy-cat.*

While playing a game with a child I may say such things as "Ooooh, are *you* lucky," "You're a lucky stiff," or "Boy, is this your lucky day." When things go badly for me I may exclaim: "Rats!" or "Gee, this is *really* your lucky day." And when he wins: "And you thought you weren't good. You're really a very good player," or (while shaking the child's hand) "Congratulations. Excellent game. You played beautifully." Shaking the child's hand provides an extra dramatic touch that strengthens the effect of the message.

When a child hesitates to tell me something or tells his mother not to tell me, I incredulously reply: "What, keeping a secret from your *own* psychiatrist?" Emphasizing the word *own* introduces an ego-enhancing element to counterbalance the possible esteem-lowering effects of the statement. However, there is an associated quality of good humor (communicated by my gesture, facial expression, and intonations) that conveys to the child that I am not bitterly condemning him for his embarrassment over his "transgression." A stance of incredulity can help the child express thoughts and feelings that he might otherwise have difficulty talking about. For example, "You mean never in your *whole life* — in the seven years that you have been alive — you not once had hateful feelings toward your brother?" Emphasizing the words *whole life* tends to add a subtle dramatic quality that the child himself often utilizes in his own talk. It is important that the therapist not be excessively condemning when expressing such surprised disbelief. It the *quality* of the communication, more than its *content*, that will determine whether or not the message will be ego-debasing.

In a conversation in which the child expresses something that I consider maladaptive (either on his part or on the part of someone else) but which he does not recognize as such, I may say, "Do you want to know what *my* opinion is about what Robert did?" Emphasizing the word *my* tends to imply that I am not necessarily right — only that I am expressing an alternative view. The therapist's always being "right" (which is usually the case) tends to undermine the child's self-esteem and is an antitherapeutic element in even the most-well-conducted therapy engaged in by the most sensitive therapist. Hopefully, other ego-enhancing experiences will outweigh this untoward effect of the treatment. If after the ensuing discussion the child and I still differ, I do not push the point — I do not get into an argument. Rather, I say, "Well, I guess we have different opinions on that. Perhaps sometime one of us may change his mind. Why don't we go on to something else?"

When a mother reports that the child has exhibited an important clinical breakthrough and is no longer exhibiting a particular pathological pattern, I will often ask him to sit next to me (and even in my seat if he is small enough) and observe as I slowly and emphatically write in his chart: "I am very happy to learn that three weeks have passed now and Ronald hasn't once picked on another boy or girl. I am very proud of him and he must be very proud of himself." I may then ask him to fetch a pen from my desk (such as a Flair pen or a Magic Marker) and I then dramatically encircle the note. Sometimes I will have him read the message aloud for further reinforcement. Similarly, when a child exhibits what I consider particularly dangerous or pathological behavior I may say, "I'm very sorry, James, but I'm going to have to put that in your chart." I will then emphatically write: "James was once again found playing with matches. I hope that I never have to write this in his chart again." These dramatically written notations serve as an added touch to whatever therapeutic approaches are being used. They add additional positive and negative reinforcement. The closer the relationships the therapist has with the child, the greater effectiveness they will have.

Magic Tricks

One of the most predictable ways to make oneself attractive to a child is to show him a few magic tricks. It is a rare child who is so recalcitrant, uncooperative, distractible, etc. who will not respond affirmatively to the therapist's question: "Would you like to see a magic trick?" Although not generally useful as primary, high-efficiency therapeutic tools, magic tricks can be extremely useful in facilitating the child's involvement with the therapist. Only five minutes spent in such activities can make a significant session. The anxious child will generally be made less tense and will then be freer to engage in higher-order therapeutic activities. The child who is very resistant often becomes less so after such an "ice breaker." The uninvolved or distractible child will usually become quite interested in them and will then be more readily shifted into more efficient therapeutic activities. In short, they facilitate attention and involvement. In addition, because they make the therapist more fun to be with and more attractive to the child, they contribute to a deepening of the therapeutic relationship which, as already emphasized, is the mainstay of the therapeutic process.

The therapist does well, in my opinion, to gradually build a small collection of the kinds of card tricks, magic boxes and cups, secret mazes, etc. readily purchased in many toy stores (preferably those specializing in "magic"). This small investment of time and money may have significant therapeutic dividends. My previous warning that the therapist should not reduce himself to the level of a clown still holds. I am not suggesting that the therapist become a magician for the child; rather, he should use such tricks on occasion, for short periods of time, for their value in facilitating more highly efficient therapeutic interchanges. The therapist interested in an excellent discussion of the use of such tricks in therapy should refer to Moskowitz's article (1973) in which he describes the aforementioned uses of magic as well as its more extensive value as a therapeutic modality.

In conclusion, I wish to emphasize that seduction of the kind I describe in this chapter is not directly effective in breaking down resistances; rather, it lessens the likelihood that they will form and serves to facilitate working them through when they arise.

Chapter Four
Parental Involvement in the Child's Therapy

In introduction, I would like to comment at length on the issue of confidentiality because it is so crucial to my subsequent discussion.

Confidentiality in Adult Therapy

I am fully appreciative of the importance of confidentiality in therapeutic work with the adult patient. If the adult fears that what he says to his therapist is going to be freely divulged to others, the likelihood that he will reveal himself fully is extremely small. Accordingly, his chances of forming a good relationship with the therapist will be seriously reduced and the probability of his gaining anything therapeutic from the experience will be meager. However, there are times, I believe, when it is appropriate for the therapist *not* to respect his adult patient's confidentiality — in deference to more vital considerations. For example, if a patient exhibits strong suicidal tendencies it is an obvious disservice to him to comply with his request that his family not be informed and their aid enlisted. Similarly, it would be an obvious disservice to others if a patient's homicidal tendencies were not revealed to those who are at risk and/or to those whose involvement will be necessary to ensure that the patient will not be permitted to act these out.

Respect for confidentiality is not, therefore, in my opinion, the highest consideration between the therapist and the patient. There are higher considerations, one of which is what would be most beneficial therapeutically. Sometimes it is therapeutically benefical for the therapist to bring in other significant figures — even against the wishes of the patient — and the sicker the patient the greater the likelihood that the therapist may have to resort to this outside assistance. Another higher consideration is the protection of innocent parties from danger.

On those rare occasions when I have had to reveal my adult patient's confidentiality, I have proceeded on the assumption that there are healthy forces within the patient that are in agreement with my action, in spite of his overt protestations over my divulgence.

A good example of this phenomenon occurred a few years ago when a patient told me that he suspected his wife of infidelity and had hired a private detective to help him determine whether his suspicions were justified. About two weeks later he called me in a state of agitated rage. The detective had confirmed his suspicions and he told me that he planned to go home and kill his wife with a gun that he had in the house. He felt that this was the only way he could "save face." He agreed, however, to come to my office en route home to discuss the matter further.

After about two hours of discussion I still did not feel secure that my patient would not act out his homicidal impulses. I confronted him with the various options that were open to me: two of which were to call the police and/or call his wife. When he raised the issue of confidentiality, I told him that more important considerations now prevailed and I would not let my pledge to preserve his confidences allow me to do nothing while another human being's life was at stake. After much further discussion I still did not gain his permission to call his wife. In spite of his protestations I did so. It is beyond the scope of my discussion here to go into detail into the ensuing events. In short, after further discussion I decided that the safest and most prudent course would be for the wife to join us in our discussions. A few hours later (after about six hours of continuous discussion) I felt that I could safely let the patient return home with his wife. (Needless to say, arrangements were first made for the gun to be disposed of.)

I believe that this patient was basically ambivalent about murdering his wife. Had he been fully resolved to kill her, he would not have called me. In his scheme of things, the only way he could preserve his masculinity was to take revenge. Healthier and more rational forces were operating, however (otherwise he would not have called me and , in addition, agree to discuss the matter en route home), and it was to these that I appealed when I would not respect his confidentiality. What I did, however, demonstrated what I consider to have been even greater respect for my patient, namely, I did everything possible to interrupt an act for which he would probably have suffered regret for the rest of his life.

Confidentiality in Adolescent Therapy

The adolescent needs, as part of his healthy growth and development, to have a separate relationship with the therapist. Having parents too deeply involved in his therapy can compromise the adolescent's maturing process and entrench his dependency — and this cannot be but antitherapeutic. Accordingly, I usually see adolescents in individual sessions. In addition, most of my adolescents are seen in group therapy because I have found this to be a therapeutic modality particularly suited to patients in this age group. Reluctant as they often are to be alone with a therapist for the interminable period of 45-50 minutes, the group offers them an opportunity to be silent at times without embarrassment or pressure to speak. In addition, their receptivity to — and even slavish dependence on — peer opinion can prove therapeutically useful. The adolescent is much more likely to take advice from a peer than from an adult. He is more receptive to confrontations from those of his own age level than from those, like the therapist, of his parents' age. The group then can be very helpful in involving otherwise resistant adolescents into meaningful therapy.

Regarding the issue of confidentiality, early in treatment (if not in the first session) an adolescent will frequently say to me: "Are you going to tell my parents the things I tell you?" I generally respond by telling the adolescent that what he tells me will be kept confidential and that I will not divulge to his parents what he speaks about in his sessions. However, I will *also* tell him that if he is involving himself in some kind of behavior that is extremely destructive *and* that he cannot stop after discussions with me and/or members of the adolescent group, I may very well have to resort to divulging what he tells me, even though he may not wish me to do so. I do not specify what kinds of things I have in mind. I don't provide the adolescent with "food for thought" or a list of things he can do and what things he can expect will be divulged. Enumerating such a list can provide the acting-out prone and/or hostile child with "suggestions" that he might not have otherwise thought of and thereby add to his difficulties. Generally I have in mind such things as severe forms of antisocial behavior in which other people may be harmed and persistent utilization of drugs with the danger of addiction. I would not include occasional smoking of marijuana in this category, but heavy use of marijuana on a daily or on a many-times-a-week basis would warrant, in my opinion, the parents' being informed. A girl who is exposing herself to pregnancies and possible veneral diseases, and who could not refrain from doing so, might very well have to be told that unless she can inhibit herself I may have to bring the parents in for whatever assistance they might provide.

My experience has been that adolescents, who may vociferously condemn me for having revealed their confidences in such situations (and this hasn't occurred often), are most often inwardly pleased that I am doing so. Frequently, if not always, they are really asking for some kind of help — for some kind of outside interference. But the adolescent cannot often place himself in the dependent state and ask for the help (because his need to maintain a facade of adult independence is so strong), but he can accept help more easily if it is forced upon him. He can thereby preserve his fragile image of self-reliance and independence by essentially saying to himself: "It is not I who asked for help like a baby. It was only after I submitted to overwhelming forces that I allowed myself to surrender. One cannot but admire my courage."

I had an experience a few years ago that demonstrates this mechanism quite well. A mother called me, quite upset that her seventeen-year-old daughter, who was in treatment with me, had called her from New York City. (I practice in a suburban New Jersey community.) The patient called from a friend's house and the mother knew the telephone number of the friend and the exact location of the friend's home. The girl said that she was running away from home, that she could stand it no longer, that she was going to live in Greenwich Village and devote herself to a life of indulgence in sex and drugs, and that she would never be seen again. However, the only thing that would get her back home was if Dr. Gardner were to commit her to the Bergen Pines Hospital (my local central receiving hospital). I told the mother that she should call her daughter right back and tell her that she had spoken to me and I had said that if she wasn't home in two hours I would, at that time, commit her to Bergen Pines Hospital. Now I had absolutely no such authority. I felt, however, that the girl was really pleading to be given an excuse for coming back. And, as I had predicted, she was home in less than two hours and was cursing me terribly and, of course, the next day she continued ranting and raving to her friends about the indignities she had suffered at my hands. I felt that she was basically quite frightened about the prospects of the kind of life she professed she wanted to lead and could not allow herself to come home and say that she had made a mistake or that she was afraid to go to Greenwich Village. By enlisting my "aid" in the way she did she could present herself as having fought valiantly and having been overwhelmed by the mighty figures around her, especially Dr. Gardner with his power to commit her to Bergen Pines Hospital. Not to have provided this girl with the threat she was begging for would have allowed entrenchment of pathological processes. The vignette has been presented not particularly as an example of a divulged confidence, but as a demonstration of the wish for help that may often present itself as a disguised wish that the therapist take action in spite of the patient's protestations to the contrary.

Confidentiality in Child Therapy

With regard to the child, I have an even stronger position regarding the limitations of confidentiality. I believe that child therapists have too readily accepted the adult model of psychotherapy (especially psychoanalysis) as applicable to work with children. I appreciate fully the numerous therapeutic techniques that have been devised specifically for children. However, much of the basic theoretical framework and therapeutic structure used in child therapy has been accepted indiscriminately from the adult model. The confidentiality issue is a case in point. Whereas adults may reveal many things to the therapist that should not be divulged, and whereas the adolescent needs to have such confidences respected as part of the developmental process, the average child (below the age of ten or eleven) has little in his life that realistically is unknown to the parents or should appropriately be kept secret from them. I am not saying that he is not entitled to his inner thoughts and his privacy, but when it comes to therapeutic considerations the advantages of their being revealed far outweigh, in my opinion, the disadvantages.

It is of interest that Sigmund Freud (1909) in his famous analysis of Little Hans, the first child to be treated by psychoanalytic techniques, did not give any consideration to Hans's privacy. Having no guidelines regarding the application of the psychoanalytic method to the treatment of children, Freud decided to have the father treat the child himself under Freud's guidance. It would have been more consistent with Freud's previous pattern to have treated the child himself. From all possible alternative approaches, he chose to have the father serve as therapist. Freud clearly states his reasons for this dramatic departure: "No one else, in my opinion, could possibly have prevailed on the child to make such avowals; the special knowledge by means of which he was able to interpret the remarks made by his five-year-old son was indispensable and without it the technical difficulties in the way of conducting a psychoanalysis upon so young a child would have been insuperable." I think it is unfortunate that most therapists have ignored this aspect of Little Hans's treatment. The psychodynamic theories that were considered by Freud to have been confirmed in Hans's treatment have almost become gospel; whereas the actual structure of the therapy — especially Freud's choice of the father as therapist and the attendant ignoring of Hans's privacy — is often completely ignored.

Although Freud was a strong proponent of confidentiality for his adult patients, there were no such considerations for Little Hans. His deepest and most humiliating secrets were to be directly revealed to his father, the person with whom one would think he would be most hesitant to discuss them. There is little evidence that Hans felt the need for confidentiality or that the therapy was an "invasion of his privacy." There is little reason to believe that Hans's treatment was in any way compromised or otherwise interfered with by his being asked to reveal himself to his father. Even in Freud's one interview with Hans, the father was present. Yet, the more ardently and strictly the classical child analyst adheres to the Freudian theories, the less the likelihood he would have such an interview.

Most therapists, regardless of their therapeutic orientation, would not instruct a parent in the therapy of his own child. First, to be a therapist requires many years of exacting training and experience. Since the parent (with rare exception) has not had such training, he is ill-equipped to conduct such therapy, and to teach him to treat his own child would be a disservice to the patient. In addition, the child's parent cannot have the objectivity which the therapist must have toward his patient if the therapy is to be successful. Yet Freud seems to have ignored these considerations. Irving Stone, in his recent novel on Freud (1971), states that Hans's father was one Max Graf, a graduate in jurisprudence, a doctorate in music, and an editor. He was one of the members of Freud's weekly discussion group and therefore had some familiarity with psychoanalytic theory. Neither Freud nor Stone describes him as having had any previous experience as a therapist. But even if he had, Freud did not believe that he would be impaired enough by lack of objectivity to be disqualified as an effective therapist (which he apparently proved to be.)

It is of interest that Melanie Klein, Anna Freud, and the child psychoanalysts who followed them — although basically accepting the Freudian theory (the differences among them notwithstanding) — did not generally utilize the parents in the treatment process. In fact, at the present time most classical child analysts, although they may get a history from the parents, confine their treatment exclusively to the child. They recognize that involvement with the parents may have therapeutic benefit; but the greater such involvement, the less they consider the treatment to be justifiably called psychoanalysis — which they consider to be the most definitive, reconstructive, and therapeutic form of therapy for those patients for whom it is the indicated treatment. Yet there is no question that Freud considered Hans to have been psychoanalyzed. A strange paradox.

Although I am in agreement with Freud that parental involvement can be useful, I am in disagreement with his statement that "no one else . . . could possibly have prevailed on the child to make such avowals." There was someone else who could probably have been even more knowledgeable than the father about the details of Hans's life: his mother. If the family was typical of other Viennese families at the turn of the century (and we have good reason to believe that it was), Hans's father probably had little to do with him. Although middle-class mothers also delegated much of the child's care to nursemaids, they were still much more in contact with their children than were fathers. Perhaps Freud's choice of the father was a manifestation of male chauvinism characterized by a basic feeling that men were intrinsically better suited to this kind of work. We know that Hans's mother had previously been a patient of Freud's; perhaps this was a consideration. But such deliberations must be speculative. My main points are that Freud recognized the value of the parent as therapist and did not consider the divulgence of the child's privacy an important consideration. The reader who is interested in further elaboration of the aforementioned aspects of Little Hans's case, as well as my views regarding other facets of Little Hans's treatment, may wish to refer to my article (1972e).

For many years I myself practiced in the traditional way and saw my child patients alone, left the mother in the waiting room, and would only bring her in intermittently or would see her in separate sessions. Over the years I became increasingly dissatisfied with this method. If something were to come up in a session that I thought would be important for the mother to know about, I would bring her in and, in the last few minutes of the session, quickly give her a rundown on what had happened and would them make some recommendations. I generally found that the mother would usually have little conviction for the recommendations because she had not been witness to the situation that brought them about and time did not often permit my elaborating on them. When I started to keep the mothers in the room I found that the child generally did not object and, in addition, the mother could carry through with my recommendations with deeper conviction. Having directly observed the events that resulted in my suggestions and having had the time to discuss them with me in detail resulted in the mothers' more frequently and effectively carrying them out. I found also that very few children expressed a desire to see me alone. They had not read the books that we have that emphasize the importance of confidentiality and had no preconceived notion that therapy was supposed to be a private matter between the child and therapist.

Once in the room, I found the mother valuable in many other ways. The younger the child, the less likely he is able to recall events that occurred since his last session. Knowledge of these is often vital to the understanding of many of the child's therapeutic productions. The mother proved to be a ready source of this important information. In analyzing the child's dreams, for example, I found the mother's assistance to be invaluable. She would often be able to tell me something about a dream element that made its meaning clear; whereas a child's associations to a dream often did not provide me with enough information for us to meaningfully analyze it. In understanding a child's self-created stories, I have also found the mother useful. The understanding of such stories is vital to meaningful utilization of the Mutual Storytelling Technique (see Chapter Five); for without a valid understanding of the child's story the therapist is ill-equipped to create a corresponding one of his own. The information given by the mother often provided just the added elements necessary for my creating a useful story. At the end of this chapter I will present clinical examples demonstrating these and other ways in which the parent has proved useful.

From these experiences and considerations has evolved the following treatment structure I use for most children below the ages of ten to eleven. The parent who brings the child generally stays in the room with the child and me throughout the session. A typical session begins with the child's being invited to discuss anything he wishes to. Generally, he talks about recent events. I try to gear him toward discussing material that I consider to be therapeutically useful. The mother joins in as indicated. Sometimes the discussion may last five minutes; at other times it may last throughout the whole session. When the point of low therapeutic return is reached, the child and I then proceed to involve ourselves in a variety of other therapeutic activities, either traditional or nontraditional (some of the latter group will be described in subsequent chapters). Sometime it is the father who brings the child, sometimes both parents, and on occasion even a sibling or two join us. (The child's permission is asked regarding a sibling's joining us. However, the request is rarely refused. The siblings are often excited about coming because they have heard about the fun things that take place in my office; and the patient is often proud to show off his special opportunity to play these enjoyable games.) Generally, the parent stays with the child throughout the course of treatment. However, if the treatment is prolonged to the point where the child reaches the prepubertal period, the whole treatment pattern is changed. Not only is the parent not then present but our involvement in the kinds of games to be discussed in this book (as well as in traditional play therapy) is discontinued. It is important for the reader to appreciate that I am not describing here *family therapy* (which, incidentally I do when indicated — either as an adjunct to a child's treatment or as a treatment program per se). The best name I can give for this treatment approach (admittedly cumbersome but nevertheless well describing what I do) is : *individual child therapy with parental observation and intermittent participation.*

I do not wish to give the impression that I rigidly force this treatment pattern on all children. There are many children below the age of ten or eleven who should justifiably be treated alone. They are, however, in my opinion and experience, in the minority and the younger the patient the greater the benefits to be derived from active parental involvement. What I consider unfortunate is the traditional view (often rigidly held) that children automatically should be seen alone and that the parental presence must inevitably be a contaminant. I believe that the ideal approach should be a more flexible one in which the alternative of active parental involvement be seriously considered. My experience has been that when one approaches therapy planning in this way most children will do best with parental involvement. However, there are definite exceptions.

The child who is overly dependent on his mother and/or the child who is overprotected by her (in severe form such relationships are often referred to as "symbiotic") needs a separate therapeutic experience from the mother. To see them together as the general therapeutic pattern may only entrench the problem. However, even in such cases an occasional joint session may be indicated to demonstrate more meaningfully the pathological pattern.

When the parent is borderline psychotic, or more overtly psychotic, and so poorly defended that he or she would not be able to tolerate the therapeutic revelations (even when symbolically expressed), then parental participation is contraindicated. Exposure of such a parent to the child's therapy is not only inhumane but any benefits the child may derive from his treatment will be more than counterbalanced by the deleterious effects of the parent's psychiatric deterioration.

At times it may be necessary to keep the overbearing and intrusive parent out of the room. However, a child may also profit from occasional joint sessions in which such a parent's behavior is pointed out and discouraged and the child is encouraged to assert himself against it. When this is first done in the therapist's presence (with his implied protection of the child from the terrible consequences he anticipates will result from his self-assertion), it becomes easier for the child to express himself subsequently outside the office. Similarly, the child who is excessively fearful of expressing hostility to a parent may need the individual sessions if he is to express any hostility at all. However, with such children, I try to reach a point where the child does become comfortable enough to express his anger directly to the parent and, as described above, this is more easily done first in the therapist's presence.

A rare but nevertheless very important situation in which the parent's presence is generally contraindicated is the one in which the parent is suffering with an incurable disease and he is using denial and other related defense mechanisms as the way of dealing with his reactions to the illness. To expose such a parent to his child's attempts to work out his own feelings about the parental illness may not only be cruel to the parent but may lessen the chance that the child will reveal his true feelings because of his probable appreciation (depending upon his age, intelligence, and sophistication) that his revelations may be deleterious to his parent.

One of the arguments often given for seeing the child alone is that the child needs to have a new special relationship formed with the therapist and that the presence of a third party compromises the formation of such a strong and deep involvement. I have not found this to be the case in most situations. I have not found the presence of the parent to compromise my relationship with the child. I do not think that one has to keep the child alone in a room in order to evolve a good relationship with him. All too often, when the child is seen alone, the child and therapist become "we" and the parents become "they." It's "us" *and* "them"; and this easily becomes "us" *vs.* "them." An artifical and unnecessary family schism may be created and this cannot but compromise the therapy. The child may find himself in the middle of a conflict regarding his loyalty — involvement with one results in feelings of disloyalty to the other. The child usually has enough problems already; he doesn't need a new one added by the therapeutic structure. With the parent in the room, however, such an antitherapeutic schism is less likely to occur. If the therapist is truly neutral, the child is likely to look upon him as someone who is deeply involved, or at least benevolently involved, with both of his parents.

Another benefit to be derived from this kind of approach is that it lessens the probability of the parents' removing their child from treatment because of their guilt over his illness. A parent generally feels guilty about bringing his child to a therapist. He repeatedly asks himself: "What did I do wrong? Where did I fail? I love him so. I tried to hard and yet look what's happened." As I have described elsewhere (1969b, 1969d, and 1970c), such guilt is, in part, related to the attempt to control a situation in which one feels helpless. For control is intrinsically involved in the notion: "It's my fault." Although other factors may certainly be operative (such as unconscious hostility toward the child), the control factor, I believe, is the more common. A common way of alleviating such guilt is that of removing the child from therapy with the rationalization that he doesn't need it. It is as if the parent were saying: "There's nothing wrong with him. He doesn't need therapy. So I have nothing to feel guilty about." Such guilt, I believe, is more constructively and realistically alleviated by the parents' actively participating in the therapy. By assisting the therapist the parent directly counteracts the feelings of impotence that are at the basis of his guilt. Psychoanalysis of this and other factors in the parental guilt may be helpful — but understanding per se has limitations. It is only when analytic insight is translated into action that meaninguful changes occur. And active parental participation provides the parent with just such an opportunity.

The parent will often feel rivalrous toward the therapist. In fact, such feelings are probably inevitable. The parents are asking the therapist to succeed in doing what they have failed at. They may observe their child to exhibit a respect for and admiration of the therapist that they do not ostensibly receive. If the child is seen alone, he may often speak to the therapist about things that he does not divulge to the parents. Such rivalrous feelings are inevitably picked up by the child and produce the aforementioned divided-loyalty conflict. If too painful for the parent they may result in the child's being removed from therapy. When the parent serves as an adjunctive therapist, many of the causes of such antitherapeutic rivalry are obviated.

I believe that one of the reasons why a therapist may hesitate to let parents observe his work is that he may be ashamed to have the parents see exactly what he is doing. If the parents are outside they may envision highly effective and therapeutic operations taking place between the child and therapist. However, if they are direct observers of exactly what the therapist is doing, they may become disillusioned. This is especially true if he is engaging in what I consider to be low-order therapeutic experiences such as building models, playing checkers repeatedly, or playing chess. The parent may justifiably complain and say something like: "For this he had to become a doctor?" "For this I'm paying all this money?" If the therapist himself is involved in higher-order therapeutic activities (some of which I will discuss in subsequent chapters), he will have less to be ashamed about and will be more receptive to parental observations. However, even when engaging in the higher-order therapeutic activities in which one is really doing effective and efficient therapy, the parent may still interpret what he sees as low-order treatment or even consider the activities a waste of time and money. Accordingly, he may remove the child from treatment; and this might not have been the case had he been sitting out in the waiting room and imagining all kinds of more sophisticated encounters. So there is a potential drawback to having the parent present; but this disadvantage, in my opinion, is small compared to the many advantages. Each therapeutic procedure has its drawbacks and active parental participation is no exception.

A related advantage to the parent's presence is that it stimulates the therapist to do his best. Being observed all the time lessens the likelihood that he will fall into slipshod and time-wasting activities with the child. This is even more true when the sessions are being tape-recorded for home listening (a practice that I will soon elaborate upon).

There are therapists who take the position that they are the protector of the child against the indignities that he suffers at the hands of his parents. I think that that is an unrealistic position for him to take — because the family environment *among those who voluntarily bring their children for treatment* is rarely that deleterious. Such an attitude contributes to the kind of family schism that I have already discussed. The therapist does best to look upon the parents as people who have tried very hard at all times to do their best in spite of their problems; but things have gone wrong because they have been misguided, and/or blinded or paralyzed by their psychiatric problems. The fact that they are coming to the therapist is a statement of their interest and affection for the child. Or, if at least one parent is coming then it's a statement of that parent's interest. Whatever problems the parents may have, scorn of them is totally antithetical to the treatment process. Parents will inevitably pick up the therapist's feelings toward them. If he is condescending, if he basically looks upon them as the criminals who have perpetrated terrible acts upon the child or who have malevolently provided him with a deleterious environment, they will pick up these feelings and either remove the child from treatment or undermine it with their responding reactions.

One last comment on confidentiality. About six or seven years ago, when I was using the audio- rather than the videotape recorder in connection with the Mutual Storytelling Technique (which I will describe in Chapter Five), a nine-year-old girl came into the session one day with her own tape recorder and asked if it would be all right to tape what was going on between us so she could listen to it at home. I told her that it was not only agreeable to me, but that I was pleased that she wished to do so. In a subsequent session she told me how her parents liked to listen to the tapes at home with her (at that time her mother sat in the waiting room) and even her sisters. She had no feeling of divulgence of privacy whatsoever.

It was from this experience that I soon came to recommend to all patients (regardless of age) that they bring a cassette tape recorder to every session, tape-record the *whole* session, and listen to the tape between sessions. The practice provides reiteration of the therapeutic messages and experiences, enhances the likelihood that what happens in therapy will become meaningful, and deepens the therapeutic relationship because of the extra experience with the therapist between sessions. For the cost of a cassette tape recorder and a few tapes (which can be used again many times over) the patient can get a much more intensive therapeutic experience. Sometimes patients will save tapes that are particularly meaningful and I have had a few fairly well-off patients who have saved the complete set of tapes from the whole course of treatment. Many of my child patients (especially the younger ones) play the tapes at home in front of siblings and/or family members. The tapes on occasion serve as a point of departure for family discussion and this contributes to the family atmosphere of open communication that I usually try to create for my patients. A father, who only rarely (if ever) comes to the sessions, has an opportunity to hear what's going on. He thereby gets some idea about what he's paying his money for and, except when specifically contraindicated therapeutically (a rare situation), he's entitled to this. In addition, it keeps the father in touch with the therapist, makes him feel less of a stranger, and thereby serves to improve the relationship between the two. The father whose only contact with the therapist is the monthly bill is not likely to involve himself meaningfully in his child's treatment. Listening to the tapes of the sessions can rectify significantly this kind of compromise of the child's therapy.

The reader may have been wondering why I have discussed in such great detail the issue of confidentiality in a book designed to help the therapist deal with the inhibited or unresponsive child. I have elaborated on this issue because I believe that children's resistance to treatment often reflects similar attitudes harbored by the parents (either overtly or covertly). The child is very sensitive and responsive to parental attitudes — so much so that their views regarding therapy most often become his. An atmosphere in which the parents are openly involved in the child's therapy is, in my opinion, the best way to reduce such parental resistance.

Reducing Resistances in the Initial Interview

In the initial telephone call I generally suggest that both parents and the child come to the first interview. Again, I appreciate that this is not a traditional practice. Many therapists see the parents alone first because they feel that they can get a better history of the child's difficulties without the child's interferences and distractions and without the parents' having to compromise what they are saying because of the child's presence. I believe that the disadvantages of the traditional approach outweigh its advantages and that having all three present at the time of first contact is preferable in most situations.

First, it is very difficult for me to get a good sense of the kind of person a child is without actually seeing him. No matter how accurately the parents may describe the child's problems, the therapist's appreciation of them is significantly reduced by his not seeing the living human being who suffers with them. In addition, the child's being in the room, even if he is distracting and disruptive, can provide vital information. In fact, his actual disruptive behavior provides information. When the child is present, one can observe firsthand how the parents interact with the child — and this is crucial information. I agree that one could observe such interaction in a subsequent interview; it isn't vital that it occur in the first interview. However, when the child (and this is especially true of children over the age of six or seven) knows that the parents are coming to the therapist and talking about him (or if he learns subsequently that the parents have been to the therapist and have spoken about him), he cannot but have the feeling that things are being said about him behind his back and that the therapist and parents share secrets about him. This can compromise the formation of a good therapeutic relationship. I think that the analogy with adult therapy holds here. Most adult therapists are very appreciative of the fact that it can be very detrimental to treatment if they have information about their patients from third parties that they cannot divulge to their patients. And if the patient learns that the therapist has such information that he is not divulging, the therapeutic relationship can be significantly compromised. And the child is no different. Whether one is six or sixty, if you're standing outside a room and there are people inside talking about you and they don't let you in, you've not only got to be curious but you also must be somewhat resentful of the people who are doing this to you. And if one of the individuals is your therapist, the chance that your relationship with him will be compromised is great. To avoid these potential sources of resistance and to gain the advantages of the joint interview I most often see all three together.

The standard practice in conducting the initial interview has been for the therapist to come into the waiting room, introduce himself to the child and parent(s), and then invite the child to come into the consultation room with him alone. One of the arguments given for separating the child from the parents at the outset is that one wants, from the very beginning, to communicate to the child that he is to have a special private relationship with the therapist — a relationship that is not shared by the parents. As mentioned, I believe the potential family schism that such a relationship can form may counterbalance the therapeutic benefits of such a relationship.

In addition, if the child shows anxiety then one supposedly learns that he has "separation anxiety." I cannot imagine any child's not being anxious in this situation. In fact, every adult is anxious at the beginning of his first psychiatric interview. He wants to be liked by the therapist. He fears that the revelations are going to bring about the scorn or derision of the therapist; he fears he may be laughed at. The situation is very highly charged and I cannot imagine anyone who is seriously considering therapy not being anxious. And the child even more so. He has little appreciation of what this new and strange experience is all about. The likelihood is that he's been told things that aren't so, e.g., "You're going to see a nice lady. She's going to talk to you." "We're taking you to a nice man who'll be playing lots of fun games with you." "We're taking you to a teacher to help you learn better." etc. But even if the child is told exactly who the therapist is and what purpose he serves, the explanation may have little meaning to him. The younger he is the less concept he has of what therapy means. Yes, he's having trouble in school and he's going to talk to this man or lady about it, but how's talking to this person (or playing games with him) going to help that?

Furthermore, the person is a stranger. To take a child, whatever his age, and ask him to go off into a room alone with a stranger must enhance the anxiety that is inevitable in such situations. Accordingly, if the child exhibits some anxiety when going off with the therapist one cannot say that he has separation anxiety — with its implication of pathology. One can only say that he exhibits the usual anxiety that most children experience in such a situation. And the younger the child the greater the probability that he would not want to go alone and the greater the chance of his being anxious. To me one of the worst experiences that a child therapist can have is his trying to force or cajole a screaming, panicky child into accompanying him alone into his consultation room. As the child desperately implores his parents not to give him up to this stranger, there may be others in the waiting room who are witnessing this specter. The observers cannot but increase the child's sense of humiliation. Once in the room, the likelihood of getting meaningful information from such a frantic child is nil. In addition, the probability of developing a good therapeutic relationship with a child after a scene like this is practically zero. A heavy price is paid, therefore, for the success in separating such a child from his parents. One way of avoiding such a nightmare is simply to invite all three people in.

Occasionally a child does not wish to come into the consultation room with his parents and me, preferring rather to remain in the waiting room. Generally, I say to such a child, "Well, if you don't wish to join us, that's okay. Your mother and father will be talking with me in my office. It's right over there (and I point to it)." I then say, "We'll leave the door open a little bit and if you change your mind and if you want to come in with us we'll be happy to have you join us." The parents and I then proceed to my office. Most often the child will tag along. His anxieties over being alone can be counted on to draw him in.

I do not try to cajole the child who is reluctant to join us; nor will I start conducting my inquiry in the waiting room in front of other people. Therapy is done in my office. Now one could say: "Why be so rigid? Why not conduct the inquiry where the child wants it, even though others are present? Have you no respect for the child?" My refusal in part relates to the fact that there are personal things that the parents do not wish to have strangers know about. And I respect their right to privacy. In addition, the diagnostic and therapeutic equipment is in my office and so my efficacy is reduced in the waiting room.

On rare occasions, a child will remain in the waiting room after his parents and I have gone into my office. In such situations, after ten or fifteen minutes, I will step outside and say, "I'm going to be closing my office door now. As you know, we'll be talking about you; so if you decide that you're interested in coming in, just knock on the door and you can come in." The closed door serves to separate the child even further and hopefully he will then be drawn in. It is a very rare child who does not come in after being told, "We'll be talking about you behind this door. If you wish to come in and listen to what we're saying about you, you're invited." (I will discuss subsequently the child who *still* doesn't accept my invitation.)

With the parents and child seated (by far the most common situation) I again veer from the traditional approach. The usual opening question to the child at this time is: "Well, what brings you here?" or "What's the problem?" or "Why have you come here?" Now there are some very good arguments for starting off in this way. The question is an open one; it doesn't draw the child into specific areas. It has no contaminants. The advantages of such a question are best demonstrated by comparing it to similar questions on a job or school application. Generally such applications have two parts. The first part gets statistical data: the applicant's name, age, address, etc. Following these easy-to-answer questions there is often a big blank space at the top of which reads: "Why do you want to go to X school?" or "Why do you want to become a such-and-such?" Of course, at that point the applicant takes pause. It may take many hours to complete the answer to this question. He may go over it with friends and relatives and finally, with a fair amount of anxiety, put down the answer.

To start off a psychiatric interview with the question: "What brings you here?" is to start off with what I consider the most anxiety-provoking question. Given at a time when the patient is already anxious over the strangeness of the situation and fears he will not be liked by the therapist, it is not likely that the therapist is going to get the best possible answer. When one attempts to get information from a person who is tense, the chance of its being accurate is small and the likelihood of the inquiry being therapeutic is even smaller. Accordingly, I generally start off with the easier factual questions — especially questions that I know the child can answer. I ask him his name, address, telephone number, age, what grade he's in, what his teacher's name is, etc. While getting answers to these low-anxiety factual questions, I am not only getting information for my records but, in addition, if there are glaring areas of discrepancy or ignorance—for instance, if a seven-year-old doesn't know his address — I am already learning something else about the child as well. Then I ask the child about his mother and father: their first names, their ages, and their occupations. I ask him if he has any brothers or sisters, and if so, their names and ages. I ask if anyone else lives in the house (housekeepers and live-in relatives can play a significant role in a child's life). This initial inquiry generally takes five-to-ten minutes. As it proceeds the child generally gets more and more answers "right" and this progressively reduces his anxiety. When I finally do come to the question of what brings him to my office, I am much more likely to get a reasonable answer. What is even more important here is that I am already starting to form a good relationship with the child by avoiding an anxiety-provoking inquiry. Confronting the child at the outset with the most anxiety-provoking question of all not only reduces the changes of getting meaningful answers, but compromises the therapeutic relationship. It is in such a setting that resistances quickly begin to arise, and these can quickly become formidable.

In this phase of discussing the presenting problems I generally shift to more active involvement by the parents. The child, for instance, may deny there are any difficulties or not know what I am referring to. I will then usually say, "Well, let's hear what your parents have to say." A parent, for example, may reply at this point: "He acts up in school and he bullies children." The child may say, "I don't. They're lying." In such cases I will turn to the parents and say, "Well, Joey says you're lying. What do you say?" And they may reply, "Joey, you know we're not lying. You've seen your report card." I will then face the child and if he still insists that his parents' complaints are not valid, I will generally not push him further on the subject. I interrupt the interchange with a comment such as: "Well, I guess you and your parents have a difference of opinion on this subject. Let's hear about other problems or other things that are going on." At that point, I try not to take the parents' side against the child. I don't want to humiliate him. I don't want to put him in a position of being told, "Okay, confess. We know you did it," because that can undermine the relationship and cause the child to be resistive to treatment. I want to try to create an atmosphere in which the child feels that all parties are given a fair and unbiased hearing. After a good relationship has been established, I will be in a better position to confront him with his deficiencies. However, even then he will do well to have had the experience that I am equally likely to discuss his parents' deficits when they become apparent.

If, while his parents are presenting some of his problems a child says to them, "Ooh, don't tell him that. I told you not to tell him that. You promised me you wouldn't talk about that," I will react with amazement: "Didn't you know that there are never supposed to be any secrets from a psychiatrist?" "You mean you're keeping secrets from your *own* psychiatrist?" I impress upon the child at that point that no secrets should be kept from me and I express it through my surprise that he would even consider withholding information about himself from me. In addition, emphasizing the word *own* represents another attempt to bring us closer and compensate for any ego-lowering he may have felt over my dissatisfaction with his attempts to hide things from me.

At times, during this phase of the interview, a parent might say to me, in a whispered or mumbled voice, "Doctor, there are certain things about him that I prefer to discuss with you alone." I usually respond that my experience has been that issues directly pertaining to the child are best discussed in his presence. I tell the parents that we will have opportunities to talk alone about things that pertain to them and I encourage them to talk about the child's problems in his presence. I want to avoid sending the child outside and thereby placing him in a situation in which he knows that we're talking about him behind his back. Such conversations produce distrust of the therapist and compromise the therapeutic relationship. I will, however, if I suspect then that it is indicated, send the child out of the room to discuss certain things that are going on between the parents that are very relevant to him but not appropriately discussed in his presence. In such a situation I will say to the child, "Joey, I would like you to have a seat in the waiting room for a little while. I want to talk to your parents about things about them. We will not be talking about you directly." Generally the child will be receptive to leaving without separation anxiety because by that time his experiences with me have been reassuring and tension-reducing.

After the inital inquiry regarding the main problems is completed (the child is brought back into my office to complete this if he has been sent out), I will generally say to the child, "We've been talking about a lot of unpleasant things up to now. Let's talk about some good things. What are you good at?" The parents too are invited to contribute their views on the child's assets. I attempt here to counterbalance any esteem-lowering resulting from the focus on the child's deficits and hope thereby to improve our relationship. We then proceed to various diagnostic activities, e.g., free picture drawing plus story, Draw-a-Person, Draw-a-Family, etc. I try to make these experiences as enjoyable as possible and do not coerce the child into responding.

At the end of the initial consultation I will generally present my initial findings and recommendations to the parents. If treatment is indicated I will recommend a full evaluation. This usually consists of about three more interviews with the child, during which time I focus primarily on him. During those three interviews the mother is most often present. However, I may send her out to see if there are any differences in the child's reactions when we are alone. I most often find there are no differences. Comparing the child's freedom to reveal himself in the two situations helps me determine whether or not I will keep the mother in the room throughout the child's treatment, or during significant parts of it, or have her stay out. My original decision regarding the mother's presence is not rigidly adhered to. If new information and/or experiences warrant my changing it, I readily do so. In addition, as part of the full evaluation, I see each parent from one to three times alone for personal psychiatric evaluations. The purpose here is not only to gain information that contributes to my understanding of what is going on with the child but also, and possibly even more important, to establish a good relationship with the parent. With the child, as well, my three interviews not only serve the purpose of gaining information about his difficulties but, in addition, provide me with the opportunity to strengthen our relationship and to set a pattern for the subsequent work. For the child who is difficult to engage, the three further interviews give me the opportunity to involve him meaningfully and to expose him to the various games and techniques that I will be using (some of which will be described subsequently).

During my interviews with the child I do not try to pressure him into providing me with testimonials regarding his problems and his motivation to alleviate them. It is unrealistic to ask a young child to make statements about the fact that he has certain problems and that he wishes to work them out or cure them or gain insight into their underlying psychodynamics. The child does not generally wish to delve into the deeper recesses of his unconscious in the hope that the insights so gained will be utilized toward the alleviation of his symptoms and the betterment of his life situation (we have enough trouble getting adults to do this). The fact that the child is coming and participating in the various activities should satisfy the therapist and he may "turn the child off" (another way of saying "increase his resistances") by tryingto gain testimonials regarding insight or motivation for change. The child comes essentially to have a good time and if the therapist is to engage the child, it behooves him to weave the therapeutic activities into pleasurable experiences. Those who try to extract from the child a statement of motivation and interest may be successful in getting one and may even be successful in obtaining an actual statement from the child listing the particular problems that he wishes to cure. However, one must be very suspicious about such testimonials. More often than not they are made because the child appreciates that the therapist wants to hear them. They are said for his benefit and carry little deep conviction on the child's part. Pressuring the child into making such statements encourages duplicity — a formidable resistance if there ever was one.

The full evaluation will generally include an interview with both parents together, and this usually takes place after the individual interviews with them. We not only discuss any marital problems they may have described when seeing me alone, but also focus on their relationships with the child. On occasion I will conduct a family interview as part of the diagnostic evaluation, especially when there are teenagers who can often provide meaningful information. When all the interviews have been completed, I collate my material and present my findings and recommendations to the parents. The information gained during the evaluation not only serves to enable me to formulate a treatment program but serves as the foundation for my therapeutic work.

A final comment about the rare child who refuses to come into my office in spite of all the aforementioned enticements: I do not believe that a person, regardless of age, can benefit from therapy when under pressure. Accordingly, under no circumstances do I try to coerce such a child into my office. I usually set a maximun of three such sessions after which I try to work with the parents alone. I do, however, recommend that I attempt to engage the child again in six months to a year; and sometimes he is then more receptive.

Treating Other Members of the Child's Family

My comments on the therapy of other members of the child's family will be confined to those aspects of such treatment that relate to the issues of facilitating the youngster's involvement in treatment and reducing his resistances. There are therapists who strongly believe that it is antitherapeutic to treat individually more than one member of a family — whether it be two siblings, or a child and a parent, or each parent. I will discuss each of these situations separately, especially as it pertains to the child's resistances.

Most often parents have not read the books that we have — books that strongly warn against simultaneously treating two siblings. When one sibling is in treatment, the question may arise whether a second sibling needing therapy should see the same therapist as his sibling or a different one. The traditional view is that it should be a different therapist because seeing the same therapist will only entrench and deepen sibling rivalries. Furthermore, many hold that the child needs to feel that the therapist is all his own; that he need not share him with other family members; and to do so dilutes and even jeopardizes the therapeutic relationship. Some children exhibit jealous feelings over having to share the therapist's affection with other patients who are neither siblings nor relatives. It is the therapist's job to help the child adjust to this reality and all therapists would agree that any exaggerated jealousies in this regard have to be therapeutically dealt with. The child has to learn to share the affection of those who are important to him and, of course, this is a crucial element in the resolution of oedipal problems. However, one might argue that the therapist's voluntarily accepting a patient's sibling into treatment unnecessarily adds fuel to the fires of such jealousy.

My experience has been that parents who don't know about the aforementioned theories tend to automatically come to me with regard to a second sibling's problems. They feel that I know the family; they have already established a relationship with me; the sibling has heard much about me (and may have even attended sessions in my office); and it seems natural that I would see the second sibling as well. In addition, the idea that they should go to someone else may be difficult for many parents to understand. Such referral involves the family's once again seeking a therapist. Even if recommended by me, the new therapist is still a stranger. The whole diagnostic process has to be repeated; whereas my seeing the child shortens it immensely. No new relationship need be established and anxieties that it will not work out are obviated. The problem then boils down to the parents' natural inclinations vs. our theories regarding the antitherapeutic effects of two siblings being seen simultaneously.

In my earlier years I referred siblings elsewhere — in spite of parents' confusion and feeble objections. I never felt they were fully convinced by my explanations regarding the detrimental effects on both children's therapy; but they had no choice but to comply. Gradually, I became more appreciative of the parents' requests and decided to take a more flexible position. I found that bringing the sibling into treatment did not produce the

intensified rivalries that I had anticipated. My experience
has been that *most* siblings need not be referred to another
therapist. However, one needs to see the second youngster
in consultation before making a decision. One cannot
decide beforehand. There are some siblings for whom I
might recommend a female therapist or one who I feel
would do better than I with the particular child. And there
is a rare situation in which the rivalries are so deep that
treating the second would be antitherapeutic. Or the other
child himself might refuse such a consultation and say, "I
don't want to see Dr. Gardner. I'd rather see someone else. I
didn't like him when we had that family interview."
Obviously in such situations, it is the child — not the family
or I — who makes the decision. These situations, where the
child needs to be referred elsewhere, are not common in
my practice. Most often the second sibling is receptive to
seeing me because he has already formed a relationship
with me. He has heard much from the first sibling about
the sessions; has seen me in family interviews; has attended
at times (and even involved himself in) his brother's or
sister's sessions; and may even have heard some of the
tapes of the sessions. Accordingly, he may have already
formed a very deep relationship with me — one that could
be a good starting point for therapy. In addition, the
parents' established commitment to the child's involvement with me obviates the previously described antitherapeutic effects of their antagonism, resistances,
rivalry, and other negative attitudes toward me and/or the
therapeutic process.

I am not suggesting that one should always treat the
sibling. I am suggesting that one should not automatically
refuse to treat the sibling; and that one should explore the
possibility of doing so. This exploration may be a little
tricky. Sensitive interviews with both the patient and the
sibling are necessary. One should be particularly concerned with neurotic reasons for refusal. Rather than comply
with these (which, like the therapist's compliance to any
patient's neurotic request, is antitherapeutic), one should

explore them and attempt therapeutic resolution (as one would with any form of neurotic behavior). For example, if a patient's resistance to his sibling's entering treatment with me is just another opportunity for hostile obstructionism, it would be antitherapeutic to comply with such refusal and a disservice to the patient not to try to work it out. I do not give my patient automatic veto power. I wouldn't put that kind of power so quickly into the hands of a child. This does not, however, prevent my being sensitive and receptive to realistic and appropriate requests that the sibling not become my patient.

I have on occasion had two teenage siblings in my adolescent group at the same time. Of course, previous consent of both youngsters was obtained. My experience has been that the arrangement has worked out quite well. Each has provided information about the other that might not have otherwise been obtained and helping one another has been ego-enhancing and therefore therapeutic for each. Of course, there have been situations when such an arrangement would have been antitherapeutic, for example, when the siblings were opposite sexed and there was a justifiable desire for privacy regarding dating experiences.

Similar arguments hold with regard to my treatment of a child patient's parent or parents. The fear of rivalry between a child and a parent for the therapist's affection and, on occasion, even the parent's feeling some jealousy toward the child is one that often deters therapists from treating individually a parent and a child at the same time. Again, I have found that the possible dangers of this situation are far less than the advantages that can accrue from such an arrangement. This is especially true when a mother is in treatment with me. I can then learn much more about the child's environment. I know much more about the things that are going on in her life that are affecting the child. Accordingly, it makes my work with the child easier and knowing intimately the child whom she may discuss in *her* treatment facilitates my work with her. There are times when I will see a father in treatment.

There are times when I will treat each parent separately (it is beyond the scope of this book to discuss the criteria by which I decide whether such simultaneous therapy is indicated or contraindicated). The parents may be in a couples' group — a therapeutic modality that I consider an excellent form of treatment for certain kinds of marital problems. It is not the group's purpose to discuss child-rearing problems; these I prefer to discuss with the parents and child as an intrinsic part of the child's treatment so he can actively participate in discussions about his behavior. (Again, it is beyond the scope of this book to detail the criteria by which I decide whether this form of treatment is indicated for a particular couple.) My groups consist of three or four couples (the number I have empirically found to be optimum), who meet with me in the early evening for an hour and a half and then the rest of the evening continue their discussions without me at one of their homes. Some of the group members have individual therapy as well — either with me or another therapist (with whom I may occasionally consult). Again, I have not found such treatment to be deleterious to the child's therapy. In fact, it entrenches the relationship with the parents and lessens the kinds of hostilities, rivalries, etc. that the parents may have toward me — reactions that may predictably increase the child's resistances and thereby undermine his treatment.

The following examples demonstrate the value of the parent's being present during the child's session. In each, a therapeutic opportunity would have been missed had the parent been absent.

Clinical Examples

A "Model Child." Tom entered treatment at the age of six-and-a-half because of a severe stuttering problem. He was markedly inhibited in asserting himself and quite fearful of expressing anger. These problems were particularly apparent in his relationship with his father. He was a "model child" both in school and at home.

Early in treatment, in a session of relatively free play, Tom drew a picture which he said was of a reservoir. The picture showed a body of water, surrounding grass, a nearby road, and a few trees. There were no people and no automobiles on the road. When I asked him to tell me a story about the picture, he stated, "A boy went fishing there and caught a few fish." That was the whole story. Further attempts to get him to elaborate on the story were unsuccessful. I did not consider the story to have too much psychodynamic significance and in an attempt to elicit further information I asked him if he had had any recent experiences that were similar. He said that two days previously he had gone fishing with his father in a reservoir. Further questions about the experience did not provide me with any further meaningful information. He merely stated that he had had a good time and that he had caught three fish.

I then asked Tom's mother if she had any ideas about Tom's picture and his comment. She related that two days previously (a Sunday) her husband had promised to take Tom fishing at 8:00 A.M. It was not until 1:00 P.M. that they finally went. During the five-hour period the patient waited patiently for his father to take him. When the mother urged him to assert himself, to ask the father to hurry up, and tell the father how upset he was about waiting, the patient refused. This pattern, she stated, was typical of Tom. In accordance with my previous recommendations, she did not intervene on Tom's behalf (as had been her practice) because I wanted him to be encouraged to assert himself and express resentment.

Following this disclosure by the mother, I entered into a conversation with Tom regarding his speaking up to his father. He denied any anger and stated quite definitely that it did not bother him that he had to wait around. I told him that I could not believe that he wasn't angry a little bit, that in all that time had not *once* felt a *little* angry at his father, and that I hoped that the time would come when he would speak up more. In the ensuing discussion, Tom did admit that he was a little angry but that he was afraid to speak up to his father. He was not able to verbalize exactly what he feared. I reassured him that I knew his father well and that I was sure that the terrible consequence he anticipated would not occur. However, only by trying would he know whether or not what I was telling him would turn out to be true. Discussions such as these contributed to Tom's gradually becoming freer to express himself — not only to his father, but to others as well. And with such freedom there was a corresponding diminition in his stuttering. Had Tom's mother not been present I would not have appreciated that the picture related to one of his central problems.

Human Relationships as Ambivalent. During the next session Tom drew a picture of a rainbow. When asked to tell me about it he replied, "It's a rainbow. There's nothing more to say about it." Further inquiry was not productive. With an orange crayon he then drew a circle, made it into a face, and then covered the facial features with orange, stating that it was an orange. He then told a story about a lady who began to eat the orange but was told by the orange the he was really a rainbow and so the lady spit it out. I appreciated that the drawing was highly symbolic but was unable to learn anything more from Tom regarding its meaning. I asked him if he had had any recent experiences with rainbows or oranges and he said no. He said he didn't like oranges and orange juice, that his mother did, but gave me no further information.

I then asked Tom's mother if she could shed any light on this matter. She said that three weeks previously, while the family was traveling in the country, they had come upon what they all agreed was the most beautiful rainbow they had ever seen. The family gazed at it in awe and there were numerous comments regarding its beauty and the exhilaration of the scene. The patient said that he had forgotten about it when I first asked him about rainbows and agreed that it was the most beautiful rainbow he had ever seen.

The information from the mother then made the child's drawing and story more meaningful. I considered the rainbow, as well as the orange (originally drawn as a face, confirming my belief that it represented Tom himself), to symbolize objects that were sources of pleasure to the mother. By transforming himself into a rainbow and then an orange he hoped to gain his mother's affection. However, the lady "spits it out." This symbolized, I believe Tom's basic feeling that even if he were to transform himself into those objects most desired (the orange) and admired (the rainbow) by his mother, she would still reject him (spit him out). The realities were that this mother was basically affectionate and devoted to this child, but she enjoyed much more her teenage children. She got little pleasure from sitting on the floor with him, reading nursery stories, or playing the kinds of games that very young children enjoy. The patient, however, saw this as massive deprivation — when indeed it was only partial. He was too inhibited to express the anger he felt toward her, and the tension and anxiety he felt over the threatened eruption of his anger played a significant role in his stuttering problem. In fact, everyone agreed that the stuttering was most prominent when he was with his mother.

With this understanding of the child's story I told one (in accordance with my Mutual Storytelling Technique, see Chapter 5) about an orange that learned that not everybody liked him all the time — that there were some people who liked him very much and some people who liked him less. In addition, this orange learned that there were times when the people who liked him very much liked him less and other times when they liked him much more. I introduced the notions that human relationships are basically ambivalent and that when someone is not providing you with the affection you want at a particular time, then you should go to others to obtain it. In addition, I introduced the idea that just because someone may not be affectionate to you at a particular time does not mean that you are totally loathesome and unlovable.

As I was telling my story the patient frenetically drew a heavy green band across the top of the picture of the rainbow and orange. Although listening intently to what I was saying, it was clear that Tom was being made anxious by my story — verifying that I was "hitting home." Without the mother's information, it was less likely that I would have been "on point" — if I could have been on point at all.

Sex and the Nonpunitive Parent. Bruce, a nine-year-old boy, was being treated for a Gille de la Tourette's syndrome — characterized by tics of the face and shoulders and coprolalia. The primary coprolalic words were "nigger shit" and "shit." There was a progressive improvement in his symptoms over five months of twice-weekly therapy. In addition, I saw his mother once weekly in individual therapy and his parents were in couples' group therapy.

In the course of treatment it became apparent that two primary issues contributed to Bruce's difficulties. One related to his fear of expressing anger toward his parents, and this was expressed indirectly through the coprolalic symptoms. The second related to an experience two years prior to beginning treatment when a teenage babysitter asked him to caress her breasts and vulva. He was quite anxious about this experience and feared that if he told his parents there would be terrible retaliations. Such fears were further intensified by his somewhat primitive housekeeper who increased his guilt considerably when he confided in her his anxiety over the experience. The symptomatic improvement was related to his increased freedom to express hostility toward his parents and his openly discussing the sexual incident and having the experience that his parents were not punitive.

About one month prior to the interview to be described the patient exhibited an exacerbation of his symptoms. All inquiries were not productive in revealing why at that time there was an intensification of his problems. His father had recently involved himself in a theatrical group and was away every evening rehearsing; however, his weekends were completely spent with Bruce. It was hard to say, therefore, whether anger at his father was contributing. In addition, he had won the right to stay up later and the parents and I wondered whether he was not getting enough sleep and whether fatigue might be contributing to his exacerbation. Although I realized that we (I say "we" because the parents and I were really working together) were "grasping at straws" in an attempt to understand why Bruce's symptoms had intensified, these were the best explanations that I and the parents could come up with.

After a month of exacerbation (during a session in the sixth month of Bruce's therapy) the mother suddenly, on "a hunch," asked the patient if he was having or if he had had any recent sexual experiences. She stated that she just had a strong feeling that that might be what was going on. She felt that he looked like he was covering up something that he was very much ashamed about. He immediately broke down, started crying, and described having played a game of "you show me yours and I'll show you mine" on one occasion about a month previously (just before the onset of the present exacerbation). He was very guilt-ridden over the experience and it had weighed heavily on his mind. A thorough discussion of the normalcy of these urges and their occasional gratification ensued. At the end of the session he was urged to discuss the matter at home with his father (without his mother's giving the latter any previous information) in the hope that his father's nonpunitive reaction would be reassuring. Following the session and his discussion with his father (who, as expected, was understanding and sympathetic) there was a dramatic alleviation of the coprolalia. In addition, there was a significant diminution of his tics. Had the mother not been present and worked along with me, it is probable that it would have taken much longer to get to the roots of this previously inexplicable exacerbation. And I have some question as to whether I would have been successful at all.

About one week later, although the patient had experienced significant improvement, he had still not returned to the point where he was prior to the aforementioned intensification of his symptoms. His mother again hazarded a guess. She had noticed that Bruce would be more symptomatic after spending time with two boyfriends who were Catholics. Both of these boys came from families in which sex was rarely, if ever, discussed. However, when it was mentioned it was only done so with intonations of disgust and other guilt-evoking remarks. On inquiry, Bruce revealed that he was indeed having lengthy discussions on sex with these two "friends" and they were flooding him with threats that he would burn in hell and suffer eternal damnation. Accordingly, a number of discussions took place in which both the mother and I attempted to communicate to Bruce our disagreement with his friends. We pointed out how unrealistic and primitive were many of the views these boys were exposed to. As a result of such discussions — spanning a two-week period — there was an even further diminution in the patient's tics. Had the mother not been present in the room, these experiences with his friends might never have been brought out and the attendant alleviation of symptomatology might not have so easily been accomplished, if accomplished at all.

Sexual Stimulation by the Mother. Roger was a ten-year-old boy who entered treatment because of tension and hyperactivity that was interfering with his schoolwork. During his second month of treatment he sat in his usual chair opposite me. Off to the side sat his mother. He opened the session by stating that he had had a dream and his mother had written it down. His mother, who was wearing a thin sweater, leaned down into her purse and said, "Oh yes, let me give it to you." She then pranced across the room, holding the slip of paper in her hand. Her braless breasts bounced freely as she approached me and I could not help noticing them. I said nothing and directed my attention to the dream:

> I was in art class with my art teacher. I had some special clay that can burn you and wet you at the same time. I was trying to build a boat with it but it changed into an ashtray. I didn't have enough clay. I wanted some more clay and the art teacher gave it to me.

Neither the patient nor his mother was able to make

any guesses regarding the meaning of the dream. I surmised to myself that the boat might represent the patient's mother, specifically her genitalia. The boat, as a receptacle, lends itself well to such symbolization and is a common representation of the female sex organs. His describing it as "wet" could further confirm this. Its turning into an ashtray could also support this explanantion. The ashtray is hot and, in addition, receives cigarettes, common phallic symbols (considering their shape and the heat they emanate). Wanting to have more clay, I felt, was a reflection of the patient's desire to intensify the sexual relationship.

With this hypothesis regarding the dream's meaning I asked the mother what kind of sexual stimulation the child might have been exposed to. She described how she considered it healthy for her to walk around naked in the home, and hardly a day passed when Roger did not observe his mother nude on numerous occasions. The mother was a woman with many seductive gestures. She described how she had once been a model and had been invited to pose in the nude for a popular girlie magazine. There was no question that the patient was being sexually stimulated by his mother and I considered such stimulation to be playing a role in his tension and hyperactivity. Accordingly, I recommended that she discontinue the practice of undressing in front of him and she accepted this advice. Had the mother not been in the room it would be unlikely that I would have pursued this line of inquiry and understood the meaning of the dream.

Getting such mothers to be less seductive is often a difficult task, especially when they are not in therapy. Often the seductivity is subtle and so deeply ingrained in the character structure that it is unreasonable for the therapist to hope to bring about significant change. The mother's gait, gestures, vocal intonations, etc. may be highly erotic and she may have little insight into the effect that she is having on males — even her own prepubertal sons. But even when insight may be gained, the chances of bringing about change in such women is small, especially because the amount of social reinforcement they enjoy is so immense. Roger's mother was in this category. I knew her well enough to know that she would have rationalized her bralessness as merely stylish and would not have appreciated the extreme seductive gratifications she was enjoying via adoption of this style. Accordingly, I confined myself at that time to discouraging only the most blatant manifestations of her seductivity, namely, her undressing in front of Roger. My hope was that, with increasing involvement in her sons's therapy, she might become more insightful and thereby receptive to looking into her seductivity.

Had the mother not been in the room with the patient I would not have been as likely to have experienced the full extent of her seductivity. Here, it was not so much what the mother told me that contributed to a deeper understanding of Roger's dream (and hence his problems) but the actual observation of the mother's exhibitionism and my own attendant titillation. The therapist does well, when he finds himself being titillated by a child's mother, to consider the possibility that the child himself is reacting similarly.

The Cold Father. Jack entered treatment at nine and a half because of disruptive behavior at school and home. There was a basic organic deficit characterized by hyperactivity and impulsivity. His father had left the home about one year previously and was most unreliable regarding his visits. When he was home he was frequently condescending toward Jack. And the anger Jack felt in response to these indignities was being displaced onto siblings, peers, his mother, and his teacher.

Near the middle of his eighth month in treatment, Jack spoke about his father's visit to the home that previous weekend. Although he tried to speak enthusiastically, it was quite clear that he was forcing the impression that the experience was pleasurable. Jack's mother, however, related how he had followed his father around all weekend "like a puppy dog." She stated that it was pathetic to see how Jack would not resign himself to his father's lack of interest. She described how whenever Jack would try to elicit his father's attention or interest he would be responded to with a "shut up" or "don't bother me." Jack became upset by what his mother said and denied that there was any validity to it.

He then described two dreams. In the first he was in a hotel in Cooperstown, New York, the site of the National Baseball Museum. (Jack was an avid baseball fan.) There he was trying to get onto a cable car of the kind seen in San Francisco. The patient could not figure out the meaning of the dream. He did describe, however, a pleasurable experience at Cooperstown with his mother and teenage siblings a week previously but could provide no further associations. Jack's mother then offered further information. She described how the whole family had gone to San Francisco when Jack was about five and this had been one of the high points of his life. This occurred long before his father had left the home and Jack often referred to the experience with great pleasure. The meaning of the dream then became clear: In response to the frustrations that he had experienced with his father the previous weekend Jack was dreaming of a return to happier days with his father in San Francisco. The more recent experience with his mother in Cooperstown was marred by his longing to regain the joys of the San Francisco trip with his father (as symbolized by his trying to get on the cable car). However, he is not successful in getting onto the cable car. This reflected his appreciation, at some level, that his father could no longer provide him with the kind of gratifications he had given him in the past.

Had the mother not been in the room I would not have understood the meaning of this dream. Its analysis is a good example of the vital role that a parent can play when actively participating in the child's therapy. Both the mother and I agreed that the aforementioned interpretation was valid. When it was presented to Jack he admitted that it might be possible but I did not get the feeling that he accepted our explanation with much conviction.

Jack then went on to relate his second dream. In it he was walking to school with a classmate and they were going to be late. There was a bus ahead and Jack wanted to run ahead and catch the bus. His friend, however, was resistive to the idea. The dream ended with neither boy reaching the bus. Rather, there was a confused discussion regarding whether they should have boarded it. Again, Jack was unable to ascertain the meaning of the dream and I, myself, could offer no specific suggestions. Jack's mother, however, stated, that in her opinion, buses appeared to be the symbol of Jack's father. When he lived at home, Jack's father commuted into New York City and returned each day in a bus to the suburban New Jersey home where the mother and children lived. Especially when he was younger, Jack would often ask if his father was on a passing bus. With this new information the dream became clear. It reflected Jack's ambivalence about joining his father. On the one hand, he desperately wants to catch up to the bus (as symbolized by Jack's pursuing it); on the other hand, he does not anticipate acceptance by his father or gratifying experiences with him so lags behind (as symbolized by his friend's [Jack's alter ego] resistance to such pursuit).

Again, when Jack was offered this explanation for the dream he passively accepted its interpretation, but I did not feel that I was "hitting home." However I did have the feeling that there was some receptivity, that some seeds were planted, and subsequent experience bore this out. Had Jack's mother not been present these advances would have been much more slowly achieved.

I believe that the material presented in this chapter departs significantly from traditional practices in the treatment of children and will be met (as it has been in the past) with some incredulity on the part of many therapists. Trained in traditional techniques, I consider myself well versed in their use. My experience with the alterations and modifications described in this chapter have convinced me that they may often (but certainly not always) be preferable. I have tried it both ways; and my suggestion to the reader is that he do so also before forming any conclusions regarding the validity of these approaches.

Chapter Five
The Mutual Storytelling Technique

Eliciting stories is a time-honored practice in child psychotherapy. From the stories children tell, the therapist is able to gain invaluable insights into the child's inner conflicts, frustrations, and defenses.

A child's stories are generally less difficult to analyze than dreams, free associations, and other productions of the adult. His fundamental difficulties are exhibited clearly to the therapist, with less of the obscurity, distortion, and misrepresentation that are characteristic of the adult's presentation. The essential problem for the child's therapist has been how to use his insights therapeutically.

The techniques described in the literature on child psychotherapy and psychoanalysis are, for the most part, attempts to solve this problem. Some are based on the assumption, borrowed from the adult psychoanalytic model, that making the unconscious conscious can itself be therapeutic. My own experience has been that few children are interested in gaining conscious awareness of their unconscious processes, let alone utilizing such insights therapeutically. Children do, however, enjoy both telling stories and listening to them. Since storytelling is one of the child's favorite modes of communication, I wondered whether communicating with him in the same mode might not be useful in child therapy. The efficacy of the storytelling approach for the imparting and transmission of values and insights is proved by the ancient and universal appeal of fable, myth, and legend.

It was from these observations and considerations that I developed the Mutual Storytelling Technique, a proposed solution to the question of how to utilize the child's stories therapeutically. In this method the child first tells a story; the therapist surmises its psychodynamic meaning and then tells one of his own. The therapist's story contains the same characters in a similar setting, but he introduces healthier adaptations and resolutions of the conflicts that have been exhibited in the child's story. Since he speaks in the child's own language, the therapist has a good chance of "being heard." One could almost say that here the therapist's interpretations bypass the conscious and are received directly by the unconscious. The child is not burdened with psychoanalytic interpretations which are alien to him. Direct, anxiety-provoking confrontations, so reminiscent of the child's experience with parents and teachers, are avoided. Lastly, the introduction of humor and drama enhances the child's interest and pleasure and, therefore, his receptivity. As a therapeutic tool, the method is useful for children who will tell stories, but who have little interest in analyzing them. It is not a therapy per se, but rather one technique in the therapist's armamentarium.

Basic Mechanics of the Method

Although drawings, dolls, puppets, and other toys are the modalities around which stories are traditionally told in child therapy, these often restrict the child's storytelling or channel it in highly specific directions. The tape recorder (either video or audio) does not have these disadvantages; with it, the visual field remains free from contaminating and distracting stimuli. Eliciting a story with it is like obtaining a dream on demand. The same method, however, can be employed — with some modifications — with dolls, blocks, drawings, and other play material.

I begin by asking the child if he would like to be guest of honor on a make-believe television program on which stories are told. If he agrees — and few decline the honor — the recorder is turned on and I begin:

Good morning, boys and girls. I'd like to welcome you once again to Dr. Gardner's Make-Up-a-Story Television Program. As you all know, we invite children to our program to see how good they are at making up stories. Naturally, the more adventure or excitement a story has, the more interesting it is to the people who are watching at their television sets. Now, it's against the rules to tell stories about things you've read or have seen in the movies or on television, or about things that really happened to you or anyone you know.

Like all stories, your story should have a beginning, a middle, and an end. After you've made up a story, you'll tell us the moral of the story. We all know that every good story has a moral.

Then after you've told your story, Dr. Gardner will make up a story too. He'll try to tell one that's interesting and unusual, and then he'll tell the moral of his story.

And now, without further delay, let me introduce to you a boy (girl) who is with us today for the first time. Can you tell us your name, young man?

I then ask the child a series of brief questions that can be answered by single words or brief phrases, such as his age, address, school grade, and teacher. These "easy" questions diminish the child's anxiety and tend to make him less tense about the more unstructured themes involved in "making up a story." Anxiety is further lessened when he hears his own voice at this point by playback, something which most children enjoy. He is then told:

> Now that we've heard a few things about you, we're all interested in hearing the story *you* have for us today.

At this point most children plunge right into their story, although some may feel the need for "time to think." I may offer this pause; if it is asked for by the child, it is readily granted. There are some children for whom this pause is not enough, but nevertheless still want to try. In such instances the child is told:

5036   Some children, especially when it's their first time on this program, have a little trouble thinking of a story, but with some help from me they're able to do so. Most children don't realize that there are *millions* of stories in their heads they don't know about. And I know a way to help get out some of them. Would you like me to help you get out one of them?

Most children assent to this. I then continue:

> Fine. Here's how it works. I'll start the story and, when I point my finger at you, you say exactly what comes into your mind at that time. You'll then see how easy it is to make up a story. Okay. Let's start. Once upon a time — a long, long time ago — in a distant land — far, far away — way beyond the mountains — way beyond the deserts — way beyond the oceans — there lived a —

I then point my finger, and it is a rare child who does not offer some fill-in word at this point. If the word is *dog,* for example, I then say, "And *that dog* —" and once again point to the patient. I follow the statemnt provided by the child with "And then —" or "The next thing that happened was —." Every statement the child makes is followed by some introductory connective and an indication to the child to supply the next statement — that and no more. The introduction of specific phrases or words would defeat the therapist's purpose of catalyzing the youngster's production of his *own* created material and of sustaining, as needed, its continuity.

This approach is sufficient to get most children over whatever hurdles there are for them in telling a story. If this is not enough, however, it is best to drop the activity in a completely casual and nonreproachful manner, such as: "Well, today doesn't seem to be your good day for storytelling. Perhaps we'll try again some other time." While the child is engaged in telling his story, I jot down notes, which not only help in analyzing the child's story but also serve as a basis for my own. At the end of the child's story and his statement of its moral, I may ask questions about specific items in the story. The purpose here is to obtain additonal details, which are often of help in understanding the story. Typical questions might be: "Was the fish in your story a man or a lady?" "Why was the fox so mad at the goat?" or "Why did the bear do that?" If the child hesitates to tell the moral of his story or indicates that there is none, I usually reply: "What, a story without a moral? Every good story has *some* lesson or moral!" The moral that this comment usually does succeed in eliciting from the child is often significantly revealing of the fundamental psychodynamics of the story. For younger children the word *lesson* or *title* may be substituted for moral. Or the child might be asked: "What can we learn from your story?"

Then I usually say: "That was a very good (unusual, exciting) story." Or to the child who was hesitant: "And you thought you weren't very good at telling stories!"

I then turn off the tape recorder and prepare my story. Although the child's story is generally simpler to understand than the adult's dream, the analysis of both follows similar principles.

Fundamentals of Story Analysis.

I first attempt to determine which figure or figures in the child's story represent the child himself, and which stand for significant people in his environment. It is important to appreciate that two or more figures may represent various facets of the same person's personality. There may, for example, be a "good dog" and a "bad cat" in the same story, which are best understood as conflicting forces within the same child. A horde of figures, all similar, may symbolize powerful elements in a single person. A hostile father, for example, may be represented by a stampede of bulls. Swarms of small creatures, such as insects, worms, or mice, often symbolize unacceptable repressed complexes. Malevolent figures can represent the child's own repressed hostility projected outward, or they may be a symbolic statement about the hostility of a significant figure. Sometimes both of these mechanisms operate simultaneously. A threatening lion in one child's story stood for his hostile father, and he was made more frightening by the child's own hostility, repressed and projected onto the lion. This example illustrates one of the reasons why many children see their parents as being more malevolent than they are.

Besides clarifying the symbolic significance of each figure, it is also important to get a general overall "feel" for the atmosphere and setting of the story. Is the ambience pleasant, neutral, or horrifying? Stories that take place in the frozen tundra or on isolated space stations suggest something very different from those which occur in the child's own home. The child's emotional reactions when telling the story are also of significance in understanding its meaning. An eleven-year-old child who tells me, in an emotionless tone, about the death fall of a mountain climber reveals not only his hostility but also his repression of his feelings. The atypical must be separated from the stereotyped, age-appropriate elements in the story. The former may be very revealing, whereas the latter rarely are. Battles between cowboys and Indians rarely give meaningful data, but when the chief sacrifices his son to Indian gods in a prayer for victory over the white man, something has been learned about the child's relationship with his father.

Lastly, the story may lend itself to a number of different psychodynamic interpretations. In selecting the theme that will be most pertinent for the child *at that particular time,* I am greatly assisted by the child's own "moral" or "title."

After asking myself, "What would be a healthier resolution or a more mature adaptation than the one used by the child?" I create a story of my own. My story involves the same characters, setting, and initial situation as the child's story, but it has a more appropriate or salutary resolution of the most important conflicts. In creating my story, I attempt to provide the child with more *alternatives.* The communication that the child need not be enslaved by his neurotic behavior patterns is vital. Therapy must open new avenues not considered in the child's scheme of things. It must help the child become aware of the multiplicity of options which are available to replace the narrow self-defeating ones he has chosen. My moral or morals are an attempt to emphasize further the healthier adaptations I have included in my story. If, while I am telling my story, the child exhibits deep interest or reveals marked anxiety, which may manifest itself by jitteriness or hyperactivity, then I know that my story is "hitting home." Such clear-cut indications of how relevant one's story is are not, of course, always forthcoming.

After the moral to my story, I stop the recorder and ask the child whether he would like to hear (and see when the videotape recorder is used) the program. Playing the program makes possible a second exposure to the messages that the therapist wishes to impart.

The therapist's attitude has a subtle, but nevertheless significant, influence on the child's ability to tell a story. Ideally this attitude should be one of pleasurable anticipation that a story will be forthcoming and surprised disappointment when the child will not or cannot tell one. The child wants to be accepted by those who are meaningful to him, and, if a productive therapeutic relationship has been established, he will try to comply with what is expected of him. Peer group influence is also important. When the child gets the general feeling that storytelling is what everybody does when he visits the therapist, he is more likely to play the game. The last factor, and probably the most important one in determining whether the child will voluntarily involve himself, is his appreciation at some level that the therapist's communications are meaningful and useful to him. If the therapist's responding communications are frequently "on target," that is, if they are most often relevant to the child's problems and situation, the child is likely to become engrossed in the game. (I say *frequently* relevant because it is unreasonable to expect that the therapist will *always* accurately understand the child's story.)

Clinical Examples

A Boy Whose Father Was Dying. James, a seven-year-old boy, was referred because of excessive fantasy play with blocks, self-involved and withdrawn behavior in the classroom, lack of involvement with peers, low frustration tolerance, and exaggerated fear of noises. His father, a lawyer in his early forties, had chronic myelogenous leukemia and had suffered a number of remissions and severe exacerbations. In each exacerbation there was a real chance that he would not survive. However, the possibility did exist that he might survive a number of years. At the time of referral the father was recovering from a two-year exacerbation of his illness and was just making arrangements to resume working on a part-time basis. His mother had devoted significant time to the father during this period. Of the father's illness, she stated, "We have to live for today. We can't tell what tomorrow will bring."

During his first session James, when asked to draw anything he wanted to, scribbled a brightly colored design. He then covered the total picture with black crayon and then scratched through the black with his fingernails to partially expose the underlying bright colors. However, in spite of his efforts, there was only minimal reexposure of the original picture. I considered the original brightly colored drawing to represent his world as it once was: happy and bright. The overlying black represented the dark cloud which had descended over his home since his father became ill. His scratching through the black symbolized his attempt to break through the specter which hung over his life and resume once again the pleasant life he once knew. However, his efforts were in vain and he was only minimally successful in viewing once again his lost world.

Near the end of the first session, James asked to play with the blocks. I was receptive to this request, especially since I suspected it would give me an opportunity to observe myself this preoccupation which his parents had described as an obsession. I hoped that he might verbalize his fantasies and thereby provide me with information about the meaning of this activity and possibly about other problems of his as well. Unfortunately, his request came so late in the session that it was impractical to allow him to begin. I promised, however, that if he wanted we could start off with block playing in the next session.

On entering for his second session James immediately emptied the bag of blocks and began playing. He painstakingly built what appeared to be a labyrinth. He then took a toy car and told me that he had built a town with many dead-end streets. Each time the car went down one of the streets James verbalized a conversation with his mother as to whether the street would prove to be a dead end. The result was always the same: all streets ultimately ended in a blind alley. And each time the patient responded in a resigned fashion: "Well, I guess it's a dead end." The parents (who remained in the room during the session) described the activity as identical to what they observed at home. They said that he could remain at the game for hours and it was clear that if I did not suggest that James and I do something else, he would have been happy to spend the whole session so engaged.

I considered the game to be a statement of how James

saw his situation. The specter of his father's possible death
hung over the whole family. Every therapeutic attempt
brought about some relief, but no cure. James never knew
how each new crisis (as symbolized by the car entering a
new street) would turn out. His experience had been that
none had ever resulted in cure (all were dead ends), but he
was still trying. The game provided him with the hope
(which was probably never to be realized) that some course
of action would ultimately be successful. Yet he was not
optimistic enough to build a city without dead-end streets
— revealing thereby his hopelessness.

When I suggested that we go to the other corner of the
room in order to play our first game of Dr. Gardner's Make-
Up-a-Story Television Program, he insisted on bringing
along the blocks. This time he built a ship with large guns.
Each time an "enemy" appeared and the ship was attacked
he cried out: "No one can hurt me. The enemy can't hurt
me." With minor variations this theme was repeated:
"Nobody can hurt me. Bang, bang." Whereas other
verbalizations in the ship game were low-keyed, those
pertaining to his invulnerability were shouted: "You can't
hurt me. Hah, hah, hah. Nothing can hurt me. Hah, hah,
hah." Sensing that this perseverated theme could also last
the whole session, I suggested he end the story so that we
could go on to another television game. He then ended the
story with a shark being scared away from the ship by the
big guns.

I considered this story to reflect James's fear of
impending doom. The "enemy" and later the big shark
symbolized his father's illness and all its ominous im-
plications. They can't hurt him, however; he can drive
away danger. The fantasy provided him with protection
from the catastrophe of his father's death. In addition, it
created the delusion that he had some control over this
uncontrollable event in his life. The defense, which
involved mechanisms of denial and reaction formation,
was a fragile one. And although each reiteration was an
attempt to strengthen it, the same need to repeat it belied

its fundamental inability to lessen his basic anxiety over his father's illness and its potential effects on him.

He then told his first story.

Patient: Once there was a person who went to a firehouse. And the fire alarm rang when the firemen saw it. This is not really a true story.

Therapist: Okay.

Patient: No, Sir.

Therapist: Hhmm.

Patient: And there was a turtle walking across the street — a tortoise. He was following the fire engines and the firemen thought they would take him home on the way to the fire.

Therapist: Wait. I'm a little confused. There was a firehouse and the fire alarm went off. Is that right?

Patient: Yeah.

Therapist: Well, did it go off because there was a fire?

Patient: Yeah and —

Therapist: Wait. And they found a turtle across the street.

Patient: A tortoise.

Therapist: A tortoise. Did the turtle have anything to do with the fire?

Patient: Uh huh. They thought they would like him and to help him, like they called him "Fire Chief Turtle."

Therapist: Oh, they wanted him to help them fight the fire.

Patient: Uh huh.

Therapist: Okay.

Patient: So they put a fire hat on the turtle and he helped.

Therapist: They put a fire hat on him. Go ahead.

Patient: Yeah and the firemen let him help. He helped the goodest and he was very careful. He was the carefulest in the firehouse so they called him "Big Chief." He can tell anybody what to do.

Therapist: Okay.

Patient: So one day he was walking across the street — the tortoise. He found a engineer working at the engineer look (sic). He thought he would help him drive the train and he worked it *better* than the engineer. He did it so safely.

So as he was so tired he went to sleep and then the day after that the tortoise saw a airport. He wanted to watch the planes go by. They sat happily. He didn't know that there was a very friendly pilot. He was afraid they were going to . . . (mumbles).

Therapist: Wait. There was a very friendly pilot and what?

Patient: And the turtle was afraid of him. He didn't know . . .

Therapist: The turtle was afraid of the pilot? He didn't know that he was friendly. Is that it?

Patient: So he went past . . . (mumbles) . . . and forgot about it.

Therapist: He went what? You mumble sometimes that I can't understand what you're saying. There was a friendly pilot and the turtle was afraid of him. Right?

Patient: Uh huh.

Therapist: Then what happened?

Patient: He just forgot about the pilot and went to sleep. But you know who came?

Therapist: Who?

Patient: The friendly pilot. He saw the tortoise and woke him up. He was a little scared. So the pilot taught him how to go on a plane so he now knows he's a friendly pilot and so he wasn't scared anymore.

Therapist: Okay.

Patient: And that pilot was really nice to him. He [the pilot] told him stories if he [the turtle] told him stories. If he [the turtle] told him scary stories he [the pilot] would tell him back.

Therapist: If this tortoise told scary stories the pilot would tell scary stories back?

Patient: Uh huh.

Therapist: Okay.

Patient: So the pilot said, "You can take a long flight on a plane." So the tortoise went on a long ride in the plane. It was really fun. And it was a small plane so they went under bridges, over bridges, over tunnels, over water. And it was a boat-plane so it could go on the water. It goes under bridges like a tunnel.

Therapist: Okay. Then what happens?

Patient: So the tortoise was really good. So one day he went — I'm gonna make him real — make him from a book now.

Therapist: What's that?

Patient: Make him partly from a book.

Therapist: I'm not clear what you're saying.

Patient: Make him partly from a book.

Therapist: Oh, you're telling a story that's partly from a book?

Patient: Not partly from a book, but it may come to a part from a book.

Therapist (to patient's mother): Do you understand what he is saying?

Mother (to patient): The story may come partly from a book?

Therapist: Is that what you are asking?

Patient: Uh huh.

Therapist: No. It's against the rules. The story *cannot* come from a book. I told you that before. Is this story from a book?

Patient: No, but soon it will come so I have to make a different part up.

Therapist: No. Finish up the story now because it's almost over.

Patient: Then he met some people.

Therapist: Go ahead. This is made up now?

Patient: Uh huh.

Therapist: Go ahead. Finish it up with a made-up story.

Patient: And some people went into it 'til midnight. These were policemen. These were four policemen. One is named Steven and Winni Minni, Minni Winni.

Therapist: Go ahead . . . Listen, we have to stop here. Now I want you to finish up the story. Okay. Finish it up. Just make an ending for it now.

Patient: But soon it'll have to come scary . . . then . . .

Therapist: I don't want to hear any more. I want you to finish up your story because we have to stop.

Patient: You're not going to tell me a story?

Therapist: I *will* tell you a story but if you make yours much longer I won't have time.

Patient: Okay.

Therapist: Now you have to decide. If you want to make your story longer then I won't have time to tell mine. But if you want to make your story shorter then I'll be able to tell mine. Now what do you want to do?

Patient: Then there was a boy named . . . um . . . Tie (sic) and another boy named Matthew.

Therapist: Go ahead.

Patient: And they took the turtle and he [the turtle] told them he could do anything so they all lived happily ever after.

Therapist: What happened with the turtle?

Patient: He just can tell everyone what to do.

Therapist: He tells a lot of people what to do.

Patient: He . . . (mumbles) . . . and has to listen. He tells like robbers to go away and God makes the robbers go away and die.

Therapist: Uh huh.

Patient: Well, that's over. It's over.

Therapist: All right. Now should I tell my story?

Patient: Yeah, but it's got to be very different than mine.

Therapist: Very different. In my story I may have the same characters or the same people or the same animals but different things happen to them. Okay?

Patient: Yeah.

The turtle (or tortoise, if you will), as the protagonist of the story, represents the patient. Although small and slow-moving, he exhibits far more competence than the fireman

("He was the carefulest in the firehouse . . .") and the train engineer (". . . he worked it *better* than the engineer.") who represent James's father. The notion is partially factual (in view of his father's illness) and partially wish fulfillment. James would like to possess adult competence to lessen the insecurity he feels about his father's frailty. Were he more competent he would be less threatened by the loss of his father. Were his father stronger he would serve as a better model for James's adult identification and James would have less of a need for fantasies of power. With both the fireman and the engineer, James attains instant skill, without any effort. Furthermore, he is made "Big Chief" of the firemen and "He can tell anybody what to do." The chief, of course, has control over his men and I considered this fantasy a manifestation of James's desire to have control over his father's life in reaction to the impotence he felt over the latter's fate.

Things are more complex with the pilot. Like the firemen and engineer, he too is a father surrogate. However, he unquestionably exhibits qualities that are this therapist's as well. We are told that the "turtle was afraid of him . . . He didn't know he was friendly." James was obviously still anxious about me in this, his second session. In addition, if the tortoise told scary stories the pilot would tell scary stories in response — a clear statement about his fears of my anticipated stories, none of which he had thus far heard. However, the pilot teaches him how to fly a plane and he then realizes that his initial hesitation was unfounded and that the pilot was friendly. This time he acquires his expertise more realistically — he is trained by the expert — but it is still the tortoise (small and slow and therefore still the child) who flies the plane. The theme of assuming his father's position still persists. Finally the pilot takes him on a long plane ride "under bridges, over bridges, over tunnels, over water." This, I considered to be a statement about his anticipated therapy as it is commonly symbolized early in treatment, namely, a journey.

James then began talking about some policemen (his father and/or the therapist) but his story became somewhat unclear. This was partially due to his utilization of typical resistance material: repetition of names and alliterations ("One is named Steven and Winni Minni, Minni Winni.") and other difficult, if not impossible, to analyze verbalizations. To break into the resistance (which was not easy, as the transcription well reveals) and to bring the story to completion (our time was almost up), I urged him (in a manner far stronger than my usual pattern) to complete his story. Under the pressure he reiterated some final important messages about the turtle: "He just can tell everyone what to do" and "He tells like robbers to go away and God makes the robbers go away and die." The statements epitomize James's desire to assume such control over the world that *he even controls God*. In this way he could prevent the robbers (who would steal his father away) from perpetrating their heinous crime. With this understanding of James's story, I told mine.

> *Therapist:* Once upon a time there was a turtle. Do you want to call him a turtle or a tortoise?
>
> *Patient:* Well, mine was a tortoise so can you call yours a turtle?
>
> *Therapist:* I'll call mine a turtle. Okay. Now this turtle wanted to go around telling everybody what to do and he thought that if he said something that God would make them do what he wanted them to do.
>
> *Patient:* Yeah?
>
> *Therapist:* So — for instance, there was a firehouse near where he was.
>
> *Patient:* Uh, it's the same.
>
> *Therapist:* No, it's not the same. It's not the same. It's a firehouse but different things happen. And he went into the firehouse one day and he said, "I know more about fighting fires than you guys and I want you to make me a fire chief and I want you to listen to all my orders."
>
> And they said, "Sorry, sorry. First of all, you're a kid and you don't know more about fires than we do and we're not going to listen to your orders and we're not going to give you a fire chief hat."

He said, "Well, I want to be a fire chief."

And they said, "Well, if you want to be a fire chief we suggest that when you grow up you go to fire school — fire-fighting school — and you learn very hard, you study very hard, and you learn how to be a fire fighter and then maybe someday you'll be a fire chief. But that's the only way you'll be able to order around firemen. No other way."

Well, this made the turtle very sad because he wanted to be a fire chief and they just weren't going to follow all his orders. Anyway, he decided that maybe he would do something else. So he looked around and he went to a freight yard where there were trains and he went over to the engineers and he said, "I want to tell you guys how to run these trains. I want to direct all the trains and I want to run these trains. I want you to listen to my orders." See, he still thought that whatever he said somehow God would listen to him and God would make all these things happen.

And they said, "Sorry, we're not going to listen to you. You're only a kid. You don't know anything about engineering. You don't know anything about running trains, and we're not going to listen to you."

He said, "Well, how can I run trains then?"

And they said, "Well, when you grow up you go to school where they teach men how to be engineers for trains and at that time maybe someday you'll run a whole yard or you'll be in the control room there and you'll be able to run all the trains, but not until that time."

Well, this made him very sad. So he was walking around near an airport and he saw airplanes there. He said, "I know what. I'm gonna control this airport." He went to the control room where the men are where they control all the airplanes. You know what that is? (Patient nods affirmatively.) And he went in there and he said, "Okay, men, I'm the chief here. I want to run all these airplanes and tell you how to fly these things."

They said, "Sorry." They told him the same things the others said. What did they say to him?

Patient: They said, "You have to all go to school."

Therapist: "You have to learn how to do that and then maybe you can control some airplanes, but not all." And this made him very sad but he gradually learned something. He learned that you can control some things and not others and if you want to control things you've got to do things to learn how to control things. You just can't control things by wishing them or thinking that God is going to make them or control things for you. And that's the end of the story. Do you know what the lessons are?

Patient: Yeah, but that's a rather really short story. Mine was longer.

Therapist: Well, sometimes I tell short stories. Sometimes I tell longer stories.

Patient: I like long stories.

Therapist: Well, did you like that story?

Patient: No, not too very much because it wasn't very long.

Therapist: Uh huh. All right. Besides it being too short was there anything about it — anything else that you thought about it?

Patient: Yeah, I wish he had a time.

Therapist: What?

Patient: I wish he had a time to be a man. Can you make up a different part?

Therapist: Oh, you want him to have time to be a man?

Patient: No, but I got to tell you something. Can you make up a part where he gets to be a pilot or something around that?

Therapist: Okay. You want to make it up or should I make it up?

Patient: You.

Therapist: Okay. Well, after this the boy realized that in order to control things . . .

Patient (interrupting): Was it turtle or boy?

Therapist: I'm sorry — excuse me — the turtle realized that in order to control things you have to work very hard over a long period of time and then sometimes quite often you can control things and you can get people to do what you want. So, he decided, what did he decide to become — a pilot, engineer, or fireman? Which do you think?

Patient: A fireman.

Therapist: He decided he wanted to be a fireman. So when he grew up he went to high school first. He studied very hard in high school so he was a good student and then after he graduated high school he went to the fire school — firemen's school — and he studied very hard there and he worked very hard there and finally one day he graduated and became a fireman. And they gave him a fire cap with a badge and a whole uniform. And they shook his hand like this (shaking patient's hand) and they said, "Congratulations, you are a fireman." And then he worked at a fireman's . . . a firehouse for a long time and he did so well that one day he became a fire chief. And when he was a fire chief he was then able to say. "Okay, men, pull out this truck. You go out this way. You go to this place. There's a fire over here." And then he ordered everyone around. But even then there were certain things that he couldn't control. Even then, even though he ordered everybody around and was the chief, there were still things that he could control and still things that he couldn't.

Patient: What couldn't he do?

Therapist: Well, he could put out a lot of fires but not every fire.

Patient: Why?

Therapist: Some fires, even as hard as he tried, he couldn't put out. But most of the fires he could. But the best way to put out a fire is to work hard at it and most often he was able to put out the fires. But every once in a while there was a fire he couldn't put out.

Patient: But how did it get out?

Therapist: How did the fire get out? Sometimes it would burn out by itself. Sometimes other firemen would come and help and then it would get put out. And sometimes the house would burn down. That was very often. Uh ... [implying negation of the previous sentence] . . . That was not very often. Most often he was able to put out the fire. But sometimes he couldn't. That's how it was.

Patient: Suppose two-hundred googol fire trucks came to the hard-to-get-out [fires]?

Therapist: What?

Patient: Two-hundred googols [Mathematics: 10^{100}].

Therapist: Even two-hundred googols.

First of all, you can't get the ... there are some fires where ... once in a while there is a fire where no matter how hard you try you can't put it out and the fire burns down the building.

Patient: Do you know how it can happen?

Therapist: How?

Patient: The longest fire engine that can reach to its front and to its back going all over the world carrying the world around.

Therapist: Hmm. Well, all I can say is that in this particular story the firemen most often were able to put out the fire. But once in a while, on rare occasions, there was a fire that came and they couldn't put it out, but that didn't happen very often.

Patient: But that may happen to our house. It might happen to our house, Mom.

Patient's Mother: Well, we have a pretty good fire department. They're pretty good putting out fires and then we're very careful about not starting fires. Aren't we?

Patient: Yeah, but how do we start the fire?

Patient's Mother: Well, by being careless — by starting the fire with carelessness — by playing with matches when you shouldn't be.

Patient: But I never play with matches. I know who plays with matches in our house. Hmm ... *hmmm* ...

hmm (singing with the implication that his mother does). Why do you do that?

Patient's Mother: Because I use them for experiments.

Patient: But you started to play with matches when you had your experiments in the bathroom.

Patient's Mother: I'm very careful about it to make sure they won't drop on the floor or anything.

Patient: Well, did it drop on the floor?

Patient's Mother: No.

Therapist: See we have to stop here, but I can say this to you that you can prevent most fires by just being very careful and not playing with matches, and when you use fire to be very careful how you use it, where you use it. And when and if a fire does start, most often the fire can be put out. But once in a while it does happen, even though everybody tries very hard, that . . .

Patient (interrupts excitedly): You know where we can go if they can't get it out? You know where we can go? To an apartment or a hotel.

Therapist: If the house burns down — and this happens once in a while — then you go live in an apartment or a hotel until they build another house. Okay?

Patient: So what if after that all the hotels and all the rooms were filled and all the houses were filled.

Therapist: No that doesn't happen. It doesn't happen. There are always other places to live. The earth is not filled up. There's always room and there's always places and if a house does burn down, which on rare occasion happens, then the people can go live somewhere else.

Patient: Or, if almost all the houses are filled if they go to someplace or somebody they know and they there sleep over their house. Can that be?

Therapist: What's that?

Patient: They sleep over their house . . . (mumbles).

Therapist: Yes they sleep at someone else's house. Right. Now the lesson of that story is that usually you can stop a house from burning down by being very careful, and if there is a fire, by learning how to be a good fireman and getting good firemen who know how to protect houses from being burned down and know how to fight fires. But once in a while, even though you try very hard, a house may burn down and if that happens you can always go to another house.

Patient: What's the name of that story?

Therapist: What name do you want to give it?

Patient: "The Turtle Be the Fireman."

Therapist: Okay. "The Turtle Who Was the Fireman"?

Patient: Yeah.

Therapist: Okay. Very good.

Patient: And mine was the . . . (long pause) . . .

Therapist: What?

Patient: Um . . . (pause) . . . "The Goodest Turtle in the Whole Wide World."

Therapist: Okay. Very good. Do you want to say good-bye to everybody.

Patient: Good-bye.

Therapist: Better sit over here and say good-bye or no one will see you.

Therapist: Good-bye.

Patient: Good-bye.

Therapist: Okay. Let's turn it off.

Patient: I want to see the TV.

Therapist: You want to see it?

Patient: Yeah.

Therapist: All right. We'll look at it a little bit.

My first message directs itself to the magic transformation to professional competence exhibited by the turtle in James's story. In mine, the turtle learns that only through slow growth and hard work can one achieve expertise. My purpose here was to discourage James from utilizing quick methods to succeed as a response to his father's ineffectiveness and possible death. In the encounter with the pilot I mentioned, for the first time, the important message:

"you can control some things and not others." I was trying to impress upon James the fact that he would ultimately have to accept his own limitations if he was to effectively deal with his father's illness and its consequences.

Returning again to the training program, I invited James to choose which career he wanted the turtle to pursue and he selected that of fireman. I often try to engage the child in making decisions at crucial points in my story to ensure that I do not diverge too far from that which is psychologically most meaningful to him. As will be seen later, allowing James to choose the fireman enabled the story to take a most meaningful direction — a course that it might not have taken had I myself chosen either the engineer or pilot as the role for him to assume. My elaboration of the length and intensity of the training program served to impress upon the patient how essential hard work is to the process of acquiring a skill. The conferring of the uniform and hat, shaking James's hand, and congratulating him on his accomplishment, was a bit of actively acting out the drama to further enhance the efficacy of my communications. (I have found dramatization to be a most potent vehicle for message transmission, especially with children in the four-to-seven-year group, and I will discuss this in greater detail in this next chapter.) The patient was obviously deeply involved at this point and actively engaged in the "ceremony."

In the ensuing discussion it became obvious that the fireman was preferred over the pilot and engineer because, as a person whose job it is to put out fires, he lends himself well to symbolizing James's primary concern at the time the story was told. The patient's obsessive, and even pathetic, desire for reassurance that firemen are invariably successful in extinguishing fires reflected clearly that fires represented calamity for him (specifically his father's illness and its potential sequelae). The fireman was selected because he has it within his power to prevent the devastating effects of fire. James would not accept my statement that there are some fires which even firemen cannot put out — so deep was his need to believe that every catastrophe, regardless of how devastating, can be controlled.

He then spoke directly of his concerns about fires destroying his own house — thereby bringing the problem "closer to home" so to speak. After being told that even his home was not immune, he switched to the issue of *preventing* fires — thereby providing himself with another method of control over the uncontrollable. Once again, I impressed upon him the fact that although most fires can be prevented or put out before extensive damage has been done, there are some which, after the best precautions and efforts, are still significantly destructive. I knew that this communication was painful to James and I did not press it without reservations. (It hurt me to confront him with such unpleasant information.) However, to deprive him of this correction of his distortions would have allowed the perpetuation of his maladaptive responses to his father's illness. He had to come to terms with the fact that certain events could not be controlled. Only after he was able to accept this could he be in a position to consider healthier adaptations.

It is a testimony to the healthy forces within this child that, without suggestions on my part about alternatives, he stated that if the house burns down, you can go to "an apartment or a hotel." In effect, James was telling me: "I accept what you say. My father may die and my protection and support (as symbolized by my house) may be taken from me. But others may be able to provide me with these necessities of life, even if not so adequately (as symbolized by the apartment and hotel)." I readily agreed with him, reinforced his solution, and so ended the program.

Magic Solution Fantasies. Mark, a nine-and-a-half-year-old boy, was referred for treatment because of disruptive and hyperactive behavior in the classroom. At home he was difficult to manage and frequently uncooperative. Initial evaluation revealed evidence of an organic component to his impulsivity and hyperactivity, but I considered superimposed psychogenic factors to be operative as well. He told this story during his second month of treatment.

Patient: Well, once there was this farmer and he liked to plant all kinds of crops, and he raised chickens and cows and horses. He liked to work out in the garden. He liked to feed the chickens and get their eggs.

One day he took an egg out of underneath a chicken and the chicken bit him. And he didn't know what to do because the chicken never bit him before. So he sold the chicken to a man and this man got mad and he sold the chicken to another man. And this person that he sold the chicken to got mad and said he didn't want it. So he gave it back to him and that man gave it back to the farmer. And then that chicken died so he was kind of glad.

So he went along with his farming and when he was planting his crops — you know corn — in his cornfields, he found like a little, whatever you want to call it, stone. And he kept it because it was kind of pretty. So when he was keeping it, he kept it in his dresser, you know. And every time when he went out to work in his crops he had the stone with him. He would put it in his pocket and every year he held that in his pocket the crops would come up just the way he wanted them to, and when he didn't have it with him something went wrong. So he always had the stone with him. And then he thought that it was a magic stone. And then one day when he was riding along in his wagon pulled by a horse, it went across the bridge and the wheel came off, you know. And the bridge started to crack. So he grabbed the stone and put it in his pocket and then just got up and walked across to the other side. And then he took the horse to the other side with him and the bridge fell out, you know. As soon as he took it [the stone] out of his pocket the bridge fell into the river. So he had to go and tell the people about it so they could put up a sign so nobody else could run into it. They put up a sign that said, "Bridge Out." And the townspeople paid to put up a new bridge.

And when the man found out that he lost the stone he was very unhappy and like he didn't tell anybody ever that he had the stone. So one time he was walking along in the same spot that he found the crop, he found the stone again. And he always had good luck forever on.

Therapist: Tell me something. Is it true that it was because the man had taken the stone out of his pocket that the bridge fell down?

Patient: Yes.

Therapist: And that if he had kept the stone in his pocket the bridge would not have fallen down.

Patient: Right.

Therapist: What about the wheel of his wagon? Would that have broken had he kept —

Patient (interrupting): Well, the wheel broke and the weight of it pushed and cracked the bridge.

Therapist: I see, but it was because he didn't have the stone that the bridge fell down?

Patient: Right.

Therapist: And what's the lesson of that story?

Patient: If you've got something you believe in, you should try to hold on to it, like you know, not try to lose it. If you really believe in it don't you know, fool around with it.

Therapist: Okay.

In the first part of the story the farmer, who as the protagonist of the story represents the patient, faces the problem of what to do with a chicken who bites him. I considered the biting chicken to symbolize those who might be hostile toward Mark. The essential problem which Mark is dealing with here is that of how to handle those who are hostile to him. He first attempts to solve the problem by selling the chicken, that is, getting rid of the hostile person and, incidentally, making a profit as well. The solution requires some comfort with duplicity in that the farmer does not inform the buyer of the chicken's alienating defect which caused him to sell it. The buyer, presumably after being bitten himself, similarly disposes of the bird to a third person. The latter, equally dissatisfied, returns the chicken to the second who, in turn, gives the unwanted creature back to the original owner. Having learned that one cannot so easily rid oneself of those who are hostile, the farmer utilizes a more expedient solution: the chicken dies. This solution, often resorted to in inferior novels, provides a quick resolution to a complex problem and generally is not particularly adaptive in reality because those who hound, persecute, and otherwise make our lives miserable do not generally die so conveniently. In fact, they often appear to live longer than those who treat us benevolently. In short, this part of the story reveals two patterns which Mark would like to utilize with those who treat him malevolently. They are both maladaptive: one cannot generally get rid of them (sell them off) and they do not generally conveniently die and thereby cease their provocations.

In addition, we are not told why, after never having bitten the farmer, the chicken suddenly decides to do so. There is no consideration of the possibility that the farmer may have contributed to the chicken's behavior by some provocation or negligence, as is so often the case in reality. The chicken, as the layer of eggs (from which most life grows), most likely represents the patient's mother. This part of the story then represents an attempt on Mark's part to rid himself symbolically of his mother who, in her attempts to get him to act in a more civilized manner, often nagged him and was "on his back."

Lastly, one must consider the possibility that the biting chicken is the incarnation of Mark's own hostility — projected outward in an attempt to disown it. His attempt to separate himself even further from his own anger by selling the biting chicken to a stranger does not prove successful and so he resorts to its total obliteration — symbolized by the chicken's death. This interpretation does not preclude my original one in which the hostility exists entirely within someone else; the story can depict both processes simultaneously.

Next, the farmer finds a magic stone which, as long as

he keeps it in his pocket, brings him good fortune. He need merely keep the stone in his pocket and his crops flourish; failure to do so causes them to grow "wrong." I considered this part of the story to reflect Mark's wish that he not have to put in any effort to accomplish things in life, especially learning in school. He did not apply himself to his studies and took an attitude of "somehow things will work out." The magic stone reflects his insecurity over things not working out and provides him with the power to bring about a favorable outcome without any effort on his part. Again, a maladaptive response to his school difficulties.

The magic stone not only causes him to prosper but protects him from danger as well. The danger depicted here is of a specific kind, namely, lack of support. The wagon, like most vehicles which one rides, generally depicts the person himself in his course through life. Here, I considered the breaking of the wagon's wheel and the falling of the bridge to depict Mark's feeling that his world was falling away from under him. His difficulties in school and at home were interfering with his gaining a sense of competence in coping with life. Both in the academic and the behavioral areas he was not acquiring the talents and skills which are necessary if one is to feel confident about coping with reality. In compensation for his feelings of inadequacy in this area, he provides himself with a magic stone which protects him from the dangerous results of his incompetence. Again, a clearly maladaptive resolution. With this understanding of Mark's story, I related mine.

> *Therapist:* Now I'll tell my story. The title of my story is "The Chicken and the Stone."
>
> Once upon a time there was a farmer and this farmer had a chicken and this chicken would lay eggs. And one day he went over to the chicken to get an egg, and the chicken bit him. He got very angry and he thought, "I know what I'll do. I'll get rid of this chicken. I'll sell this chicken to someone else." He also thought, "Maybe it will die. Then I won't have any problems with it."
>
> So another man came along and he said, "Would you like to buy a chicken?"

And the man said, "Well, tell me about this chicken. Is he a good chicken? Is he kind? Does he bite?"

The farmer said, "Well, he may bite."

"Look," the man said, "I don't want a biting chicken."

And the farmer didn't know what to do because there he was stuck with this chicken. He said, "Gee, I wish this chicken were dead."

The second man said, "Look, here you have a chicken that's biting. You want to get rid of him. You want him to die. Is that the only way you know how to solve a problem with a biting chicken? You know, you can't solve life's problems by killing off or selling off the people who are bothering you. You've got to work it out with them. You can't get rid of people so easily and you can't even get rid of biting chickens so easily. So I suggest that you try to figure out some way of solving this problem with the chicken."

Well, he talked to the chicken. (In my story this chicken talks.) And he found out that there were things which he was doing which were bothering that chicken and that's why the chicken bit him. And when they were able to settle that problem and he stopped doing the things which bothered the chicken, the chicken stopped biting him and then the chicken continued to lay many more eggs and he then no longer wished to get rid of the chicken to sell him and he no longer wished that the chicken were dead.

Now, one day this farmer was working in his cornfields and he found a very pretty stone. It was very shiny and very pretty. And he said, "I wonder if this is a magic stone. I'd sure like to have a magic stone. My crops haven't been doing too well lately. So he rubbed the stone and he hoped that the crops would do better. But nothing happened. The crops still were poor.

But one day he was in town and he was in a general store buying provisions and the owner of the store noticed that the farmer was rubbing the stone and holding it in his pocket. And he said, "What are you doing there?"

The farmer said, "Oh, that's my magic stone. That gives me luck."

He said, "Has it ever given you luck?"

The farmer replied, "Well, no, but I'm hoping it will make my crops better."

And the man in the store said to him, "Well, I never heard of a magic stone." He said, "What are you doing with your crops? Are you using any fertilizers and things like that?"

The farmer said, "Well, not really. I really don't believe too much in them. It's a lot of extra work putting in those fertilizers and it costs money."

And the man said, "Well, I think that the reason why your crops aren't doing well is that you're not taking care of them well enough. You're not putting in fertilizers." And he asked the farmer some other questions about what he was doing and it was clear that the farmer was not doing everything that he could. And the man in the store said, "Instead of rubbing a magic stone I suggest you get to work on your farm and start taking good care of your crops. I think there's a better likelihood that they'll do well than if you rub a magic stone."

And the farmer thought about what the man had said and he decided to try him out. So he got the fertilizer and he started to work harder on his crops, and sure enough that year he had a better crop than he had ever had before. Well, although the farmer was impressed with what the storekeeper had said, he wasn't fully sure that the stone still wasn't magic.

And on his farm there was a bridge which was somewhat old and weak, and he used to look at it and say, "I wonder if I should fix it up one of these days. Na, I'll rub my stone. It will keep it going." So he used to rub his stone every time he'd pass that bridge in order to keep the bridge solid. But one day as he was riding his wagon across the bridge a wheel broke and his wagon fell down and sure enough the bridge broke as well, even though he had had his magic stone in this pocket. And there he was in the water — his horse jumping around very scared, the wagon broken even more than it had been, the farmer sitting in the water all wet, and his wagon broken even more, and the bridge completely crushed. And there he was with the magic stone in his pocket! And as he sat there, he realized that this stone really wasn't magic. Finally it took *that* to make him realize and after that he decided to build a new bridge. He threw away the stone and he built a new strong bridge and that was the end of his belief in a magic stone. And do you know what the lesson of that story is?

Patient: Don't count on something else to do your work for you.

Therapist: Right! That's one lesson. That's the lesson with the magic stone. What's the lesson of the part with the chicken and the egg and the biting?

Patient: You should fix your own problems now if you can, or else somebody else will fix them for you.

Therapist: Well, *that* and if you have a problem with someone it's not so easy to get rid of them.

Patient: Try to figure it out.

Therapist: Try to figure it out with them. You can't kill them off, you can't sell them generally. Human beings are not like chickens. You can't just sell them or kill them so easily. If you try to, you know, you'll get into a lot of trouble. So the best thing is to try to work the problem out with the person. The end. Wait a minute. I want to ask you something. Do you want to say anything about this story?

Patient: No.

Therapist: Did you like it?

Patient: Yeah.

Therapist: Any particular part?

Patient: The part where he found the stone and it was pretty and shiny.

Therapist: Uh huh. Any other part?

Patient: No.

Therapist: Did you learn anything from this story? Did this story teach you anything?

Patient: No.

Therapist: Not at all?

Patient: Well, yeah.

Therapist: What does it teach you?

Patient: Well, you should kind of figure out your own problems and don't count on other people to do stuff for you.

Therapist: Okay. What about magic? What does it say about magic?

Patient: Magic — well, if you've got a magic stone make sure it's really a magic stone and then go counting on it. (laughs)

Therapist: Do you think there are such things as magic stones?

Patient: No. (laughs)

Therapist: I don't believe so either.

Patient: You can keep them as a good luck charm — as a pretty piece, but not as a magic stone.

Therapist: Do you think a good luck charm really brings good luck?

Patient: Hhmmm, not really.

Therapist: I don't think so either. No. Okay. So that's the end of the program today. Good-bye, boys and girls.

In my response to the patient's chicken story I told one in which the chicken symbolizes a hostile person rather than the patient's own projected hostility. I felt that the former meaning was the most pertinent to the patient at that time. To introduce the latter into the same story might have "overloaded" him with my communications and thereby made them less effective. In addition, the child is usually more talented than I in forming a story in which the same figures depict many themes simultaneously. When I wish to respond with a story which deals with more than one issue which has been portrayed simultaneously in the child's story, I relate them as either separate events in one story or two separate stories. (For example, "Would you like to hear another story about that fox?")

Whereas the first buyer in Mark's story gullibly buys the chicken without asking questions, in my story he inquires about the chicken's habits — especially whether he bites. I attempted thereby to communicate that buyers in reality may not easily be taken in by the seller's duplicity. I hoped to let Mark know that one doesn't easily get away with lying and in this way lessen his tendency to lie in order to achieve his ends. The farmer then tells the truth and hopefully serves as a model of honesty for the patient. Thwarted in his attempts to get rid of the malevolent chicken, the farmer expresses the wish that it die. Again, reality considerations reign and the chicken remains very much alive. At this point the buyer becomes more directly the transmitter of my healthier communications and adaptations. He advises direct inquiry into the difficulties in the farmer-chicken relationship in the service of resolving them in ways more appropriate than those already attempted by the farmer.

Accordingly, the farmer invites the chicken to express his grievances ("In my story this chicken talks.") rather than act them out with biting. The chicken does so and the problems are resolved. Because the patient's story did not specify the nature of the chicken's source(s) of irritation, I made only general reference to them. Had I wished to get more specific I would have first asked Mark why the chicken bit the farmer. The information so gained could have served to provide me with specifics for my story. But I already had so much information to work with by the time Mark finished his complete story that I decided not to add any more material. Again, overloading can reduce the child's receptivity to the therapist's stories. My main message then was that if someone is hostile toward you, rather than trying to get rid of him by separation or death, try to work out the problem through civilized inquiry and nonviolent action.

In my story the magic stone does nothing to improve the farmer's crops. My advice to utilize more realistic and predictably effective methods is transmitted through the owner of the general store. The farmer is receptive to this advice and, although it works, he still does not give up his hope that his stone will perform magic. We are generally more attracted to easy methods and solutions than to difficult and complex ones and the farmer is not immune to this human frailty. It takes a more dramatic proof of the impotency of his stone to convince him of its worthlessness in controlling natural events. Rub the stone as he might, his wagon wheel broke, the bridge crumbled under his weight, and he tumbled into the water damaging his wagon even more. The written transcription does not communicate the sense of drama and excitement which I tried to convey as I related this incident in the story. The patient's involvement confirmed that he was swept up in the tale. It is in such moments of drama that the therapist's messages are most meaningfully communicated.

At the end, rather than tell the moral myself, I asked Mark what he understood to be the lesson. In this way I can often determine whether my messages have been truly understood because a statement of the moral requires a deep appreciation, on an abstract level, of the story's fundamental meaning. His responses revealed that he had basically understood my main points but that he was not so readily giving up his belief in magic. Therapy, like many other things in life, is a slow process if it is to be meaningful. One cannot expect radical changes toward health with one story. But each one can serve as a small step toward that goal.

A Very Bored Young Lady. Roberta, a ten-and-a-half-year old girl, was brought to therapy because of facial tics, nail biting, emotional inhibition, preoccupation with thoughts that she is inadequate, and impaired self-assertion. She was easily teased by friends and would not fight back. She poorly communicated her thoughts and feelings and became withdrawn and somber in situations that would arouse emotions — especially anger. At such times she might become aloof, tired, and would yawn frequently.

Her parents had been separated for about two years at the time of referral, but had not yet made a decision regarding either divorce or reconciliation. Each dated others and she frequently met the dates of her parents. They denied that this might have any untoward effects on her and took the position that this was the reality of their lives and she would have to adjust to it somehow.

Roberta told this story during her second month in treatment:

> *Patient:* I don't know how to start it. Would you start it?
>
> *Therapist:* Okay. Once upon a time . . . a long time ago . . . in a distant land . . . far away . . . there lived a . . .
>
> *Patient:* A dragon.
>
> *Therapist:* And this dragon . . .
>
> *Patient:* His name was Ronald.
>
> *Therapist:* . . . was named Ronald. Go ahead. And one day this dragon named Ronald . . .
>
> *Patient:* . . . went swimming.
>
> *Therapist:* . . . went swimming. Yeah, go ahead.
>
> *Patient:* And water got up his, um, thing that the fire comes out of his nose.
>
> *Therapist:* Yeah.
>
> *Patient:* And he couldn't breathe fire anymore. And so he went to his doctor and he told the doctor that he couldn't breathe fire anymore and he didn't know why. And the doctor looked up in his nose and saw that there was water and he drained all the water and Ronald could shoot flames again.
>
> *Therapist:* Uh huh.
>
> *Patient:* And he was happy for ever after.
>
> *Therapist:* Okay. And the lesson of that story? (Patient starts biting fingernails.)
>
> *Patient:* I don't know.
>
> *Therapist:* Hh hmm. Well, what do we learn from that story? What's the moral?
>
> *Patient* (still biting fingernails): I don't know.
>
> *Therapist:* Can't think of any?
>
> *Patient:* Nope.
>
> *Therapist:* Okay. Now it's my time to tell a story.

I considered the dragon to represent Roberta herself and its inability to breathe fire an expression of repressed hostility. The fire, with its potential for massive destruction, well lends itself to symbolizing anger. Similarly, water — as the most potent antagonist to fire — lends itself well to the symbolization of those forces that squelch anger. The doctor's removing the water from the dragon's nose symbolizes Roberta's desire that the inhibitory forces be removed. However, such removal is done without any active participation on Roberta's part. She need only passively lie back and the doctor solved the problem himself. With this understanding of the patient's story, I related mine.

> *Therapist:* Once upon a time there was a dragon and this dragon's name was Ronald (patient still biting fingernails). And one day this dragon found that he couldn't shoot the flames out of his nose anymore and when he would try they wouldn't come out. Now on that very same day he happened to go swimming and some water did get up into his nose and he thought that this was the reason why he probably couldn't breathe (patient blinking, still biting fingernails) flames anymore.
>
> So he went to a doctor and the doctor looked in his nose and the doctor said, "Well, that water that you described as being the cause of all of this is not there anymore. That water has dried out (patient blinking and still biting fingernails) and that isn't the reason why you can't shoot those flames out."
>
> And the dragon said, "Well, what is it then?"
>
> He said, "Well, I think that you're afraid to breathe fire anymore. I don't know what has happened to you but for some reason you are frightened. I see nothing physical about this. There's nothing . . . I think it's psychological. That's how I see it. You're probably afraid to breathe out those flames."
>
> What do you think the dragon said?
>
> *Patient:* "I'll try it. I'll like it."

Therapist: Well, what do you think happened then?

Patient: He tried to blow fire and it worked.

Therapist: Yeah. Well, actually what happened was it wasn't that easy. He was scared of letting out the fire. He had developed the idea that even if someone bothers you or if some enemy attacks you that to breathe out the flame is bad or wrong or nice people don't do that; (patient nonchalantly brushing off shoes with her hand) even in self-defense it's wrong for a dragon to breathe flame.

Patient: So why was he given the flame to begin with?

Therapist: That's right (patient inspecting sole of her shoe). He was a dragon who was given the flame to begin with and in spite of the fact that he was given the flame to begin with, he still had the idea that it was wrong to breathe it out. Now what do you think of that?

Patient (in bored fashion): I don't know.

Therapist: Do you think it was a wise idea or not?

Patient: To not?

Therapist: Pardon me.

Patient: What do you mean?

Therapist: What do you think about that dragon's idea that even though he was born with the flame and the capacity to use it that he didn't?

Patient: Oh, (yawning slightly) I don't think it was a good idea.

Therapist: Hh hmm. Well, that's right. (patient playing with necklace locket) It wasn't and what he did was he began to realize that he would have to start getting some practice in breathing out flames because he had gone for some time now being scared to breathe them out.

So when some other animal came along and bothered him or a person or another dragon, (patient examining fingernails) he first let out a little bit of flame and realized that he did have the flame. And he was kind of scared. (patient biting fingernails) His knees were knocking and his teeth were chattering and he was very frightened at first. But he began to realize that each time he let out the flame it became easier and that he wasn't taken advantage of anymore. See, during the time when he wasn't breathing out his flame he was taken advantage of and people would do things to him because they knew that he wouldn't let out his flame. (patient yawning while clapping her hand over her open mouth) But once he started to let out the flame he began to see that . . . Is this story bothering you? Is it boring you?

Patient (almost inaudibly): No.

Therapist: Huh?

Patient: No.

Therapist: Were you listening to it?

Patient: Yes.

Therapist: Okay. (patient yawns again) At any rate, once he started to breathe it out he realized it wasn't so bad and he realized also that people would stop taking advantage of him.

And do you know what the lesson of that story is?

Patient: No.

Therapist: Well, try to figure it out. What did this dragon learn?

Patient: That if you have something, if you are given something, you should use it even if you think it's wrong.

Therapist: Uh huh. But did he change his mind about thinking that it was wrong?

Patient (playing with necklace locket while looking down at it): Hhmmm. I think so.

Therapist: How did he change his mind? What did he realize?

Patient: I don't know.

Therapist: What did he come to realize?

Patient: That if you have something you should use it (sighs deeply, while stroking abdomen).

Therapist: Hh hmm. And what was the purpose of the flame for him?

Patient (speaking through a yawn): To protect him.

> *Therapist:* Right. Okay. You don't seem to be too enthusiastic about this game. You seem kind of bored.
> *Patient:* Hhmm.
> *Therapist:* Is that right?
> *Patient:* Yeah.
> *Therapist:* Why are you bored?
> *Patient* (smiling): I knew you'd say that. Um, because I am. No reason. I just am (stroking stocking).
> *Therapist:* Hh hmm. Okay. Do you want to watch this?
> *Patient* (in bored, condescending tone): I don't care.
> *Therapist:* Okay. Fine. Let's watch it then.
> *Patient:* Is your clock right or is it a little fast?
> *Therapist:* No, that's the right time (patient again looks down at her necklace locket and starts playing with it).

The written transcript cannot convey the attitude of extreme ennui that pervaded as I got further along in the telling of my story. The patient sat back with a deadpan expression on her face and yawned profusely. At times she covered her mouth and at other times did not. Although her eyes remained open, I would not have been surprised had she closed them at any point. It was clear to me that her boredom served as a defense against her appreciating the true significance of my message, viz., that, although it may be anxiety-provoking, letting out one's resentment is far more adaptive and effective than suppressing it. Although she paid lip service to appreciating my moral and, ostensibly, gave the "correct" answers to my questions, it was clear that she was fighting against both herself and me in fully appreciating their significance.

The transcript does not convey an even more important phenomenon: the infectiousness of Roberta's ennui. Just as laughter and depression can be transmitted to others — others who have no reason themselves to be experiencing these emotions — Roberta's boredom brought about a moderate state of boredom within me. The transcript does not communicate the feeling of fatigue which I experienced near the latter third of my responding story nor can it communicate the inner pressure I had to place upon myself in order to push the conversation. I could not know how aware Roberta was of the effectiveness of this mechanism. It not only served to defend her from the anxiety elicited in the conversation, but essentially put a wet blanket on me, the transmitter of the anxiety-provoking material. It was an effective psychological smoke screen blown in my face and I don't think I could have gone on much longer with the interchange. It was not simply a feeling of being insulted by her yawns; it was more a feeling of overwhelming fatigue that gripped me. My attempts to focus on this defense mechanism were futile. Each time I broached the subject of her being bored, she denied that she was and I did not feel that pursuing this issue further would have been productive. The interchange closed with my feeling that I had not been successful in getting my message through, although I could not be sure. Her final comment about the clock going too fast (with the suggestion that the time had passed too quickly and that possibly she wanted more at some deep level) gave me a little hope that perhaps something had gotten through after all.

The reader who is interested in further information on this method may wish to refer to one of my general articles describing the method (1969a, 1971d, 1972c, and 1974d), my cassette tapes (1970f and 1973e [the latter contain actual recordings of therapist-patient interchanges]), or my full-length text describing the method (1971a). In addition, he may wish to refer to articles in which I describe its utilization in the treatment of a variety of clinical disorders: oedipal problems (1968a), post-traumatic neurosis (1970d), psychogenic coughing (1970e), anger inhibition problems (1972b), and psychogenic problems secondary to minimal brain dysfunction (1973b, 1974b, and 1974c). Becker (1972) and Schooley (1974) have found the technique useful in the treatment of the untoward psychological reactions of children hospitalized because of physical illness.

Chapter Six
Dramatization of the
Therapeutic Communications

Just as the Mutual Storytelling Technique was developed from the observation that children naturally enjoy both telling and listening to stories, the idea of dramatizing them arose from the observation that children would often automatically (and at times without conscious awareness) gesticulate, impersonate, intone, and enact in other ways while telling their stories. I found that when I introduced such theatrics myself the child became more involved in my stories and receptive to their messages. Whereas originally I introduced the dramatic elements *en passant*, that is, in the process of telling my story (just as the children tended to do), I subsequently formalized the process by inviting the child to reenact our stories as plays following our telling them: "I've got a great idea! Let's make up plays about our stories. Who do you want to be? The wolf or the fox?" At times I would invite the mother and even siblings to join us. (We often face the problem of having a shortage of available actors.) We see here another way in which mothers can be useful in the child's treatment. (A little encouragement may be necessary at times to help some mothers overcome their "stage fright.") Of course the therapist himself must be free enough to involve himself in the various antics that are required for a successful "performance." He must have the freedom to roll on the floor, imitate various animals, "ham it up," etc. He has to be able to be director, choreographer, writer, and actor — practically all at the same time. He may have to assume a number of different roles in the same play, and quickly shift from part to part. Such role shifts do not seem to bother most children nor reduce their involvement or enjoyment. Nor do they seem to be bothered by the therapist's "stage whispers," so often necessary to keep the play running smoothly.

The therapist who can create with the child such performances has a very valuable tool at his disposal. The enjoyment the child may derive from such plays can be immense. Accordingly, they can serve to entrench the child's involvement in treatment. In addition, such dramatizations enrich the therapeutic communications. One is not only transmitting the message verbally; rather one is adding a host of nonverbal stimuli (physical, kinesthetic, visual, tactile, and at times even olfactory and gustatory). Such multisensory exposure increases vastly the chances of the therapist's "being heard." And they help immensely in getting his messages to "sink in."

Clinical Examples

"Let's make up a play about your story. I'll be the frog and you'll be the boy who pulls off his leg. Okay?" Adam, an eight-year-old boy with minimal brain dysfunction, exhibited significant social perceptual difficulties. It was very difficult for him to place himself in another person's position and this caused him much pain and rejection in social situations. Intellectual impairment (his IQ was about 85) and difficulty in conceptualizing and abstracting resulted in his failing to appreciate and learn many of the subtleties of social interaction. Many of these appear to be learned almost automatically by normal children. Children with minimal brain dysfunction may find this their most crippling problem and it behooves the therapist to appreciate this when he works with such children. In Adam's case it was the primary focus of his treatment.

In session one day his mother reported that on the previous day Adam had pulled off the leg of a frog that he had caught in his backyard. I immediately responded with disgust: "Ych, that sounds terrible!" Although I knew that my response was going to lower Adam's self-respect at that point, I felt it was the price that had to be paid for a little superego development. I then asked Adam if he would like to play a game in which I am a frog and he is a boy who wants to pull off my leg. He hesitantly agreed. I lay on the floor and invited him to try to pull off my leg. My moans were immediate: "Ooooh, that hurts! Please stop. Please, my leg is going to come off. Ahhhh — ." I asked the patient what the boy then did. He replied that he stopped because he didn't want to hurt the frog any longer. "That's right," I replied. "When the boy realized how much he was hurting the frog, he stopped pulling its leg." I then asked Adam if he would like to play a game in which the boy doesn't stop after the frog screams out and he pulls off the leg and the frog dies. He agreed. This time, in spite of my bloodcurdling cries, the boy pulled off the frog's leg. "Now my leg is off and I'm dead," I mumbled as I lay stiffly on the floor. "Try to bring me back to life," I whispered to the patient as if giving stage directions (a maneuver commonly required in such plays). In spite of the patient's attempts to revive me (these included poking, pulling, artificial respiration, and a little feigned mouth-to-mouth resuscitation), I remained stiff and prostrate, all the while mumbling, "Even that doesn't help. When you're dead, you can never be brought back to life." The game ended (as such games usually do) with questions: "How does a frog feel when someone tries to pull off its leg?" "What can happen to a frog if someone pulls off its leg?" "Can a dead frog be brought back to life?"

One might argue that the above approach is a little too strong and that it might create intense feelings of self-loathing in the child. I can only reply that I do not believe that this has been my experience. Whatever transient lowering of self-esteem the child may suffer in such a game (and I grant that he certainly may) is more than compensated for by the ultimate enhancement of his self-worth that results from his heightened sensitivity to the pains of others and his ceasing to inflict unnecessary and wanton pain on those around him. Lastly, if such a game is indeed too ego-debasing to the child, he himself can usually be relied upon to refuse to play it or to discontinue it if it gets too "hot" for him. It is grandiose of the therapist to consider himself to know beforehand whether a healthy communication is going to be devastating to a patient. I tend to try it out and respect the patient's defenses when they exhibit themselves.

The reader should appreciate that I am fully aware that this child's cruel act related to hostility that was being redirected from other sources onto the frog. One cannot focus simultaneously on many of the multiple factors which usually contribute to a pathological act. Here I chose to direct my attention to the egocentricism issue (the child's inability to project himself into the situation of another living thing) and his ignorance of certain aspects of social reality.

"This damn magic wand is no good." George, another boy with minimal brain dysfunction and borderline intelligence, entered treatment at eight-and-a-half-years of age. He was quite immature in many ways and was overprotected by his mother. His view of the world of magic was very much like that of the five-year-old and his magic-cure expectations were strong. Near the end of his second month in treatment he told this story.

Patient: The name that I'm gonna have — I'm gonna have two names of the story each.
Therapist: Go ahead.
Patient: One name is gonna be "Little Ducklings"

and the second name is gonna be "One of the Ducklings Turns into a Grown Man." There's only gonna be one duckling.

Therapist: Okay.

Patient: There's the mother, the father, the brother.

Therapist: Okay. Now do you want to start the first story? Go ahead.

Patient: I said there's going to be two names and that's the story.

Therapist: Oh, just one story with two names?

Patient: Yeah.

Therapist: Okay. Start the story.

Patient: And two lessons.

Therapist: And two lessons. Okay. This is a story, one story with two names and two lessons. Go ahead. Let's hear.

Patient: Once there's a duckling. He said, "Ooh, how did I get changed into a duckling? I was a person all my life. How — how could this happen? How did this happen? I must even act like a duck now so a fairy godmother will come and save me. Quack, quack, quack, quack." But no fairy godmother came. So he said, "Quack, quack, quack, quack, quack" and he was begging for his fairy godmother.

Therapist: Okay, then what happened?

Patient: Then he said, "Quack, quack. Oh, I wish a fairy godmother would come. Quack, quack, quack, quack." And he was quacking so hard that he flew over to the water and fell in.

Therapist: Okay. Then what happened? This is a very good story.

Patient: Then he said, "Caw, caw, quack, quack, coo, coo, quack, quack," and he was . . . (mumbles) . . . up.

Therapist: And he was what?

Patient: Burning up.

Therapist: He was burning up. Why was he burning up?

Patient: Because he said, "Quack, quack, quack, quack, quack!" Like that.

Therapist: Okay. Then what happened?

Patient: Then he said, "Quack, quack, quack." (patient speaking in singsong manner) "Oh, I wish a fairy godmother, a fairy godmother." That's a little song the duckling made up.

Therapist: Okay. Go ahead.

Patient (sings again): "Oh, I wish a fairy godmother would come and get me out, would come and get me out, would come and get me out." And he was going, "Quack, quack, quack, quack, quack!" And then he turned into a horse!

Therapist: He turned into a horse! Yeah. Go ahead.

Patient: Then he said, "Boy, what happened with me? I was a duckling before. I used to go heeee, heeee. I hope a fairy godmother comes this time. Heeeeewwwwww, quack, quack." And then he changed back into a duck because he went "quack, quack" by accident.

Therapist: Uh huh. Then what happened?

Patient: And then the fairy godmother *really* came and said, "Huh! What, what. I thought I heard somebody calling me. I don't see anybody. Hhmm. Must be my magic wand ... (mumbles) ... by accident.

Therapist: Wait a minute. The fairy godmother said, "What, I thought I heard somebody calling me," and then she said what about a wand?

Patient: And then she said, "Hhhmmm! My magic wand probably made him disappear." But the duck was really in the pond under the water.

Therapist (interrupts): She thought that her magic wand made the duck disappear. That's why she didn't see him in the pond. Go ahead.

Patient: "Ooh, oh, oh, oh, I tricked her."

Therapist: Wait a minute. I don't understand that. Who's talking now?

Patient: The duck.

Therapist: And what did he say?

Patient: "Ooh, I tricked that fairy godmother by accident. I'll go get her. Fairy godmother, quack,

quack. I'm a duckling. Change me back into a person."
But the fairy godmother was in the clouds.

Therapist: So what happened then?

Patient: Then he was there again and when the fairy
godmother came again she saw him turned into a
horse. And she said, "Hey, what happened, horse? You
were quacking before. Don't you know how to make a
horse sound? A horse goes, 'Heeehawww,
heeehawww.' You went 'quack, quack, quack' and
clapping your hands. I'm not gonna help you. Keep this
magic wand and try yourself." And then the fairy
godmother went away.

Therapist: And then what happened? (Pause) So the
fairy godmother went away and wouldn't change him
into a person?

Patient: No, because she was so mad at him. He didn't
know how to make a horse sound. He changed before
the fairy godmother came there.

Therapist: Oh, the fairy godmother was mad because
he changed from a duck into a horse?

Patient: Yeah, and she heard him quacking.

Therapist: Oh, she heard him quacking and then he
turned into a horse. Okay, and then what finally
happened? So the fairy godmother got angry at him
and went away. Then what finally happened?

Patient: Then the magic wand worked on him and
that's the end.

Therapist: It worked on him. And what happened
when the magic wand worked on him?

Patient: It flew back — it was um — it flew back to the
fairy godmother.

Therapist: What happened to the duck or horse?

Patient: He turned back into a boy before it went ...

Therapist (interrupts): Oh, he turned back into a boy.
Oh, I see. Okay. And the lesson of that story?

Patient: Two lessons, remember?

Therapist: What are the two lessons?

Patient: Never (long pause).

Therapist: Never what?

Patient: Never be mad at a duck!

Therapist: Never be mad at a duck? And the other lesson?

Patient: Don't think there's no such thing as fairy godmothers. There's, there's a lesson that goes with that also. And the third lesson is: Don't believe in fairy godmothers because there's no such thing and if you heard a duck quacking and it changed into a horse it was really the duck and don't be mad at it.

Therapist: I see.

Patient: That's the lessons.

Therapist: Okay. Now it's my chance to tell a story.

This story is typical of that told by many children with minimal brain dysfunction. It is somewhat disorganized and the patient does not concern himself with whether his listener understands what is going on in it. Frequent questioning is required if the therapist is to surmise the story's psychodynamic meaning. In analyzing such a story it is best to think about main issues and general trends and not get bogged down in minutiae. The main thing that happens in this story is that a boy is turned into a duck and in that state he has the power to change himself into a horse. Finally, after a few somewhat confusing experiences with the fairy godmother, he is turned back into a boy. George had a speech defect for which he had received some therapy. In addition, his lower lip protruded somewhat and occasionally saliva dripped from it. (Characteristically, his mother was ever at hand to catch the saliva and it was not until I recommended it that she taught George how to use a handkerchief and to think about his tendency to salivate.) His depicting himself as a duck related, I believe, to his speech deficit as well as to his protruding lip. The horse, with his odd vocalization, also lends himself well to symbolizing the patient and his speech defect.

The story also depicts some hostile interchanges between the duck-horse and the fairy godmother: the duck tricks the fairy godmother by making a quacking sound and then changing into a horse; the duck hides from the fairy godmother so that she cannot find him; and the fairy godmother throws her wand at the horse. I decided that these elements, although important, were less readily analyzable because they were represented in such a confused fashion. I chose, therefore, to focus on the aforementioned theme and related this story.

Therapist: Once upon a time there was a duck and he was just a duck. He was a real duck. He never was a person.

Patient: What's the name of the story?

Therapist: The name of my story is: "The Duck and the Fairy Godmother." Okay? No, excuse me. I'm going to change the name: "The Duck and the Old Lady." Okay?

Patient: (laughs)

Therapist: "The Duck and the Old Lady" is the name of my story. Once upon a time there was a duck. And he was just a duck, a plain duck. He was a very nice duck but he thought it would be better not to be a duck. He thought it would be best to be a person. So he used to go around saying, "Quack, quack, quack, quack, quack quack," hoping he would find a fairy godmother. And he would sing a song and the song would go. How did the song go?

Patient (in singsong manner): "Quack, quack, quack, quack, quack, quack."

Therapist: He'd go, "Quack, quack. I wish I saw a fairy godmother." He'd go, "Quack, quack, quack, quack, quack, quack, quack. Fairy godmother! Where's the fairy godmother?" No fairy godmother came.

Patient: Talk slow. The duck talks so fast, I can't hear you.

Therapist: He would say, "Quack, quack, quack."

Patient (joins in): "Where's my fairy godmother?"

Therapist: "Where's my fairy godmother?"

Patient: And he was shaking his hands . . . (mumbles)

. . .

Therapist: But he couldn't find any fairy godmother.

Then one day he saw an old lady. She was walking by the river.

Patient: Did that old lady — was that old lady really a wicked witch?

Therapist: No.

Patient: Or a good witch?

Therapist: No, she was just an old lady, but this old lady . . .

Patient (interrupts): Did she have a wand?

Therapist: This old lady used to think that she was a fairy godmother. She thought that maybe there was such a thing as a fairy godmother and she thought . . .

Patient (interrupts): You told — you told this the other day except it didn't have a duck in it.

Therapist: No. This is a different story. Do you want to hear my story?

Patient: Yes, but the other day you told it about the old woman.

Therapist: Yeah, but this is a different story about an old woman. Okay? Do you want to hear this one?

Patient: Yes.

Therapist: So the duck went over to her and he said, "Quack, quack, quack, quack. Fairy godmother, will you change me into a person?"

And she thought that she had magic powers so she said, "Okay." (waving imaginary stick over patient's head) And she had a wand — she had a stick and she said to the duck, "Magic . . . magic . . . duck . . . duck, quack three times and I'll change you into a person. Quack three times." Okay, you make believe you're the duck.

Patient (while therapist rotates imaginary stick over his head): "Quack, quack, quack."

Therapist: And she waved it around and do you know what happened?

Patient: What?

Therapist: The duck still remained a duck!

Patient: (laughs)

Therapist: And she said, "Say quack again. Say quack harder."

Patient (yells): Quack!

Therapist: Harder!

Patient (yells louder): Quack!

Therapist: Harder!

Patient (yells again): Quack!

Therapist: Harder!

Patient (screams): Quack!

Therapist: And he still stayed a duck. And she got very angry . . . "Ooh, this magic wand! (striking the imaginary wand against a table) I'm hitting this magic wand. This magic wand (makes angry sounds) is no good! We'll try it again! Now you say quack again three times. Go ahead. Magic wand . . . "

Patient (while therapist is waving wand again over patient's head): "Quack, quack, quack."

Therapist: And he still remained a duck. And she got very . . . "This damn magic wand!" (angrily breaks the imaginary wand over his knee) And she took it and threw it away. (flings the wand away) She said, "Wait, I'll get another magic wand." She came back with another one and she said, "I'm going to say a new thing (waving wand over patient's head). Abracadabra, hokus, pokus, turn this boy (sic, therapist's error) into a person. He's a duck!" What happened?

Patient: He still remained a duck?

Therapist: Right! And she said, "I can't stand these magic wands. Umph!" And she took it and she broke it on her knee (breaks wand on knee) and she threw it away! (throws wand away) She was very mad.

As she was standing there, a man came along and he saw her.

Patient: Who was that man?

Therapist (jumping up and down): And she was jumping up and down screaming and crying, and this man said to her — who was this man? He was just a man walking by, an old man. And he said, "What are you so mad about old lady?"

She said, "My magic wands don't work. I want to turn this duck into a boy, into a person."

And the man said, "There's no such thing as a magic wand."

And she said, "You know, I'm beginning to see that."

Patient (interrupts): In the other story there was a woman with a magic wand like that, but there was no man; there was an owl. There was no duck.

Therapist: Right. In the other story there was a wise old owl. Right.

Patient: And the boy.

Therapist: What's that?

Patient: And in the other story there was a boy who wanted to be turned into a duck, I think.

Therapist: Well, it was a different story, but let's talk about this one. Anyway, so this man said, "There's no such thing as magic wands."

And the old lady said, "You know, I'm beginning to see that. I thought that I would like to be a fairy godmother and do this duck a favor and turn him into a boy.

And the man said, "Well, why would you want to turn him into a boy? He's a perfectly fine duck!"

And the duck said, "No, I'm not! No, I'm not!"

And the man said, "Why? What's wrong with you?"

He said, "I don't speak too well."

Patient (laughs): Heeoh. He doesn't speak too well.

Therapist: Yeah. And he said, "That's the reason why you want to turn into a person? You can *learn* to speak well."

And the duck said, "No, I can't! No, I can't!"

What did the man say?

Patient: "Yep, you could."

Therapist: And what did the man say as to how he could learn to speak well?

Patient: By going to a speech teacher.

Therapist: Right! So what do you think the duck did?

Patient: Go to a duck speech teacher.

Therapist: He went to a duck speech teacher. He left

the old lady who he realized could not really change him into a person. He was a duck. And he went to the speech teacher and then after that, it was very hard and it took a long time, but after that what happened?

Patient: He, he, he — oy, yoy yoy — he ... (mumbles)

. . .

Therapist: He what?

Patient: He, he ...

Therapist: What happened after that?

Patient: He ...

Therapist (interrupts): Forget something?

Patient: He ... uh ...

Therapist: What happened after he went to the speech teacher?

Patient: He (long pause) ...

Therapist: Come on, you can ...

Patient (interrupts): He could talk well.

Therapist: Right! Very good! He could talk well. He practiced very hard and then after that did he keep wishing then he would be a person?

Patient: No.

Therapist: He was happy he was a duck. And the lesson of that story is what? What are the lessons of that story? Can you figure them out?

Patient: How many ... (mumbles) ...

Therapist: The first lesson. What's the first lesson?

Patient: Uno (Spanish: *one*) lesson is ...

Therapist (interrupts): Uno lesson.

Patient: Never think you can change your magic wand into a person or a duck.

Therapist: Right. There's no such thing as magic. There's no such thing as a magic wand. Okay. Come over here. What's the second lesson?

Patient: Number dos (Spanish: *two*) lesson is never cry — eey, yie, yie.

Therapist: Never cry. That's not a lesson. Sometimes people cry. That's perfectly all right. All right. Let me tell you the second lesson. The second lesson of that story is: If you are a duck and you have some trouble speaking, the best thing you can do is to what?

Patient: Is to go to a duck speech teacher or a regular speech teacher.

Therapist: Right. And practice hard and after that you'll be able to speak well.

Patient: The end.

Therapist: The end.

Patient: Could we stay here all day until I want to go home, until I get tired?

Therapist: Well, we'll stay a little while longer.

Patient: Goody!

Therapist: Right. Do you want to watch this program?

Patient (running to turn on TV monitor): Good-bye!

Therapist: Good-bye, everybody.

The purpose of my story is obvious. I attempted to impart the notion that there are no such things as magic cures and that a more practical and predictably effective course toward overcoming one's handicaps is through constructive action. The written transcript cannot completely convey all the theatrical elements that I introduced in order to enhance the patient's interest in my story and encourage receptivity to my therapeutic messages. The therapist who is able to "ham it up" in this manner provides his patient with a valuable therapeutic adjunct. The child was swept up by my wild gestures and readily participated in the little play. His statement at the end: "Could we stay here all day until I want to go home, until I get tired?" confirms quite well the kind of enthusiasm that such dramatization can evoke.

When I started my story I was not completely clear about exactly how I was going to develop it. I did know, however, that it was going to center on a denial of the efficacy of magic. When a child asks me to tell the title of a story I generally provide one that epitomizes the story's primary theme or message. In this case, the patient's question caught me a little bit off guard because I had not yet precisely formulated my story. Accordingly, I gave the title "The Duck and the Fairy Godmother." I immediately recognized that this title implied that there would actually be a fairy godmother in the story. Accordingly, I quickly retracted the title and substituted "The Duck and the Old Lady." The therapist should not hesitate to change his mind in the course of his storytelling if he suddenly realizes that he can do better for his patient by doing so. It is unrealistic to require of ourselves that we create, on the spur of the moment, polished theatrical performances or cohesively written stories. In the split second between my stating the first title and then retracting it, I decided that my story would include an old lady who aspired to be a fairy godmother but who was unsuccessful. Hence, when I presented the second title I specifically omitted any reference to magic.

Another problem that I faced in formulating this story was that of what to do with the duck. As described, the duck well lent itself as a symbol of the patient because of his speech problem and his salivating, protruding lip. To portray the patient as a duck in my story might entrench this pathological personification and might thereby be antitherapeutic. However, to depict the patient as a boy would then rob me of the opportunity to deal with the magic transformation issue in a manner that was close to the patient's representation of the problem. If the therapist's story gets too remote from the patient's it becomes less therapeutically effective. I decided, therefore, that the advantages of maintaining the duck outweighed the disadvantages. In addition, the child's ability to create a fantasy that most efficiently and effectively synthesizes the symbols is far greater than that of the therapist. I believe that we lack the ingenuity not only of our child-patient's unconscious, but of our own unconscious as well. We ourselves cannot consciously create a dream as rich and as efficient as that which can be created by our own unconscious. The efficiency and ingenuity of our unconscious processes to utilize simile, metaphor, allegory, and efficient and innovative symbol fusion far surpasses that of our conscious mind. Therefore, I do not try to reconcile all elements of my story nor do I strive for one-hundred percent consistency. In this case I chose to be a little inconsistent (and even possibly a little antitherapeutic) in order to preserve the duck symbol for the larger purposes of my story, that is, to present a story which focused on the patient's magic cure delusion.

In the early part of my story the patient interrupted to point out that there were similarities between the story I was telling and a story I had told during a previous session. He was referring to a story in which a wise old owl was the conveyor of my therapeutic messages and that story as well dealt with the magic cure theme. His recognition of the similarities well demonstrates that the messages I communicate in my stories do sink in and are remembered.

"We can't seem to find the fairy godmother." This principle is again demonstrated by the sequence presented below which took place nine days later. On this day, instead of only the patient and his mother appearing for the session, his father and two younger siblings (his six-year-old brother and four-year-old sister) also appeared in the waiting room. The father was about to take the younger siblings out for a walk while the patient and his mother were in session with me. I invited the father to bring the children in because of my previous experience that their participation might be useful. The children were quite enthusiastic about the idea because they had heard from their brother such wonderful tales about the exciting things that go on in my office. Also, they had listened to some of the audiotapes that were made during their brother's sessions and had enjoyed what they had heard. George's father, however, was somewhat hesitant to come in because he felt the younger children would be disruptive. Accordingly, I told the younger children that they could come into the room as long as they behaved themselves and that if they did so, they might be allowed to participate in some of the games that George and I played, but I could not promise for certain that they would be invited to join us. The children were quite cooperative and did not interrupt George when he told this story on the television program.

Therapist: Good morning, boys and girls, ladies and gentlemen. Today is Friday, the 20th of April, 1973, and I am happy to welcome you all once again to Dr. Gardner's Make-Up-A-Story Television Program. Our guest today is now going to tell us another one of his own original made-up stories. You're on the air.

Patient: The name of the story is: "Animals Who Can't Talk and Animals Who Can Talk."

Therapist: "Animals Who Can't Talk and Animals Who Can Talk." Okay. This sounds like a very good title for a story. Go ahead.

Patient: Once there were two animals and they couldn't talk and on the farm and on that farm there were cows who couldn't talk and all animals who couldn't talk. And there was another farm far, far away — there was another farm — and on that farm animals could talk and those animals said to the other animals, "Buh, buh, buh, buh," and the other animals didn't understand those animals.

Therapist (interrupts): Excuse me, the animals who could talk or the animals who couldn't talk said, "Buh, buh, buh?"

Patient: The animals who could talk.

Therapist: Who could talk said, "Buh, buh, buh." Go ahead.

Patient: And the — what am I up to?

Therapist: You're up to — there were two farms. One farm had animals who couldn't talk and one farm had animals who could talk. And the animals who could talk said, "Buh, buh, buh," to the animals who couldn't talk. That's where you're at. Right?

Patient: (nods affirmatively)

Therapist: Now go ahead.

Patient: Then the animals who couldn't talk said (scratches ear) — didn't say anything, just went like this (arms outstretched, shrugs shoulders, palms up,

and has wistful expression on face). That's all. And they
— the animals who could talk — didn't know what that
meant. And then finally the animals who could talk
thought that they were saying it wrong. Instead of
saying, "Buh, buh, buh," they said, "How come you
can't talk?"

Therapist: Go ahead.

Patient: And then the animals who couldn't talk said
(moves lips), just opened their mouths.

Patient's mother (gestures that therapist look at
patient).

Therapist: Do that again. I wasn't looking. Your
mother said I missed something. What about the
animals who couldn't talk? What did they do?

Patient: (moves lips and mouth without sound
coming forth)

Therapist: Okay. Then what happened?

Patient: And then the animals who could talk said, "Ha!
You still can't talk and I way trying to make you talk.
I'm going to get a fairy godmother." And he just sat
there and he didn't call for a fairy godmother. He didn't
wish for a fairy godmother.

Therapist: Who didn't wish for a fairy godmother?

Patient: The animals.

Therapist: Which ones?

Patient: The ones who could talk, to make the ones
who couldn't talk, talk.

Therapist: Oh, the ones who could talk wanted to get
a fairy godmother in order to make the ones who
couldn't talk be able to talk. Is that it?

Patient: (nods affirmatively)

Therapist: Okay, then what happened?

Patient: When he was just standing — sitting on the
porch waiting for a fairy godmother . . .

Therapist (interrupts): Who was standing waiting for
a fairy godmother?

Patient: Uh (pauses).

Therapist: Who was waiting for the fairy godmother?

Patient: . . . (mumbles) . . .

Therapist: Who?

Patient: The ... (mumbles) ... peeg ... or the giraffe.

Therapist: A peeg?

Patient: A pig!

Therapist: A pig! Was this one of the pigs who could or couldn't talk?

Patient: Who could.

Therapist: Who could talk.

Patient: Or it could be a giraffe.

Therapist: A giraffe who could talk. So a pig or a giraffe was waiting for the fairy godmother. Okay.

Patient: And they just sat there doing nothing. They were looking up in the sky saying, "What happened to my fairy godmother? I probably didn't wish for one or say it out loud." And then he began to scream, "Fairy godmother" so loud that all the animals who could talk and couldn't talk ran away.

Therapist: Why did they run away?

Patient: Because he screamed so loud.

Therapist: Then what happened?

Patient: And then he said ...

Therapist (interrupts): Who's he?

Patient: And then the pig said, "Oh, wow, I really screamed loud that time. I scared all the animals who couldn't talk away. That's the name of the animals.

Therapist: What?

Patient: Couldn't Talk and Could Talk.

Therapist: Okay. His screams scared away all the animals who couldn't talk. Then what happened?

Patient: Then he said (in singsong manner), "Oh, I wish for a fairy godmother, a fairy godmother," and he sang and sang until he believed, until somebody, until he realized there's no such thing as a fairy godmother.

Therapist: Okay. You mean she never came?

Patient: No.

Therapist: Then what happened?

Patient: The end.

Therapist: Well, I have a question. What happened to

the animals who couldn't talk? What happened to them?

Patient: They had to go to a teacher.

Therapist: Hh hmm.

Patient: They went like this (makes grimacing facial expressions) and the teacher couldn't understand what the animals were saying.

Therapist: So what happened then?

Patient: I'm all done.

Therapist: Well, did they learn to talk?

Patient: Yes. They said — they tried hard like this (makes facial contortions) and they made a couple of sounds: "Buh, buh, buh, yup, yup, yup," and then they started talking loud (voice gets louder): "Yup, yup, yup, yup, yup." And they talked so loud that they grew up to be a giant.

Therapist: Uh huh. I see. Okay. Is that the end of the story?

Patient: Yes.

Therapist: And what's the lesson of that story?

Patient: There are two lessons.

Therapist: What are the two lessons?

Patient: Never sit there but if you want a real fairy godmother don't believe in fairy godmothers. My third lesson is: There's no such thing as fairy godmothers.

The story well demonstrates how my messages from the sequence of nine days previously had been remembered by the patient and were retold in his story. One could argue that such repeating is not specifically therapeutic and that the child might be doing it merely to ingratiate himself with me. There is no question that this was probably going on. However, there is also no question in my mind that such repetition for the purpose of ingratiating the therapist is part of every patient's cure, regardless of age. Hopefully, the patient will reach the point that his new ways of thinking and doing things will be done for their own sake, rather than merely for the therapist's. In addition, I believe that George repeated my story because of his appreciation, at some level, that it had validity and that it offered him more promise for improvement than fairy godmothers.

Because the story had so many healthy elements, I decided not to alter it in my responding story. Rather, I decided to entrench the message by its repetition in the dramatic mode. The presence of George's younger sibling provided me with a source of willing recruits for participation in my planned theatrical performance.

Therapist: Okay. Now I'll tell you what. I think that was such a good story that instead of my making up a story, what I think we ought to do is let's make up a play. Okay? Do you want to make up a play in which we'll make up a play about your story? Do you want to do that?

Patient: What does that mean?

Therapist: Well, what we'll do is we'll act it out. We'll tell your story and we'll play the parts of different animals — you and me. Okay? Do you want to do that?

Patient: (nods affirmatively)

Therapist (points to sister and brother sitting in another part of room): Do you want your brother and sister to be in the play?

Patient: (nods affirmatively)

Therapist (speaking to brother and sister): Would you like to be in a play?

Voice heard from out of camera range: Yes.

Therapist: Okay, come on over here. We'll make a play now. I'll show you how we'll do it. (Sister Sue and brother Bob walk over to where patient and therapist are sitting. Therapist starts moving furniture around.) Let's make a play in which we have two farms. Come over here (motions to Sue and Bob to come closer). These are our two guests on our program today (has Sue and Bob face camera). These two guests are going to be in the play (moves microphone to side).

Patient: But how are you going to be by the microphone?

*Therapist:*The microphone will pick up our voices.

Now here's what we're going to do. We're making believe that there are two farms. Okay?

Patient: (nods affirmatively)

Therapist: On one farm the animals can't talk and on the other farm the animal can talk. Now, let's make believe, first of all, the animals who can talk. Let's make some animal sounds (points to patient). What kind of animal sound do you want to make? What kind of animal sound?

Patient: (just stares in space)

Therapist (to patient while Sue and Bob just remain standing motionless): What animal sound do you want to make?

Patient: What kind of a sound . . .

Therapist (interrupts): Any sound.

Patient: does a giraffe make?

Therapist: I don't know. What kind of sound could a giraffe make?

Patient: (still pondering, while other children are still standing motionless)

Therapist: I don't really know. What's your guess? (after a pause) Well, Pick an animal whose sound you know.

Patient: A pig.

Therapist: Well, how does a pig go?

Patient: Oink, oink, oink, oink.

Therapist: Okay, so you'll be the pig. (turns to Bob) Now what animal do you want to be?

Bob: Dog.

Therapist: You'll be the dog. What sound does the dog make?

Bob: Ruff, ruff!

Therapist (turns to Sue): What animal do you want to be?

Sue (in low voice): A dog.

Therapist: A dog. What sound does a dog make?

Sue: Ruff, Ruff!

Therapist (to all three children): Okay, now, now all the animals make sounds. Let's make believe first we're the animals on the farm making the sounds. Okay, every animal make his own sound! Go ahead. Let's do it. (joins in with them) "oink, oink, ruff, ruff."

Patient: "Oink, Oink."

Sue: Ruff, ruff.

Bob: Ruff, ruff.

All: Oink, oink, ruff, ruff, oink, ruff, oink, ruff, etc.

Therapist (to Sue): Okay, let's hear you.

Sue: Ruff, ruff, ruff, ruff.

Therapist: Okay, Now those are all the talking animals. Now — turn around (twists Bob around toward camera) so everybody can see you on television. All right? Now (places Sue in one spot) you stand over here. Okay. Now you (places Bob on his left side) stand over here so you'll be seen on television. Now, so those are the animals who *can talk.*

Now, then, there are other animals who can't talk. They just go like (makes strained facial expression), "Mmmmmmmmmm:" Okay (points to Bob), you do that. (Bob tries to imitate therapist).

Patient (to therapist): I hear noise out of you.

Therapist: Yeah, but I'm not saying (points to Sue) Go ahead, you try words to do it.

Sue: (just stares at therapist)

Therapist (grimaces and strains face again, trying to evoke some kind of sound): Go ahead (pointing to patient), you try to do it.

Patient: (makes contorted and strained facial expression)

Therapist (joins patient and makes straining expression and sounds again): Now (placing right hand on Sue's shoulder and looking directly at her), you do that.

Patient (interrupts): They should be . . .

Therapist (interrupts while still looking at Sue): Go ahead.

Patient: . . . like this (strains face and clenches hands).

Therapist (again has strained facial expression as he joins in with patient): "Mmmmmmmmmm," and they just can't talk. Then the animals — now the other animals come along and say, "Let's get a fairy godmother to help those animals talk." So let's call out for the fairy godmother. (shouts) "Fairy godmother."

Bob (joins in with therapist): ". . . godmother."

Therapist: Go ahead. Call out for her.

All children: "Fairy godmother."

Therapist (joins in): "Fairy godmother.Would you help those animals talk? (looks around at all the children) Go ahead, do it (points to patient). Yell out for the fairy godmother.

Patient (shouts): "Fairy godmother. Will you help those animals talk?"

Therapist (pointing to Sue): You say it.

Sue (in rushed, garbled voice): "Fairy godmother. Will you make those animals talk?"

Therapist (pointing to Bob): What about you?

Bob (shouts): "Fairy godmother. Will you make those animals talk?"

Therapist: All right. Let's look up there. (They all look up at ceiling.) Do you see any fairy godmothers up there?

Patient: No.

Bob: (points toward window): Look up there — nothing!

Therapist: Let's yell louder. Maybe she'll come.

All shouting together: "Fairy godmother!"

Therapist: Yell louder. Maybe she'll —

All (shouting even louder together): "Fairy godmother!"

Therapist (showing increasing anguish): "Fairy godmother, fairy godmother." (looks all around) Do you see any fairy godmother?

Bob (turning around toward window and holding curtain open in one hand): No, might be coming.

Patient: Just lights.

Therapist (talking to Bob and then turning toward window and puts hand on curtain): Do you think she may be out the window here? Let's look out.

Bob (as he separates curtain and looks out): She may be coming.

Therapist (to Bob): Well, look out here. Do you see any fairy godmothers out there?

Bob (looking out of window): No.

Patient and Sue: (looking out window from where they are standing)

Therapist (to patient and Sue): Do you see any fairy godmothers?

Sue: (nods head negatively)

Patient: I only see the light but no fairy godmother.

Therapist: Let's try once more. Maybe she'll come.

All (shouting loudly together): "Fairy godmother! Fairy godmother." (look all around and up at ceiling)

Therapist: Will you come down and make the animals talk?" (with dismayed expression on face) I don't see her. Do you see her?

Children: (seem completely absorbed and interested in what therapist is saying)

Therapist: Now what's going to happen? Now here are all the animals — let's make believe that we're all the animals who can't talk. Okay? (makes strained facial expression)

Children: (imitate facial expression)

Bob: (bends down for a second and pretends he's a dog)

Therapist: "We can't talk." Then what are those animals going to do? (directs attention toward patient) What's going to happen now? What are they going to do?

Patient: I think the other animals will tell where they know a good speech teacher.

Therapist: Right! So all the animals who can't talk go to a speech teacher. (looking at all three children) Who wants to make believe that they're the speech teacher? Who wants to be the speech teacher.

Patient: (raises hand)

Therapist (pointing to patient): You be the speech teacher. Okay, we three are animals. (begins strained facial expression and makes garbling sounds again, and points to Bob) You do it.

Bob: (makes garbling sounds)

Therapist (points to Sue): Okay, you do it.

Sue: (nods head up and down, smiling, tries to imitate garbling sounds)

Patient (looking apprehensive): What should I do?

Therapist: Well, what does a speech teacher do ?

Patient: Help people?

Therapist: All right. So what are you going to do?

Patient: Help.

Therapist: Okay, How are you going to help us speak?

Patient: By teaching you how to.

Therapist: Okay, make believe that you're the speech teacher teaching us how to.

Patient: Now say "Moo."

Therapist (pointing to Bob): You try it first. You try to say "moo."

Bob: "Moo."

Therapist (all excited): Hey, he said "Moo!" (pointing to Sue) Now you try it. (talking to patient) Teach her to say something.

Sue: "Moo."

Patient: Say "Good."

Sue: "Good."

Therapist: Okay, now tell me to say something.

Patient: "Good", "bad," and "hat."

Therapist: What is that again?

Patient: "Good," "bad," and "hat."

Therapist: "Good" "bad," and "hat." Okay. (with strained facial expression) 'G...g...g" It's very hard — you see, it's very hard to learn how to speak. It isn't easy. "G...g...goo...goo...good." Hey, I said it . Hey, I can start to speak! (talking directly to patient) Now you say to the children, "It takes a lot of practice and you've to to work very hard."

Patient: It takes a lot of practice and you got to work very hard.

Therapist (looking around at all three children): So, all of us, let's say we work very hard for a long time and we're all learning, and we can speak now. Okay?

Patient: (nods affirmatively)

Therapist: Okay. So everybody speak. Speak! Moo, moo.

Bob: Oink, oink.

Therapist: Oink, moo, meow, oink.

Bob: Ruff, ruff.

Therapist: Ruff, ruff, ruff, meow.

Sue: (seems to be too entranced to join in making animal sounds)

Therapist: Hey, we're all speaking! Thank you very much, speech teacher (shakes patient's hand) for teaching us how to speak. (shakes hand again) Thank you very much. Let's shake this speech teacher's hand.

Bob: (shakes patient's hand)

Sue: (shakes patient's hand)

Therapist: Okay. And that's the end of the program. Let's say good-bye. The end.

Bob and Sue: (wave good-bye)

Patient: So short?

Therapist: So short?

Patient: Yes.

Therapist: Do you want to make it longer?

Patient: No.

Therapist: Do you want to add a part?

Patient: Noooooo!

Therapist: Okay. Do you want to watch this?

All: Yes.

Therapist: Raise your hand if you want to watch this. (patient and Bob raise hands)

Sue: (just looks amused and pensive)

Therapist: Okay, we'll watch.

Again, the written transcript cannot fully convey the children's involvement in the play. They were all genuinely swept up in it and found it exciting and absorbing. The patient's comment at the end, "So short," was only final confirmation that he was having a good time and that the experience was a meaningful one for him. I added nothing new in the way of content; rather, I attempted to entrench the healthy message from his story in a powerful and absorbing manner. This experience marked a turning point in his therapy for following it there was very little talk of magic. This is not to say that there was absolutely no talk about magic; it is unrealistic to expect to remove such an attractive adaptation entirely. In fact, it is probable that none of us give up such hopes completely no matter how old we get. The important thing was that it was no longer a primary mode of adaptation for George.

The Girl Who Jumped Around Too Much. Sally, a six-and-a-half-year-old girl with minimal brain dysfunction, was asked to discontinue dance lessons because of her hyperactivity, distractibility, and interference with the learning of the other students. She was very restless in the dance class and would not attend to the teacher. Instead, she ran around the class, bumped into other children, and exhibited other disruptive antics. A few months later the class gave a recital and, of course, Sally was not a participant. However, because her five-year-old sister was in the recital she was invited to see it.

Sally was transfixed throughout the dance recital and for weeks afterward sang fragments of the songs that were presented and imitated segments of the dances. It was during this period that she presented material in her play that clearly related to her feelings about her dance lessons and the recital. She began with the dolls and the dollhouse and told a story about a robber which I will omit because it is not directly relevant to the issues I wish to focus on here. Her transcription starts at the point where she introduced the dancing school experience.

> *Patient*: Then when the robber was gone they had to go to dancing school. And then the biggest girl — the biggest girl was gonna be the assistant.
> *Therapist*: Hh hmm.
> *Patient*: There's only one dancing teacher and the biggest one is the assistant.
> *Therapist*: All right. Go ahead. Then what happened?

Patient: (fidgets in chair)

Therapist: What happened there?

Patient: (just staring into space, swinging legs)

Therapist: Huh. What happened?

Patient: Then they left and the assistant, the older child, walked in and all the other children. Then you know what? Then there was (moves doll figures around on table in front of her) a boy there who wanted to this boy's friend and he let go of it. He wanted to be the girl's friend. And this boy has to be the dancing teacher's friend — I mean the dancing assistant. And there was a girl (moves girl figure toward playhouse on table) and she jumped around (bangs figure on table) and pushed in between the children (still moving figures around).

Therapist: Hh hmm.

Patient: And then the teacher — and then the assistant put her out the door (moves figure outside of playhouse). Then later on in the year when the recital came, the Daddy said, "Could I use this child for the recital?" And so he said — and so all the children and the dancing assistant (moving figures around as she is talking) said, "No."

Therapist: Why? Why did the dancing assistant say no?

Patient (continually moving figures around on table): Because she jumped around.

Therapist: What happened then?

Patient: Then she had to sit in the audience.

Therapist: Uh huh. And how did she feel in the audience?

Patient (still moving figures around): Sad.

Therapist: Then what happened?

Patient (moving figures around): Then — then when the recital was all over, then the girl — then the girl tried tumbling school.

Therapist: All right. What happened in tumbling school?

Patient (intensely concentrating on moving other

figures about on table): All the other children from dancing school were there.

Therapist: Uh huh. Okay.

Patient (still moving figures about): And even the assistant was there.

Therapist: Okay. And what happened there in tumbling school?

Patient (waving arms up and down): They tumbled and the girl didn't even run around.

Therapist: She didn't!

Patient (still waving arms up and down): So later in the week — year — when the recital came they — this one be a leader.

Therapist: She became a leader! Oh boy!

Patient (excitedly singing): And threw her hat up into the air!

Therapist: Uh huh! Oh boy! And what else?

Patient: And then the other children— the other children didn't want to be a leader. Then they were in the class and then she was all finished (moving figure around) with her . . . (mumbles) . . .

Therapist: She was all finished with what?

Patient: Her leader act.

Therapist: Her leader act. Okay.

Patient (moving figures): And then — then — and then big clowns — and then the assistant baby wanted to be — so (concentrates on taking figures out of playhouse) they came out — they came — they came out — and got a — (waves arms back and forth) and got a trophy. And they sang (sings while moving arms alternately up and down and moving body from side to side), "Every show must have an end, have an end, have an end. Every show must have an end. Every show must have an end, have an end, have an end. Every show must have an end, da la de da."

Therapist: Okay, is that it? Is that it?

Patient: Yeah.

The sequence clearly makes reference to the patient's disruptive behavior in the dance class. The experience of being asked to leave the room was an actual one . In fact, this was a frequent occurrence prior to the teacher's asking the mother to take Sally out completely. The idea of transferring to a tumbling school was clearly a healthy adaptation on Sally's part. There, her hyperactivity would be less noticeable and she could channel her energies into more constructive directions. The sung sequences ("And threw her hat up into the air," "Every show must have an end . . . ") were taken directly from the recital and reflect the patient's deep response to the performance. Although she saw it only once, she remembered verbatim significant segments.

In accordance with the above understanding of Sally's story, I responded.

Therapist: Do you want to make a play out of that story you just made? Do you want to make a play out of it?

Patient: What is a play?

Therapist: A play. A play is, you know, we'll act it out. We'll take the different parts. Okay?

Patient: Okay.

Therapist: All right. Who do you want to be now? Do you want to be the girl and I'll be the teacher or shall I be the girl and you'll be the teacher? What part do you want to be?

Patient (as she gets up from the chair): The girl.

Therapist: You want to be the girl? Okay.

Patient (excitedly jumps up and down, moves arms up and down, and has smile on face as she goes midway across the room to the couch and then sits on it).

Therapist (getting up from chair by table): Okay, I'll tell you what. I'll be the teacher. Come over here.

Patient: (starts to move across room toward therapist)

Therapist: Okay, let's make believe that this is the dancing class first. Okay?

Patient: (stands facing him about three feet away and nods head affirmatively)

Therapist: (kay. Come over here. Come closer (motior ing to patient to come nearer to him). Everybody dance and you mustn't run around or annoy the other children or else I'm going to have to send you outside the room Okay? Okay, everybody, let's see you dance."

Patient: (puts hands on waist and twists body all around while standing in place; has back toward camera)

Therapist: Okay. I'll tell you what. (walks over to patient and switches places with her so that she is facing camera and therapist is semi-facing camera) Why don't you stand over here like this and I'll be the teacher over here? "Now let's see you dance."

Patient (practically repeats same dance motion of putting hands on waist and twisting body all around while standing in place as she did previously).

Therapist: Okay. "Are you going to bother the other children?"

Patient (lifts arms up and down): No.

Therapist: "Good." Shall I make believe I'm a girl bothering other children?

Patient (excitedly): Yes.

Therapist: Okay. (walks over to patient and stands by her side) Let's say I'm next to you in that class and you're trying to dance. Go ahead, you try to dance.

Patient: (dances in place, lifting arms and legs)

Therapist: And I'm going to go around (bumping into patient and running around her), ha, ha, ha. I'm going to run around and I'm going to bother her. "Get out of my way." (dances all around patient who is laughing happily and amused by the whole thing) I run around and I bother all the children. And then the teacher says to me — she says (in stern tone), "You are very bad. You have to go out of this room because you're bothering everybody!"

Patient: (excitedly jumping up and down, giggling and laughing)

Therapist: So I go (moves toward door and in crying,

pleading voice). "Please don't send me out of the room. Oh, please."

Patient (so engrossed and amused that she is jumping up and down and laughing).

Therapist (changes position with back toward camera and switches back to stern tone of teacher): "You're very bad because you're running around and you're not listening to what I am saying!" So what happens?

Patient (excitedly makes a suggestion): She sends you out.

Therapist (goes to door, has left hand on doorknob, back toward camera and patient, pretending he is crying): "Oh, I don't want to go out. (opens door and goes halfway out) Oh, I don't want to go out (making crying, pleading, begging sounds). Please let me come back in." (closes door)

Patient: (all the time thinking the situation is hilarious and continously laughing and jumping up and down in place even after therapist leaves room)

Patient's Mother (watching play from chair out of camera range): Go let Dr. Gardner back in the room.

Patient (who has stopped all action for a moment): Okay.

Therapist (knocking on the door from the outside; voice is still pleading): "Please let me come back in the room. (more knocks and in begging tone) Please let me come back. I promise I'll be good."

Patient (jumping excitedly again up and down and laughing at the same time): Okay. (then stops action and stands in front of door closet waiting for therapist to come back in)

Therapist (as he comes back into room): So does the teacher let the boy come back? Oh, first make believe I'm a girl. Does the teacher let the girl come back?

Patient (hands behind back standing in front of closet, in serious tone): Yeah.

Therapist (standing next to patient): So what

happens when the girl comes back? Let's say the girl is back. What does she do?

Patient: I don't know.

Therapist: Is she good? Does she run around and bother the other children? Does she listen to the teacher or what?

Patient: I don't know.

Therapist: Well, what happens is . . . Well, this child, this little girl didn't listen. Once she came back into the class — let's say you're starting to dance again (motions to patient to dance). Go ahead, you start to dance.

Patient (following instructions, dances in place, lifting one leg at a time and has arms crossed in front of her).

Therapist: Well, instead of dancing like she was supposed to, she start running around the room again (immediately runs gleefully around the patient and makes loud sounds) and she didn't listen to the teacher and she just pushed around (bumping into the patient who has begun to laugh excitedly again) and wouldn't let anybody dance. And so what did the teacher do?

Patient (excitedly): Send her out.

Therapist: The teacher said what?

Patient (jumping up and down and laughing): You try to go out.

Therapist (pretending he's crying and in mournful voice): "Oh, I'll have to go out of the room again. (opens door and as he's leaving) Oh my, goodness . . . I'll have to go out of the room again."

Patient: (still very excited and thoroughly engrossed — laughing all the time and jumping up and down in place)

Therapist (knocks on door and begs to be allowed to come back into room): "Please let me come back in. Please, please."

Patient (after hesitating a moment to see what was going to happen next): Okay.

Therapist (entering room again): Well, what happened was that the teacher said that she can't stand the class anymore and this girl couldn't stay in the class. And that was it. Now, what happened at the end of the year when they had the big recital?

Patient: (staring into space)

Therapist: Where was this girl? Was she on the stage in the recital?

Patient: Yeah.

Therapist: No. Where was she?

Patient (jumping up and down): In the audience.

Therapist (as he moves toward chairs in front of table where session first began): Let's make believe she's sitting in the audience. All right? She is sitting in the audience. (sits down on chair).

Patient: (has excitedly crossed the room midway, jumping and hopping around away from where therapist is sitting)

Therapist: She is sitting in the audience. Am I the girl sitting in the audience?

Patient (stops action for a moment and looks at therapist): Yeah.

Therapist: And are you on the stage?

Patient (dancing in place): Yeah.

Therapist: Were you the good girl?

Patient (still dancing in place): Yeah.

Therapist: And I'm the bad girl. Right? I'm the one who wouldn't listen to the teacher. So you're in the recital. Okay? (motions to patient) Come over here. Over here. (Phone rings and while therapist answers it, patient is singing, clapping, and dancing in place. Then she goes around in a circle, jumps down on the floor, and does a half-somersault. Therapist finishes short conversation over phone and directs attention to patient.) All right. come on. We have the recital now. There's a recital. You're on the stage. Okay?

Patient: (nods while dancing around)

Therapist (starting to cry): And I'm the girl sitting here in the audience.

Patient: (dancing and jumping around in a circle and making gleeful sounds)

Therapist (crying louder): "Look at all those kids having fun and I have to sit here. Oh my."

Patient: (getting further carried away and swept up with play; laughing and jumping around)

Therapist: What are you doing? Are you dancing on the stage?

Patient: (drops to floor and tries to do a somersault, which is only half-successful; gets up and jumps around, making her own music)

Therapist: What are you doing? Are you dancing on the stage?

Patient: (seems to be too caught up "performing" to answer therapist's questions)

Therapist: Okay, what am I doing here — the girl in the audience?

Patient (finally walks over to couch, which is located a few feet from therapist's chair, and sits down): Sitting.

Therapist: And how do I feel? (motions to patient) Come over here.

Patient (bouncing up and down on couch from sitting position, oblivious to therapist's instructions): Sad.

Therapist: And how do I feel?

Patient: Sad.

Therapist: And what am I thinking?

Patient: You were in the . . . (mumbles) . . .

Therapist: Am I thinking what? What am I thinking? (motions again to patient) Come over here.

Patient (still bouncing up and down on couch): You were thinking you were in the recital.

Therapist: I am thinking that I was in the recital?

Patient: Yeah.

Therapist: But am I in the recital?

Patient (still bouncing on couch): No.

Therapist (beginning to pretend he's crying): "No I'm sitting here very sad. Oh, I wish I could be in tha recital."

Patient: (gets up from couch and dances around ir circle, humming or singing a tune)

Therapist (watches for a few seconds): Come here. I want to ask you a question.

Patient: (heads toward therapist and looks at him for a moment and then heads for couch but doesn't sit down)

Therapist: "What can I do so that I can be in the recital next year?"

Patient (walking and dancing around): Try tumbling school.

Therapist: Tumbling school? What do I have to do there?

Patient (still moving around): Tumble.

Therapist: Uh huh. All right. Let's make believe it's tumbling school. Okay?

Patient: (nods while moving around)

Therapist: Okay, here I am (getting up from chair) in tumbling school. Do you want to be in tumbling school? (motions to patient to come to him) Okay, come on, we're both in tumbling school. (patient stands by therapist's side) The teacher is teaching us how to tumble. Okay?

Patient: (waiting to be told what to do)

Therapist: Okay, let's do some tumbles. Go ahead. Do a tumble.

Patient: (lifts arms up above head and positions body as if if she is about to do a cartwheel)

Therapist (imitates patient's stance and looks like he's about to do a cartwheel too): Go ahead.

Patient (runs forward instead of tumbling): Pretend you're doing it.

Therapist: Okay, I'll pretend I'm doing it. Like that (goes forward as if about to tumble). Okay, you over here.

Patient: (gets back into position as if about to tumble again, but this time she does a half-cartwheel)

Therapist (pretends he tumbles but he spins body around; makes whirling sound; motions to patient): Okay, now come on over here. Now the teacher says (in stern voice), "Now everybody listen and be quiet." Now what do I do? What do I do?

Patient (moving up and down in place): I don't know.

Therapist: Am I quiet? Do I listen to the teacher or do I run around and bother the other children?

Patient: Run around.

Therapist: Well, this year I think I've learned my lesson. Last year I couldn't be in the dance recital so this year I'm going to be very careful to listen to the teacher so whenever she says anything I'm not going to run around and bother the other children, and I'm going to listen to what she says. All right?

Patient (in low voice): All right.

Therapist: So what happens at the end of the year?

Patient: A recital (starts to walk away from therapist).

Therapist: Am I in the recital?

Patient (faces therapist): Yeah.

Therapist: Okay, let's make believe that this is the recital.Okay?

Patient: (walks back and stands by therapist's side)

Therapist: Okay. "Here I am (gleefully takes a step to the side, still facing patient) in the recital. Oh boy! I'm in the recital! It's so much fun! Am I glad that I didn't run around."

Patient: (jumping up and down excitedly in the middle of the room)

Therapist: "Am I glad that I listened to the teacher. (motions to patient) Come here. Let's be in the recital together."

Patient: (eagerly runs over to therapist and stands by his side, singing merrily)

Therapist: Okay. What should we do in the recital now?

Patient (singing and puts hand on head): Throw your head up in the air (throws hand in air as if waving a hat and then jumps up and down excitedly).

Therapist (copies patient's motion of pretending he's throwing head up in the air while singing): "Throw your head up in the air." Okay. Now what?

Patient (thinks for a second and then positions herself again as if about to do a cartwheel with hands outstreched above her head and one foot forward): Now.

Therapist (imitates patient's motion as if he is about to do a cartwheel too): Like that. Okay.

Patient (as she does an actual chartwheel): Pretend to do this.

Therapist: Okay, I'll pretend to do this. (pretends to cartwheel, spinning body around) "Oooh, it's hard! Wow! This is a fun recital!"

Patient: (jumps excitedly around, making her way to therapist's side)

Therapist: "Am I glad I was good last year. Am I glad that I didn't run around among the other children. Am I glad I listened to the teacher. This recital is fun!" Okay, it's the end of the recital. Shall we say good-bye?

Patient (has walked over to couch and sits down with a bounce): Yeah.

Therapist (motioning to patient to return by his side): Come on. Let's say good-bye.

Patient (walks over to therapist and half-facing camera and therapist, waves left hand): Good-bye.

Therapist: Do you want to watch this program on television?

Patient (as she makes her way to couch, which she bounces on): Yeah.

Therapist (walking out of camera range): Okay.

Although I have tried to include all the actions taking place, the transcript cannot truly communicate the dramatizations. Most prominent was the patient's excitement and its associated hyperactivity. Although my story was designed to help the patient reduce her hyperactivity, the very excitement of the dramatization tended to enhance it. However, the jumping up and down was related to the excitement of making the play and similar agitation would be seen with nonhyperactive children in similar circumstances. Actually, I introduced nothing new in my play; rather, I tried to reinforce the healthy messages exhibited in Sally's story. There was no question that the playacting modality is very attractive to children and messages communicated in this way are certainly attended to and, I believe, incorporated into the child's psychic structure.

Chapter Seven
The Talking, Feeling, and Doing Game

There are many children who, in spite of the various facilitating and seductive techniques that we may utilize, may still be unable or unwilling to express to us their underlying fantasies (whether in stories or less organized form) or provide us with high-order material for meaningful therapeutic interchange. And there are others (also very common) who may involve themselves for short periods of time in such interchanges and then "clam up" or "cool off" with the result that a major part of the session is spent in low-efficiency or even therapeutically worthless activities. I have found the games to be described in this and succeeding chapters effective in drawing the majority of such children into what I consider a high order of therapeutic involvement.

The Talking, Feeling, and Doing Game,* is similar in appearance and format to many of the standard board games with which practically all children are familiar

*Manufactured by Creative Therapeutics, 155 County Road, Cresskill, New Jersey, 07626.

(Figure 1). The game begins with the child and therapist placing their playing pieces at START. Each in turn throws the dice and moves his playing piece along a curved path of squares. Depending upon the color of the square on which the piece lands, the player selects a Talking Card, Feeling Card, or Doing Card. The questions or directions on the cards in each stack range from the very low anxiety-provoking (so that practically any child will be able to respond) to the moderately anxiety-provoking. If the child does respond (and the most liberal criteria are used — especially for the very inhibited child), he receives a token reward chip.

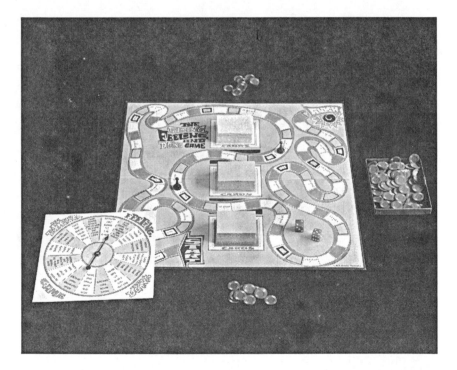

Some of the low-anxiety Talking Cards are: "What is your address?" "What present would you like to get for your next birthday?" "How old is your father?" "How tall are you?" "How old is your mother?" "How much do you weigh?" "What is your lucky number? Why?" "What is your telephone number?" "What kind of work does your father do?" Each of these questions can readily be answered by most children. The inevitable token reward fosters further involvement in the game.

Some typical relatively higher anxiety-producing Talking Cards are: "Make up a message for a Chinese fortune cookie." "Suppose two people were talking about you and they didn't know you were listening. What do you think you would hear them saying?" "Say something bad about your mother." "People are a mixture of both good and bad, that is, everyone has good and bad parts. Say something good about someone you don't like." "Of all the animals, which one is your favorite? Why?" "What things come into your mind when you can't fall asleep?" "Someone passes you a note. What does it say?" "What's the worst thing you can do to someone?" "If you could make yourself invisible, what would you do?" "A girl was the only one in the class not invited to a birthday party. Why do you think she wasn't invited?" "Make believe that you're looking into a crystal ball that can show your future. What do you see?" "Make believe a piece of paper just blew in the window. Something is written on it. Make up what is said on the paper." Most children, in my experience, will attempt to answer these questions. None are as anxiety-provoking as the free fantasy requested in the Mutual Storytelling Technique. If the child does not feel comfortable responding, he is not pressured; his only negative reinforcement is the failure to receive the reward chip. The therapist may, on occasion, similarly not "be able" to respond in order to protect the child from feeling unworthy about his inability to answer. (I will elaborate below in greater detail on the therapist's responses.)

Some typical low-anxiety Feeling Cards are: "What food do you hate the most? Why?" "How do you feel when you stand close to someone whose breath smells because he hasn't brushed his teeth?" "How do you feel about taking baths or showers?" "How do you feel after you've made in the toilet?" "How do you feel when someone tickles you?" "How do you feel when someone hits you?" "What's something you could say that would make a person feel good?" "What do you think of someone who doesn't wipe himself after he goes to the bathroom?" "A boy got sick on the day of the class picnic and so he couldn't go. How did he feel?" "A boy was sent to his room for hitting his sister. How did he feel as he was sitting there alone? What was he thinking?" "On the last day of school a boy learned that he would have to repeat the same grade. What had happened? How did he feel?" "Tell about something you did that made you very proud." "What do you think about someone who picks his nose and then wipes the mucus on something?" "How do you feel while you're eating ice cream?"

Some typical relatively higher anxiety-producing Feeling Cards are: "All the girls in the class were invited to a birthday party except one. How did she feel? Why wasn't she invited?" "What's the worst thing a child can say to his mother?" "Everybody in the class was laughing at a boy. What had happened?" "A child has something on his mind that he's afraid to tell his father. What is it that he's scared to talk about?" "Everybody in the class was laughing at a girl. What had happened?" "How do you feel when you learn something bad about someone whom you love?" "What do you think about a boy who sometimes plays with his penis when he's alone?" "What do you think about a girl who sometimes plays with or rubs her vagina when she's alone?" "Tell about something you did that you are ashamed about." "A child is ashamed to tell his father about something. What is it?"

Some typical low-anxiety Doing Cards are: "Make believe you're blowing out the candles on your birthday cake." "With your finger draw a circle in the air." "Make a funny sound with your mouth. If you spit you don't get a chip." "Scream as loud as you can. How do the people feel who have had to listen to you?" "Stick your finger in your ear. You won't mind doing this if you have clean ears." "Stick your finger in your belly button." "Stick out your tongue at someone." "Make believe you're throwing a ball." "Nod your head, clap your hands, and stamp your feet — all at the same time." "Make believe you're doing a good thing." "Breathe in and out five times, without spitting. You do not get a chip if you spit. You do not get a chip if you breathe in anyone's face." "Make believe you're eating ice cream." "Dance around the room." "Hold your arms over your head and clap your hands."

Some typical relatively higher anxiety-producing Doing Cards are: "Make believe you're speaking to someone on the phone. Whom are you speaking to? What are you saying?" "Make believe you're opening a letter that has been written to you. What does it say?" "Make believe someone grabbed something of yours. Show what you would do." "Tell about something that makes you angry. Act out what you would do if that thing were happening right now." "Make believe you're having a bad dream. What's the dream about?" "Make believe you're picking up an envelope that you find while walking down the street. There's a note inside but no name on the front. You open it up. What does the note say?" "What is one of the stupidest things a person can do? Show someone doing that thing." "Make believe you're saying something nasty to someone. To whom are you talking? What are you saying?" "What is the most selfish thing you ever did? Make believe you're doing that thing now." "What is the bravest thing you ever did? Make believe you're doing that thing right now." "You're standing in line to buy something and a child pushes himself in front of you. Show what you would do." "You're standing in line to buy something and an adult pushes himself in front of you. Show what you would do." "Make believe you're doing a bad thing."

The child's responses are generally revealing of those psychological issues that are most meaningful to him at that time. The information so gained serves to guide the therapist in providing responses to his own cards that would be most pertinent to the patient. Of course, other information the therapist has about the patient contributes further to his ability to provide relevant and therapeutically beneficial responses.

Throughout the play any of the issues brought up by the cards can serve as a point of departure for discussion between the therapist and patient. It is preferable for the therapist to try to create an atmosphere of relaxation in order to encourage slow conversation rather than quick competition for the accumulation of reward chips. The therapist must use his discretion in deciding how much discussion is indicated for each patient. As is obvious, the Talking Cards tend to elicit responses of a cognitive nature, the Feeling Cards responses that are emotional, and the Doing Cards responses that require some action. In each case the first goal is to loosen up the child's inhibitions in these areas. The topics chosen cover the wide range of issues usually dealt with in most children's therapy. The cards are so designed that they can be read by most third graders. Late first- and second-graders will often enjoy trying to read the cards with the help of the therapist. And younger children (not old enough to read, but old enough to appreciate game structure) will enjoy the game with the therapist's reading their cards to them. Because there are so many cards (96 in each stack), and because the general atmosphere is usually one of discussion over each card, there may be weeks (and even months) before the child may select the same card again. When that occurs he usually is at a different point in treatment, different issues may be meaningful, and he therefore generally provides different responses.

The winner is the person who has the most chips after both players have reached FINISH. The game is designed to take about thirty to forty-five minutes (this includes play and discussion). If less time is available, then play can proceed until the allotted time is up. The winner is the one who has accumulated the most chips when the designated time is over. The winner then gets a prize. I have a conspicuously located, transparent plastic box of inexpensive trinkets and objects (the kind children can obtain from gum-ball machines), and the winner can choose his prize from the box (Figure 2). Often the object chosen by the child is of psychological significance and a discussion of the choice and the child's comments about the object can be therapeutically useful. In addition, a few children have saved these prizes at home and started a collection. I believe that in these cases it represented a desire to maintain contact with me between sessions and served thereby to strengthen the therapeutic relationship.

It is important for the therapist to communicate to the child that it is perfectly acceptable not to respond to a card. The therapist himself may want to do this at times either because he may not feel it appropriate for him to reveal to the child certain personal material that is suggested by the card or because he wants to lessen any embarrassment the child may have over not being free enough to respond to a number of cards. On the other hand, one of the game's purposes is to provide the therapist with an opportunity to reveal personal things about himself to the degree that he considers it therapeutically indicated. All too often, therapists try to encourage children to reveal themselves yet strictly refrain from similar personal expression. Not serving as good models themselves, they thereby lessen the likelihood of success in getting the child to reveal himself. It is not so much what the therapist reveals, but the process of his revealing that is therapeutic. Often the therapist may choose not to respond with self-revelatory material but rather to provide a response that is more directly relevant to the child's problems. No matter what kind of response the therapist chooses to give, his primary consideration should always be: "What response would be most therapeutic for this child?"

The path also contains squares that instruct the player to GO AHEAD and GO BACK varying numbers of spaces. If a player lands on a square marked SPIN, he spins a spinner which may provide him with extra tokens or instruct him to give up tokens (either from the bank or other player) or to go forward or backward a certain number of spaces. The spinner has proved particularly attractive to children and they generally become quite excited when they land on SPIN — even though there is a chance that they may lose chips or go backward. In addition, there are cards in each of the three stacks that instruct the player to take an extra turn or lose his next turn. All these elaborations, although they do not generally result in the elicitation of psychodynamic material, do add excitement to the game and thereby enhance the child's interest and involvement.

Although the game is primarily designed to draw out the inhibited child and to engage the uncooperative child, it can also be useful in the treatment of the child who is free to express himself. After a period of more revelatory therapeutic experience, such children usually need some less revealing (and thereby less anxiety-provoking) therapeutic exposures and this game can provide them.

Although primarily designed to be used in the one-to-one therapeutic situation, the game can be used in child group therapy as well (preferably for small groups of three to five children). When so utilized the therapist can use a child's response as a point of departure for group discussion. The game is particularly useful in child group therapy because it provides intrinsic structure in a situation that traditionally tends to become unstructured (the children tend to become playful, rambunctious, distracted, etc.). In addition, it facilitates discussion of problems in a setting in which such conversations are usually difficult to accomplish because of the reticence of most children to engage in them.

Generally, the material elicited when utilizing the Mutual Storytelling Technique is closer to pure dream and free fantasy than that revealed in The Talking, Feeling, and Doing Game. The "Make-up-a-Story Television Program" is so structured that there are no specific stimuli around which the stories are told. Traditional play materials such as dolls and puppets, although valuable and frequently effective catalysts for story elicitation, do contaminate the story and tend to "draw" the child's projections into specific directions. The cards in The Talking, Feeling, and Doing Game are similarly contaminating. However, I believe that the "push" of the unconscious material to be released in a form specific for the child's needs at that particular time is far stronger than the "pull" of the evoking stimulus and its power to significantly alter the projected material. Accordingly, the "channeling" of the projections is not, in my opinion, very significant.

My experience has been that the game is useful in children up to puberty. The adolescent usually finds the game "childish." This, I believe, is more related to the inhibitions that tend to befall youngsters during this period than to the fact that the game is beneath their level of maturity. Whether or not this is so, the adolescent generally does not wish to play the game (with the exception of those with significant problems such as borderline intelligence, minimal brain dysfunction, or psychosis) so that its use, effectively, ends at puberty.

Clinical Examples

Enhanced Competence and Reduced Anger. Fred,

a six-and-a-half-year-old boy with minimal brain dysfunction, had coordination difficulties that interfered with his playing ball, drawing, and effectively performing in various physical activities. A presenting complaint was his striking out at other children without provocation. On a few occasions, he tried to choke others or use "judo" quite maliciously. There was good evidence that such episodes would often occur when he observed others to be more competent than himself. While playing The Talking, Feeling, and Doing Game the following interchange took place:

> *Therapist*: Your card says, "Make believe you're throwing a ball." Okay, let's see you [do that] but don't move too far away. Throw it over here so you'll be on TV. Go ahead.
> *Patient*: (pretends he's throwing a ball)
> *Therapist*: Okay. How are you at throwing balls?
> *Patient*: Good.
> *Therapist*: Let me talk to you about that for a minute. Stand up for a minute. You know, some kids are better at throwing balls than others. Did you know that?
> *Patient*: Yep.
> *Therapist*: That not everybody is the same. Some kids are very good at throwing balls and some kids aren't too good. Did you know that?
> *Patient*: How could you be not good?
> *Therapist*: Some kids are born that way. They're born that they can't throw balls too well.
> *Patient*: What happens if they do throw balls?
> *Therapist*: Well, if they do — sometimes if they are born and they can't throw too well and they practice very hard with someone let's say like a gym teacher or with their father or with a big brother or a teenager or somebody like that — then they can get better and then they can throw as well as any other kid. But did you know that there are some kids who aren't as good as others with that? Did you know that?
> *Patient*: . . . (mumbles) . . .

to his father. He was not able to verbalize exactly what he feared. I reassured him that I knew his father well and that I was sure that the terrible consequence he anticipated would not occur. However, only by trying would he know whether or not what I was telling him would turn out to be true. Discussions such as these contributed to Tom's gradually becoming freer to express himself — not only to his father, but to others as well. And with such freedom there was a corresponding diminution in his stuttering. Had Tom's mother not been present I would not have appreciated that the picture related to one of his central problems.

Human Relationships as Ambivalent. During the next session Tom drew a picture of a rainbow. When asked to tell me about it he replied, "It's a rainbow. There's nothing more to say about it." Further inquiry was not productive. With an orange crayon he then drew a circle, made it into a face, and then covered the facial features with orange, stating that it was an orange. He then told a story about a lady who began to eat the orange but was told by the orange the he was really a rainbow and so the lady spit it out. I appreciated that the drawing was highly symbolic but was unable to learn anything more from Tom regarding its meaning. I asked him if he had had any recent experiences with rainbows or oranges and he said no. He said he didn't like oranges and orange juice, that his mother did, but gave me no further information.

I then asked Tom's mother if she could shed any light on this matter. She said that three weeks previously, while the family was traveling in the country, they had come upon what they all agreed was the most beautiful rainbow they had ever seen. The family gazed at it in awe and there were numerous comments regarding its beauty and the exhilaration of the scene. The patient said that he had forgotten about it when I first asked him about rainbows and agreed that it was the most beautiful rainbow he had ever seen.

The information from the mother then made the child's drawing and story more meaningful. I considered that he had a definite impairment in this regard. I did not embarrass him by confronting him with this denial; rather, I spoke in general about other boys who had such problems. Most children will readily discuss a problem of their own in the guise of speaking about a third party and the above interchange is an excellent example of this phenomenon.

I tried to emphasize the point, so important to repeat for children with minimal brain dysfunction, that no one is good at everything and that everyone has imperfections. I then emphasized the importance of practice in order to rectify the deficiency as well as lessen the jealousy one has of the more proficient. I then focused on the anger which is an intrinsic part of jealousy. Lastly, I focused on the inappropriateness of the acting-out of the anger and the reduction of the anger that can result from practice and its ensuing competence. In the interchange at the end of our discussion the patient clearly revealed his understanding of my messages. Fred, however, still had a long way to go toward alleviating this problem His deficiency in the physical realm was apparent; but he was receiving instructions from a gym teacher and his father.

Pain Inflicted on Others (Dramatically Portrayed). The game continued.

Therapist: Okay, my card says, "Make believe you're having a bad dream. What's the dream about?" Okay. I'm having a dream. I'm having a dream about somebody who knows judo coming over and picking on me instead of just using the judo to defend himself. I'm just walking along innocently and not doing anything and all of a sudden this kid comes over to me and he starts using judo on me. He gets me to the ground and he starts choking me. And I'm having the dream. (Therapist simulates choking himself with his own hands.) "Ahhhhh, stop it, stop that. Stop picking on me! You're using judo on me. I didn't bother you. Don't do that!" (Simulates waking up) Whew, that was some bad dream. Well, I get a chip for that. Right?
Patient: Right.
Therapist: Okay, now here's what your card says:

"Make up a message that you would put you into a bottle which you would throw into the ocean." What would put on such a message?

Patient: "Don't let anybody do judo on you."

Therapist: Why not?

Patient: It could be dangerous.

Therapist: Right! What can happen to a person if judo is used on him?

Patient: It could kill.

Therapist: Hh hmm. Now what is judo supposed to be used for?

Patient: Protecting yourself.

Therapist: What about picking on someone else with judo?

Patient: No.

Therapist: Right. Okay, you get a chip.

In the response to my card I used the request to make up a bad dream as an opportunity to enact a scene in which I am being attacked by someone who is using judo on me. Although, strictly speaking, judo does not involve choking one's opponent, the patient did choke a classmate under the guise of using judo on him. By simulating choking myself I attempted to enhance the efficacy of my message through dramatization and nonverbal communication. I tried to emphasize the point that judo should not be used on innocent parties; only on those who attack one. Fred listened attentively to what I was saying and was intently observing what I was doing.

In the next card that Fred selected he incorporated my message into his response. He verbalized the dangerousness of judo and in the ensuing discussion repeated my message that judo should only be used to protect oneself. In the course of therapy the child exhibits varying degrees of conviction with regard to the repeated messages. Such repetition is part of the process of incorporation and it plays a role in alteration of behavior. The interchange ended with my giving Fred a reward chip — a further attempt to entrench and reinforce his healthy response.

Lessons in Social Perception. A subsequent inter-change occurred.

Therapist: Okay, your card says, "Laugh hard and loud." Go ahead.

Patient (laughs gleefully): Ah hhaaa hhhaaa.

Therapist: Okay, I want to ask you a question about that. Are you supposed to laugh hard and loud like that in school?

Patient: No.

Therapist: What about out on the playground?

Patient: Yes.

Therapist: Right. What about at home?

Patient: Yes.

Therapist: Yes, sometimes. What about when you're sitting at the dinner table?

Patient: No.

Therapist: Right. There are times that it's a good thing to laugh hard and loud and other times (reaches over to hand patient a chip) . . .

Patient (interrupts): No, let me! (takes reward chip)

Therapist: Okay. You take your red chip reward.

I used the opportunity given by Fred's loud laughing to enter into a discussion on where and when it is appropriate to laugh loudly. The reader should note that in such discussions I try to elicit correct responses as much as possible from the patient, rather than lecture to him. However, when his responses are inappropriate it then becomes necessary for me to be somewhat didactic. Such didacticism is vital in the treatment of all children, but especially those with minimal brain dysfunction. It is far more palatable when given by a benevolent individual whom the child respects. And the child's receptivity is further enhanced when the communications are imparted in the context of a game.

The game then continued.

Therapist: Okay, Now it's my turn. My card says, "How do you feel when someone hits you?" When someone hits me, especially when I don't expect it, it hurts a lot. I've been hit sometimes when I didn't even know the person was going to hit me. I wasn't ready or prepared and it really hurt sometimes. Once somebody tried to choke me and once somebody hit me in the belly. I didn't even know they were going to do it and it really hurt bad. I remember when I was a little kid that happened a few times and I cried and it was very painful. It hurt me a lot and I wouldn't be friends with that boy. I stayed away from him. I didn't want to play with him or anything. And the kids who saw it — the kids who saw him pick on me that way — they too were very mad at him because they saw how much it hurt me. What do you think about that?

Patient: How did they know it hurt you?

Therapist: They could tell, I was ready to cry; it hurt so much. It hurt a lot.

Patient: Well, why didn't you pick on them back?

Therapist: Well, I did try to fight back as one should do if somebody picks on you first. You try to fight back or you tell them to go away and stop it. Or you tell them you're going to call the teacher or something like that. Or you try to get him off you. But they could tell it hurt when somebody tries to choke you or hit you in the belly . . .

Patient (interrupting): Would they be your friends?

Therapist: Not after that I wouldn't be friends with that boy. I wouldn't . . .

Patient (interrupting): No — the people who saw!

Therapist: Oh, yeah, the people who saw would be my friends, but they wouldn't be friends with the boy who started up, started to choke me. They wouldn't be friends with him. Not at all.

Patient: I know how you could do it. You could call their mother.

Therapist: That, yeah. But one could do that and she might talk to the boy but even so that boy would not be somebody that I would want to be friendly with. Not at all. Would you want to be friends with a kid who does a thing like that?

Patient: No!
Therapist: Right. Okay. So I get a chip. Right.
Patient: Right.
Therapist: Okay.

Fred had a significant problem in lashing out at other children. He did not seem to appreciate the impact he had on others and the pain they suffered. The normal child of his age generally had a greater ability than Fred to project himself into another person's situation. Fred seemed to be fixated at a more egocentric level of cognitive development and it was therefore difficult for him to project himself into another's situation. My elaboration of the pain I felt as a child when picked on by a bully was an attempt to help Fred appreciate the effects of one's striking another person.

In addition, I tried to impress upon Fred that such antisocial behavior brings about the alienation of others. He tried to divert attention from this issue by talking about how a bullied boy could protect himself by reporting to his mother. I agreed that that might be an effective course of action; however, I quickly went back to the issue of social alienation. The child with minimal brain dysfunction is often deficient in appreciating the consequences of his behavior.

Aesthetic Sensitivity and the Work Ethic. A subsequent interchange took place.

Therapist: My card says, "Name your favorite song. Why do you like that song so much?" My favorite song is "America, the Beautiful." Do you know why I like that song so much?
Patient: Why?
Therapist: There are two reasons why I like that song. The first reason is that when I sing that song it makes me think of very beautiful things — of beautiful mountains, and valleys, and clouds. There are many parts of this country that are very beautiful.
Patient: What's a valley?
Therapist: A valley is between two mountains. And so when I sing that, I think of that. Then I think of

another thing, about our country, America. And that is that the people of America can do many things that people in other countries can't do. They have a lot of chances if they want to work hard at something to get a lot of things. If they want to work hard they can be what they want very often — not always — but very often. America gives people a chance to do that and that's one of the things I love about America. Do you want to say anything about that?

Patient: You get a chip.

Therapist: Okay

Patient: This time you get a *red* chip.

Therapist: Okay. Thank you very much.

Much of the work in trying to help the child with minimal brain dysfunction enhance his social perception focuses on deficits. There are times, however, when one should try to enhance assets. Here, I try to enhance Fred's appreciation of natural beauty. To the degree that one can help a patient enjoy healthy pleasures, to that degree one enhances his self-esteem. And the enhancement of self-esteem serves as a universal antidote to the wide range of psychogenic symptoms. My hope in discussing my reactions to the song "America, the Beautiful" was to impart in Fred a similar appreciation.

In addition, I took the opportunity to make a comment about the work ethic. A deep commitment to the work ethic is vital for the child with minimal brain dysfunction. He must work harder in many areas to accomplish what the normal child can with less effort. And the therapist should take every opportunity to encourage commitment to this principle.

On Spitting and Breathing in Someone's Face. The game then continued.

Therapist: My card says, "Breathe in and out five times without spitting. You do not get a chip if you spit. You do not get a chip if you breathe in anyone's face." Okay. (Therapist breathes in and out five times.) Now why do you think it says you don't get a chip if you spit?

Patient: It's not nice. You get a chip.

Therapist: Wait a minute. I get a chip, right. I did it. But why do you think it says, "You don't get a chip if you spit?"

Patient: Um, it's not nice.

Therapist: Why isn't it nice?

Patient: You could hurt them if spit goes in their eyes.

Therapist: Yeah. How does it make people feel if somebody else's spit goes in their eye?

Patient: Terrible.

Therapist: Yeah. You feel bad. And it also says you don't get a chip if you breathe in anyone's face. What about that? Why do you think it says that? Why do you think they wrote that down there?

Patient: You wrote it down.

Therapist (laughingly): Right. You're right. I wrote it down.

Patient: Why did you write it?

Therapist (laughingly): You're a pretty smart fellow.

Patient: Why did you write it?

Therapist: Why do you think I wrote that down?

Patient: Well, I don't know.

Therapist: Well — why do you think? It says here, "You do not get a chip if you breathe in anyone's face." That's what is says there.

Patient: Because it's not nice.

Therapist: Why? What happens if you breathe in someone's face?

Patient: Their germs will get in you.

Therapist: You can get germs. Right. How do they feel? If someone breathes in your face, how do you feel?.

Patient: Sad. You get a chip.

Therapist: Okay. Very good. You know we have to stop here. I just want to say one other thing about that. Breathing in someone's face makes him feel bad. Spitting in someone's face makes him feel bad and hitting someone makes him feel bad. Right?

Patient: Right.

Therapist: We talked about that before. That's why I put that down on that card — to help remind people that when you do that — when you breathe or you spit in someone's face it hurts their feelings. It makes them feel bad.

Patient: What does it mean when you get a chip?

Therapist: What does it mean? Well, the chip is like a reward. It's a prize. Now we're going to see who wins the game because we have to stop here. How many chips do you have? You count your chips.

Patient: One, two, three, four, five, six, seven, eght.

Therapist: You have eight and I have seven chip. So you're the winner. Congratulations! You're going to get a prize. We're going to go over and get a prize. Let me congratulate you on winning the game. Okay. And let's stop the game for today.

The above segment is an excellent example of the kinds of interchanges the therapist should have with the child with minimal brain dysfunction in order to enhance his social perception. The card itself provides a little lesson in social perception and the ensuing discussion was designed to capitalize on every aspect of the card's message.

My main intent was to try to help the patient project himself into the position of another person — to see the world through his eyes — to appreciate his pains and discomforts.

In the course of the interchange I frequently pointed to the words on the card, hoping to enhance their efficacy through the appeal of the written word. At times, when a child reports an improvement in some area or tells me about his having accomplished something important, I will carefully write it down in my notes, clearly stating each word. This has the effect of enhancing the child's pride in his accomplishment. On the other hand, if the child has done something particularly socially alienating, with great misgivings I will sadly inform him that I have to write that down in his chart. With a somber attitude I will record the transgression. My hope here is to inculcate some guilt, some appreciation of the severity of the misdeed. Used judiciously (if used frequently it loses its potency) this practice can help strengthen the child's superego. Those who hold that the purpose of therapy is solely to lessen guilt are misguided and are sadly misinterpreting psychoanalytic theory. There are times when the therapist should encourage the enhancement of guilt and not to do so is to deprive the patient of an important therapeutic experience.

      Thinking Ahead. Less than two months later, while playing the game, the following interchange occurred.

> *Therapist*: Okay. Your card says, "What is the most painful thing that can happen to a person? Why?" You know, what's one of the worst things . . .
>
> *Patient* (interrupts): Um, a car accident. You can get killed.
>
> *Therapist*: Right . Now are you talking about a person getting hit by a car or a person in a car driving the car?
>
> *Patient*: A car accident.
>
> *Therapist*: Which?
>
> *Patient*: Um, damaged.
>
> *Therapist*: You mean two cars hitting one another?
>
> *Patient*: Yeah.
>
> *Therapist*: And who can get killed?
>
> *Patient*: The people that are in there.
>
> *Therapist*: Uh huh, Now what's the best way to prevent that from happening?
>
> *Patient*: Uh. Be careful.
>
> *Therapist*: Be careful. Right. So that if you're a driver of a car what do you have to do?
>
> *Patient*: Be careful.
>
> *Therapist*: Be careful. What do you have to do while you are driving?
>
> *Patient*: Um, I don't know.
>
> *Therapist*: Well, you have to watch very carefully where you are going. Right?
>
> *Patient*: Right.
>
> *Therapist*: And what about if you're a person crossing the street? What do you have to do?

Patient: I don't know.
Therapist: Well, do you have to be careful if you are crossing the street?
Patient: Yeah.
Therapist: Why?
Patient: You could get runned over.
Therapist: Right! Okay. You get a chip for that.

I used Fred's car accident response as a point of departure for emphasizing some of the untoward consequences of one's not paying attention. Used judiciously, apprising the patient of the negative effects of his behavior can be therapeutic. It is only when such confrontations become excessive that they may have an antitherapeutic and ego-debasing effect. There can be serious consequences to distractibility, and not confronting the patient with them is a disservice to him. Too often, children with minimal brain dysfunction wish that there were no consequences to their inappropriate behavior. Witholding information regarding such consequences is a disservice to the patient.

The Bully and Social Alienation. The game continued.

Therapist: My question is: "If you became mayor of your city . . . " Do you know what the mayor is?
Patient: Hhmm.
Therapist: What's the mayor?
Patient: Um . . . (mumbles) . . .
Therapist: That does what?
Patient: President of the town.
Therapist: President of the town! A very good way of saying it. Right. He's the guy in charge of the town. Right. (reading card) "If you became mayor of your city what would you do to change things?" Well, I would — in the schools I would change things so that if anyone were to beat up a kid I would have him taken out of the classroom so that he wouldn't hurt the other children. To somebody who is a bully I would have a

special rule that a bully has to be taken out of the class for at least two hours after hitting someone so to help him remember not to hit other children. That's what I would do.

Patient: That's what I would do.

Therapist: You would do the same thing?

Patient: Yeah.

Therapist: Good. Okay. Fine. I get a chip for that.

Here, I directed my attention to Fred's hostility problem. He was striking out at other children in the classroom and did not seem to fully appreciate the effects he was having on others. I believed that Fred's anger was primarily related to the frustration he felt over his neurological impairments. My hope was that his educational program (which included special physical training as well) would ultimately result in his feeling less frustrated over his impairments and he would then be less angry. Until that time came, however, Fred had to helped in other ways. Here I appealed to conscious control and the warning that there may be unpleasant repercussions for those who maltreat others. When discussing disciplinary measures I often use the phrase, "to help him remember." It has an appeal to most children and is, I believe, a good way of explaining a disciplinary measure.

Competence and Anger. In my next interchange with Fred I directed myself to the more crucial elements underlying his hostility.

Therapist: Okay. Your card says: "What's something you could say that would make a person feel good?"

Patient: Um.

Therapist: Sit over here. You're off — you're going to be off television.

Patient: If someone got hurt, um, I would, I would, um, ask them if they were all right.

Therapist: If someone got hurt?

Patient: Yeah. I would try to make friends with them.

Therapist: Hh hmm. Okay. How might a person get hurt? What kind of a thing would get a person hurt?

Patient: If someone hit them.

Therapist: If someone hit them. Right. And what would you say to make them feel better?

Patient: I would um, defend them so that they wouldn't get hit again.

Therapist: What would you do?

Patient: Beat them up.

Therapist: You'd beat up who?

Patient: The person who did that.

Therapist: The person who hit?

Patient: Yeah.

Therapist: What do you think about a person who hits?

Patient: Bad.

Therapist: Why would a person hit? What kinds of things would make a person want to hit?

Patient: Um, someone was bothering him.

Therapist: That's one thing. What about a person who isn't bothered by anybody, let's say somebody who just goes around hitting, who isn't bothered by anybody. What might make him want to hit?

Patient: Um, I don't know.

Therapist: I know one reason. Do you want to know what it is?

Patient: Yeah.

Therapist: For instance, sometimes there are kids who don't do very well in school. Excuse me, that noise will come over the microphone and they won't be able to hear our voices. Anyway, let's say there is a kid in school who isn't doing very well in school. He isn't studying very hard or he has some trouble learning. So instead of studying hard he just sits around, doesn't do very much work, and then he does poorly and he feels very sad about that and very angry about that. And he may go around hitting kids. Did you know that?

Patient: Yeah.

Therapist: There are kids who do things like that. That would be one kind of a thing that would make a kid want to hit. Do you want to say anything about that?

Patient: No.

Therapist: Okay. You get a chip for that answer.

Patient: No!

Therapist: Right. Not a chip, excuse me. We're keeping score. Okay, you write down *one* for that. Okay. Good.

It is clear that here I direct my attention to what I consider to be the most crucial element in Fred's bullying. Hopefully, by encouraging a strong commitment to schoolwork Fred would be more effective academically and in the physical realm, and would thereby be less frustrated and angry. I could not be sure that my message was getting through. There were times when Fred's responses indicated that he "received" this message, but there were other times when he was not particularly receptive.

      Civilized vs. Uncivilized Methods for Hostile Release. In the next interchange I had a further opportunity to discuss Fred's hostility problem.

Therapist: Okay. Your card says, "What is one of the stupidest things a person can do? Show someone doing that thing."

Patient: Killing someone. (imitates someone shooting a gun) "Boom, boom."

Therapist: Hh hmm. Okay. I would consider that a stupid thing certainly. Now I want to ask you a question about that.

Patient: What?

Therapist: Why would someone want to kill someone?

Patient: Because they didn't like them, because some people feel that if you don't like someone the thing to do is to shoot them.

Therapist: Uh huh. Is there any other thing you can do if you don't like someone besides shooting them? Anything else besides that?

Patient: . . . (mumbles) . . .

Therapist: What?

Patient: War.

Therapist: War?

Patient: Yeah.

Therapist: Besides war. If you don't like somebody, is there anything else besides war and shooting, anything else you can do?

Patient: (silent)

Therapist: Anything else?

Patient: ... (mumbles) ... Why do you keep on telling, asking me?

Therapist: I keep asking you these questions because I want to find out what other ideas you may have on a subject and maybe by talking about it maybe I can give you some of my ideas. For instance, in this particular thing, I think that there are other ways of doing things when you don't like someone other than killing him. What do you think you might do?

Patient: ... (mumbles) ...

Therapist: Pardon me?

Patient: Just stay away.

Therapist: Stay away! That's certainly one thing you can do it you don't like someone. You can stay away. What other thing can you do? See how many things you can think of of what you can do if you don't like someone. Excuse me, that noise is going to come over the mikes. Go ahead.

Patient: Um. Those are all the reasons.

Therapist: I'll give you a hint. You use a part of your body that's in your head. It's between here (pointing to top of head) and here (pointing to chin). What part of the body?

Patient: Brain.

Therapist: You use your brain, that's true. What else?

Patient: Your heart.

Therapist: No. Is your heart...? Where's your heart?

Patient: (points to heart).

Therapist (pointing to head): Is that between here (pointing to top of head) and here (pointing to chin)? No. It's a part of your body between here and here that you can use if you have trouble with someone and you don't like them. What you can do to try . . .

Patient (interrupts): Holes in your head.

Therapist: No. Do you know what the answer is?

Patient   1: What?

Therapist: Your *mouth*. What can you do with your mouth?

Patient: Tell them that you don't like them.

Therapist: Right! Tell them and talk to them and try to solve the problem with them. Right. Okay. You get a point for that.

Here, I encourage Fred to use civilized communication before acting out his anger. Actually, Fred's response to the card revealed his own appreciation that killing is "one of the stupidest things a person can do." I used his response as a point of departure for further emphasizing the value of verbal methods of resolving conflicts.

Self-projection. A subsequent interchange in the same game then occurred.

Therapist: "What do you say to someone whose foot you stepped on by mistake?"

Patient: Hh hmm.

Therapist: This is my question. I would say, "I'm very sorry. I hope I didn't hurt your foot. I hope it doesn't hurt you." Because I would know that when you step on someone's foot it can hurt them. Do you know that?

Patient: Yeah.

Therapist: Did anyone ever step on your foot? Hhmm?

Patient: Not anymore.

Therapist: Not anymore. Did anybody ever step on your foot?

Patient: I don't remember.

Therapist: You don't remember?

Patient: No.

Therapist (incredulously): In your whole life you don't remember anybody stepping on your foot?

Hhmm? Well, anyway how do you think it feels if someone steps on your foot?

Patient: Owwwwww.

Therapist: It hurts. Right! Right! That's right. You know there are two ways of stepping on someone's foot. One way is by mistake like it says here, "What do you say to someone whose foot you stepped on by mistake?" And what's the other way?

Patient: On purpose.

Therapist: Right! The opposite of *by mistake* is *on purpose.* Right. And does it hurt a person if you step on their foot on purpose?

Patient: Yes!

Therapist: Right. Both ways hurt. Right. Okay. Good. You can put me down for a point.

Crucial to socially acceptable behavior is the ability to project oneself into another person's situation. In fact, it may be the crucial element in adjusting healthily to other individuals. Taking off from the card in which the issue of stepping on someone's foot is raised, I attempted to strengthen Fred's social sensitivity. Although in this interchange he appears to have understood my points, there was no question that he still had a long way to go in improving his behavior in this realm. He struck children, often without provocation, and was not completely sensitive to the pain he was inflicting on others.

The Power of Prayer. The game continued.

Therapist: Your question is: "Do you believe in God? Why?"

Patient: No, I don't.

Therapist: You don't. Hh hmm. Why not?

Patient: Uh — uh.

Therapist: What's your reason?

Patient: Because I know there's no such thing as God.

Therapist: Hh hmm. Okay. Let me ask you this question. Do you know why some people who pray ... ? Do you know what praying is?

Patient: (shakes head negatively)

Therapist: Praying is talking to God and hoping — let's say you have a problem or you have some trouble ... some people, they pray to God and they hope that God will help them with their trouble. What do you think about that?

Patient: It won't work.

Therapist: What do you think *does* work if you have trouble.

Patient: Do better.

Therapist: Try to do better. Right. Try to figure it out yourself. Right. And — look we have to stop here today. We can watch a little bit of this.

I used the question about God as a point of departure for discussing prayer. There are some religious children who believe that through prayer their learning disabilities will improve and even disappear. However, even the most religious child should be introduced to the concept of: "God helps them who help themselves." The more common attitude, however, is not one of leaving the problem to be solved by God, but rather sitting back and hoping that the problems will just go away. Although Fred was applying himself, there was room for improvement in this area and my discussion was an attempt to encourage his further commitment to his academic tasks.

A Personal Revelation by the Therapist. Morton entered treatment at the age of nine because of disruptive behavior in the classroom. Although there was a mild neurological problem present (he was hyperactive, impulsive, and distractable), his primary problem centered on his relationship with his father. Morton's parents were separated and his father often did not show up for planned visits, or when he did he was often late. In addition, he was not the kind of man who basically enjoyed being with his children. Morton's anger was intense, but it was displaced onto his mother, teacher, and peers. While playing The Talking, Feeling, and Doing Game, the following conversation took place.

Therapist: My question is "What's the worst thing that ever happened to you?"

Well, I would say that one of the worst things that ever happened to me occurred when I was a teenager. There was a girl in my class in high school who I liked very much. I guess at that time I would say that I loved her. And I thought about nothing else but this girl, and I kept thinking about her and I stopped studying. All I could do was walk around and think about her and I don't think she cared for me too much. She wanted to be friendly with me, but she didn't like me anywhere near as much as I liked her. And I met her around June or so or May. I really got hooked on her and started thinking about her all the time, and she didn't treat me very nicely. And it wasn't until the end of August when she sent me a very painful letter in which she spoke about how much she didn't like me. And I discussed this with a friend of mine and he kind of knocked sense into my head and told me that I was crazy if I answered that letter. And after that, it was hard, but I didn't answer it and I stopped seeing her and I gradually got over it. But it was very painful to me and it was too bad that I didn't realize that it was a foolish thing . . .

Patient (interrupting): I got the message.

Therapist: What's the message?

Patient: Like you loved the girl so much, but she didn't love you!

Therapist: Right. And so what do you do in such a situation

Patient: Just ignore her. That's all I can think of. Other things? I don't know.

Therapist: Well, what should you do?

Patient: Don't let it bother you.

Therapist: Uh huh. Try to get wise, not trying to get something . . .

Patient (interrupts): Yeah, yeah, yeah, yeah, yeah! (throws dice)

Therapist: Okay. Good.

In my initial response to the card I related a real incident that occurred to me during my high school days.

There are those who believe that the therapist should strictly refrain from revealing things about his personal life to his patients. They hold that the therapist should be a blank screen upon which the patient can project and that such revelations can only contaminate treatment. In addition, they claim that the patient is not coming to hear about the therapist but rather he is coming to talk about himself.

I believe that such revelations, *judiciously utilized,* can be therapeutic. I do not agree that they must necessarily be antithetical to the purposes of treatment. The "blank screen" concept certainly has merit as does the warning that the therapist should not use the patient's time talking about himself because he may thereby be neglecting his patient. However, I believe that there are times when such revelations can be therapeutic.

Generally, we encourage our patients to express themselves and to free themselves from the inhibitions that impede them in this regard. However, often the therapist does not serve as a good model in this regard. In extreme cases, such as classical analysis or in strict forms of nondirective therapy, the therapist may never reveal his own feelings. He thereby serves as a poor model for his patients in this area regardless of what other benefits they may derive from the treatment. No matter how we may try to avoid it, our patients, I believe, still use us as a model for their behavior. Hopefully, the qualities that they emulate and introduce into their own life patterns will serve them well. Accordingly, the therapist does well, at appropriate times, to exhibit emotions in order to help his patient do so as well. The crucial problem is that of when it is appropriate and when it is not. I believe that it would be inappropriate to contrive situations in order to provide the therapist with a justification for such emotional expression. The contrived and artificial quality of such expressions cannot but be sensed by the patient and they will, therefore, engender disbelief and even distrust. Also, it would be inappropriate if the therapist's revelations contain significant neurotic material. These can be injurious to the patient and may tend to involve him in the therapist's neuroses. Such revelations can be appropriate when they serve to encourage healthy adaptations by the patient. For example, they tend to lessen the idolization of the therapist that so often occurs when he does not reveal much about himself. Revealing on occasion one's own deficiencies and problem areas can make the patient feel less unworthy when he compares himself to the therapist. All too often the patient has the view of the therapist as a perfectly healthy human being; whereas he views himself, in comparison, as loathesome and animallike. Judiciously revealing some of his own deficiencies — at the right time and at the right place in treatment — tends to lessen this antitherapeutic disparity. One of the purposes of treatment is to enhance the patient's self-esteem because low self-esteem is at the root of practically every psychogenic problem.

Such revelations can also be therapeutic when they serve to communicate a message that would be healthy for the patient to incorporate. Like the responding story, they can transmit important therapeutic messages in a way that does not produce significant anxiety. Like the self-created story, the patient need not focus on his own deficiencies; rather he is talking about the defects and the problems of other people, whether they be in the therapist's self-created story or in his relating an event from his own life.

In general, the therapist does better to reveal an incident in which he demonstrates a deficiency on his part, rather than a better way of handling a situation than the patient. The latter type of revelation tends to lower the patient's self-esteem, whereas the former does not.

I believe that my responding revelation about the incident that occurred when I was a teenager was of therapeutic benefit to the patient. While talking about my own experience, I was really encouraging him to take a more realistic attitude toward his father. By my relating the course of events that led to my own resolution to discontinue trying to get affection from someone who is not going to provide it, I was encouraging him to act similarly with his father. At the same time, I revealed to him that I too am susceptible to similar problems and I hoped thereby to lessen the aforementioned antitherapeutic idolization that so often occurs in treatment.

"**Fields' Rule.**" A subsequent interchange occurred.

> *Therapist:* Okay, my card says, "Make believe a piece of paper just blew in the window. Something is written on it. Make up what is said on the paper."
>
> It says on the paper, "If at first you don't succeed, try, try again. If after that you still don't succeed, forget it. Don't make a big fool of yourself." That's what it says on the paper. What do you think of that?
>
> *Patient* (laughing): That's a good one.
>
> *Therapist:* Okay.

My response is a quote from W. C. Fields who is alleged to have made the statement. In my *The Boys and Girls Book about Divorce* (1970a, b) I have elaborated on this message and made it into a chapter entitled "Fields' Rule." The message here is essentially a reiteration of my previously described experience with my teenage girlfriend. This time, however, the patient did not resist the message and stated with enthusiasm, "That's a good one."

Thinking Ahead. Martin entered treatment at age seven because of poor school performance in spite of extremely high intelligence. He was sloppy in the classroom, would not do his homework, and was generally disruptive. Both in school and at home he was hyperactive and distractible; however, there was no organic basis for these symptoms. Rather, I considered them to be a manifestation of tension and anxiety. Martin's parents had separated about six months prior to his coming to treatment and there were many unexpressed feelings regarding his parents' separation and their continuing difficulties. Specifically, the parents were deeply embroiled in divorce litigation and this was clearly affecting Martin. At the beginning of his third month of treatment, while playing The Talking, Feeling, and Doing Game, the following interchanges took place.

Therapist: "What is one of the smartest things a person can do? Why?"

I would say one of the smartest things a person can do is to think in advance what the consequences are...do you know what "consequences" means?

Patient: What?

Therapist: What will happen if he does something. In other words, when you're going to do something think in advance whether it's going to cause trouble or not or whether there's a possibility that what you are doing may cause trouble. And a smart person thinks in advance whether there's going to be trouble or not.

Patient: Oh!

Therapist: And then he tries to avoid doing those things which might cause trouble. That's my opinion. What do you think?

Patient: Okay.

Therapist: What do you think. Have a seat or else you won't be on television.

Patient: You get a chip.

Martin was very attentive to what I was saying and I was quite sure that my message "sunk in." However, his general level of activity was still quite high and at the end he moved away from the view of the television camera.

My comment was a general bit of advice which hopefully could serve Martin in many areas. I was particularly thinking about his schoolwork where he did not appear to concern himself with the consequences of his disruptive behavior in the classroom.

Affection Must Be Earned. When the patient took his next card the following conversation occurred.

Patient: "Name three things that could make a person happy."

Therapist: Hh hmm. Go ahead.

Patient: That someone should give them a great big kiss. That's one.

Therapist: All right. Okay.

Patient: Number two. Someone could say, "I love you."

Therapist: All right.

Patient: Number three. Someone could say or someone could um (pauses) . . .

Therapist: Go ahead.

Patient: "You're a nice person."

Therapist: Okay, so the three things are that someone would give a person a kiss, someone could say, "I love you," and someone could say, "You're a nice person"?

Patient: Yes. (kicking)

Therapist: Okay. Excuse me, could you stop kicking there please because that noise will come over the microphone and we won't be able to hear ourselves when we watch this on TV later.

Patient: Okay. (still kicking)

Therapist: Okay. Now — you're still kicking. I have something to say about that. I would say that if a person wanted those things to happen to him, to be kissed, for someone to say, "I love you," and for someone to say, "You're a nice person," he has to work for that. Do you know what I mean?

Patient: Yeah.

Therapist: He has to try to be nice so that people will love him and want to kiss him. Otherwise, they'll try to run away from him and go in the opposite direction.

Patient: Yeah.

Therapist: So things like that don't just happen. Do you know that?

Patient: Right.

Therapist: Okay.

Here, I tried to impress upon Martin the fact that his wishes would only come true if he were to behave in such a way that people would react in accordance with them. Like most children (and probably most adults as well) Martin wished to be loved without applying himself or developing ingratiating personality traits.

Again, Martin's hyperactivity revealed itself with his kicking noises. My comment attempted to communicate to him that he himself would suffer certain consequences over his kicking, namely, that the noises coming over the microphone would impair our watching the program that was being made of our playing the game.

Revelation of the Therapist's Imperfections. The game continued.

Therapist: Okay, my card says, "What sport are you worst at?"

I think the sport I am worst at is basketball. I'm really a loser when it comes . . .

Patient (interrupts): Yeah, I'm not so good at basketball either.

Therapist: Uh huh. What sport are you best at? What's the best one?

Patient: (doesn't answer)

Therapist: Hmm? What's your best sport?

Patient: Well, my best sport is uh . . . mmmm . . . (looking to his mother) what is my best sport?

Therapist: You think of the answer.

Patient: Well, my best out of all I like best . . .

Therapist: All right, what do you like best?

Patient: Oh, that's easy. That's easy. Bowling!

Therapist: Uh huh. You like that the best?

Patient: Yes.

Therapist: What's your highest score?

Patient: I never did bowl in a real bowling alley.

Therapist: Uh huh. What kind of a bowling alley did you bowl in?

Patient: I have a toy bowling alley at home.

Therapist: Uh huh. Oh, you like that very well?

Patient: Yes.

Therapist: Okay.

Patient: And my friends think that Mrs. S. has a bowling alley where you bowl a little ball, and they have to hit the pins and then the pins go up.

Therapist: Okay. Good. All right, I get a chip for my answer.

Most patients, regardless of age, tend to look upon the therapist as being extremely successful in all areas of functioning. Although this may be helpful in certain aspects of therapy, it can also be detrimental. To look upon the therapist as someone who is perfect, or almost perfect, may lower the patient's self-esteem because of the unfavorable comparison. Accordingly, when appropriate and when I believe it will be therapeutic, I admit deficiencies to my patients. Here, the card "What sport are you worst at?" provided me with just such an opportunity.

I then used the subject of one's ability at sports to ask the patient about the sport that he was best at. In this way I hoped to enhance his self-esteem by getting him to talk about something he did well.

A Touchy Subject. The game then continued.

Therapist: Read it now.

Patient: "What is the most selfish thing you ever did? Make believe you're doing it."

Well, I don't know anything, but I'll do something.

Therapist: Well, first say what it is and then you do it. What is this selfish thing?

Patient: Well, to grab things away from people.

Therapist: For instance, what did you do ... like what did you grab from somebody that was selfish?

Patient: Well, I don't know, but I'm just saying ...

Therapist (interrupts): No, you have to tell something that really happened.

Patient (getting agitated): Well, I don't know anything.

Therapist: Okay, so you don't get a chip then.

Patient: Oh. Well, could I take another card?

Therapist: Well, no, no. You have to try to think. Everybody, once in a while, does selfish things. No one's perfect.

Patient: I know.

Therapist: So what selfish thing did you do?

Patient: I don't know.

Therapist: I could think of something selfish you did.

Patient: What?

Therapist: Should I help you?

Patient: Okay.

Therapist: Your mother told me about it just before — before we started the game. Now what was the first thing she was upset about when she came into the office today?

Patient: I forget.

Therapist: I'll give you a hint. It has something to do with a thing starting with the letter "c."

Patient: I don't know.

Therapist: The second letter is "a."

Patient: The third letter?

Therapist: "r."

Patient: I don't . . .

Therapist (interrupts): What's the word?

Patient: I don't know!

Therapist: What's the word.

Patient: I don't know.

Therapist: What does c-a-r spell?

Patient: Car.

Therapist: Okay, the selfish thing has something to do with car.

Patient: Um.

Therapist: What am I talking about?

Patient (exasperated): I don't know.

Therapist: Ah, I think that you're — I can't believe that you don't remember after all that long talk that we had.

Patient: Oh, yes, I broke the car and don't want to pay the money.

Therapist: You broke the car. How did you break the car?

Patient: Well, I dented it or Philip dented it, but we were both just as responsible and I have to pay some money and I don't want to pay it.

Therapist: What's going to happen?

Patient: I have to pay it!

Therapist: All right, what was the selfish thing?

Patient: I didn't want to pay it, I guess.

Therapist: That's selfish and what was the other selfish thing?

Patient: I don't know.

Therapist: The other selfish thing was not thinking about the fact that this was a new car — one day old — a brand new car and you did not think about how your mother would feel if you dented it or scratched it or something like that.

Patient: Well, I didn't know it was going to happen.

Therapist: Yeah, but you weren't careful. You weren't considerate of her property.

Patient: Oh.

Therapist: Do you think that's selfish?

Patient: No . . . (mumbles) . . .

Therapist: Do you think not wanting to pay is selfish?

Patient: Well, no, I did want to keep my money.

Therapist: Yeah, but you said you didn't want to pay.

Patient: Right.

Therapist: Or at least pay part of it. Do you think that that is selfish?

Patient: Well, it cost $22.50. That's a lot of money.

Therapist: Yeah, but that's only half of what it's going to cost. It's going to cost her $45.

Patient: Uh, um.

Therapist: Hmm? Do you think it's selfish not to want to pay part of it?

Patient (in a low voice): No.

Therapist: Okay, so you don't think that's selfish, so I guess if you don't think that's selfish then I guess you don't get a chip. The card asks about a selfish thing.

Patient (in low voice): I still want one.

Therapist: Do you want to think of something else? Do you want to just skip your chance again?

Patient: No.

Therapist: Okay. I guess we have a difference of opinion regarding whether that is selfish or not. See, my opinion is that there are two selfish things there. What are the two selfish things *I* think are in there?

Patient: That I wasn't considerate of the car and that I don't want to pay the money.

Therapist: Right, but you don't think either one of those things are selfish?

Patient: No.

Therapist: Okay. I guess we have a difference of opinion.

Prior to the session, the mother complained bitterly that Martin and his friend Philip had jumped all over her new car and scratched it. As can be seen from the interchange, Martin did not wish to discuss this issue. His card gave me a good opportunity to go into it, but he resisted all the way in recognizing his mother's justification for resentment and requiring him to pay part of the expenses.(Philip's parents as well were being consulted regarding what obligation they and/or Philip were going to assume.) Because Martin did not agree that these were selfish things he did not get a reward chip. In discussing with a child an issue that we do not agree upon, I do not allow a conflict to develop. Rather, after two or three rounds in which each of us expresses himself, I will conclude the discussion with a comment such as, "I guess we have a difference of opinion. Let's go on." And this is what I did in this case. It is antitherapeutic to attempt to coerce a patient into accepting an interpretation. In such situations one usually gets a statement of agreement but no real conviction that the therapist's position is valid.

Humor and Social Perception. The game then continued.

Therapist: "Make a funny sound with your mouth. If you spit you don't get a chip." Hmmm. It's tough to try to do without spitting. (makes funny loud sound)

Patient: You spitted.

Therapist: I think that I spit.

Patient: Yeah.

Therapist: Uck! I don't get a chip.

Patient (laughs): I could make a funny sound.

Therapist: Do you think you can do it without spitting?

Patient: Hh hmm.

Therapist: If you can do it without spitting you get a chip. I'm going to see if you spit.

Patient (makes funny sound).

Therapist: That is a funny sound, right. Okay, you get a chip because you can do it without spitting.

The game includes a number of cards that are designed to elicit humorous and enjoyable interchanges between the therapist and the patient. These are part of the seductive process mentioned in previous chapters and are vital if the child's interest is to be maintained. In addition, in this particular card there is included a lesson in correct social behavior.

Affection Gained from an Acquired Attribute vs. Affection Gained from Innate Traits. The game then continued.

Therapist: "What's the best color eyes to have? Why?" Well, I don't think that there's any one color better than the other. I think that people are born with different color eyes and it really doesn't make any difference what color eyes you have, and one is neither better than the other. People are born different. What do you think?

Patient: Well, I think that's right. I'll get you a chip.

Therapist: Okay. Why don't you sit in your chair because you're going to kick that wire. Here sit over here.

Patient: Oh.

Therapist: Okay.

My response was designed to communicate the message that one should judge people on the basis of acquired attributes rather than innate characteristics. Those who are deficient in the former area may try to compensate by exaggerating the value of traits in the latter. Again, we see Martin's hyperactivity and my response.

"What's the worst thing a child can say to his mother?" We then continued.

Therapist: Okay, you go now.. What does your card say?

Patient: "What's the worst thing a child can say to his mother?" Oh, that's easy. "You're stupid."

Therapist: Hhmhh. Can't you think of something worse?

Patient: "I hate you."

Therapist: Hh hmm.

Patient: "I hate you, stupid."

Therapist: Hh hmm. Did you ever have any thoughts like that about your mother?

Patient: No.

Therapist: Never in your whole life?

Patient: No, I don't!

Therapist: I can't imagine. I can't imagine in your whole life — in your *whole* life — how old are you now?

Patient: Seven.

Therapist: In seven years you have never *once* thought that you hated your mother?

Patient: No!

Therapist: Never *once*?

Patient: Not that I hate her.

Therapist: What's the worst thought that you ever really had about her in your *whole* life of seven years?

Patient: I don't know, to tell you the truth.

Patient's Mother: I bet you thought I was stupid sometimes.

Patient: No.

Patient's Mother: Because I do stupid things.

Patient: Well, sometimes you do stupid things, but I never think you are stupid. But sometimes you've done a few stupid things.

Therapist: But you never once had the thought that you hated your mother.

Patient: Noooo.

Therapist: Never once? I don't think you really hate her all the time, but even once a little bit.

Patient: No.

Therapist: Really? Okay, because most kids on

occasion, once in a while, when something happens they really get mad at their mother and they may say something like they hate her or they think it.

Patient: Oh.

Therapist: You've never had that?

Patient: No.

Therapist? What do you think about a child who would have such a thought?

Patient: Well, I think his mother would have done something that he really wouldn't have liked.

Therapist: Right, that's true.

Patient: And it got him very very mad.

Therapist: Right. Do you think that there's something wrong with a child who would have such a thought like that?

Patient: I don't know.

Therapist: I agree with you that, you know, sometimes a mother will do something that will get a kid really angry and then he'll have that kind of thought.

Patient: Oh.

Patient's Mother: When he's gotten really angry he's barricaded himself in sometimes and pounded on the door and nailed himself in his room.

Therapist: Hh hmm. When that happens do you hate your mother?

Patient: No.

Therapist: Hh hmm. You don't. Okay. I was just wondering whether you had such thoughts because most kids do at times have thoughts like that.

Patient: Oh.

Therapist: Even though they don't hate their mother all the time.

Patient: Oh.

Therapist: But I find there's nothing wrong with that, you know, you have it once in a while.

Patient: Oh.

Therapist: Okay, you get a chip.

> *Patient:* Thanks.
> *Therapist:* Okay, now I go.

I used the card as an opportunity to enter into a discussion on the subject of inhibited anger — a subject that I considered to be particularly pertinent to Martin's difficulties. I felt that the anger he harbored toward his parents (especially because of their separation) was being displaced onto peers and his teacher. My attempt in this interchange was to help him get in touch with his angry feelings and to decrease his guilt over them so that he could express them more appropriately. He was listening intently to what I was saying, but it was clear that my ideas were somewhat alien to him. However, my experience has been that over a period of time such communications help a child become less repressed regarding his angry feelings.

The interchange in which I described some incredulity regarding Martin's never having had hateful thoughts toward his mother contains a term that I have found helpful in communicating with children. Specifically, the term "your whole life" is one that facilitates communicating with children at their own level. The expression of incredulity also served to help Martin become free in expressing any hateful feelings that he might have been aware of but embarrassed to express.

Although the value of the mother's being present in the room has been emphasized throughout this book, here is an example of her presence serving somewhat as a contaminant. When I was requesting that Martin try to provide the answer to my question about the worst thought that he had even had about his mother in his *whole* life, she provided a specific answer, namely, that he might have thought that she was stupid. I quickly went back to my question in order to pursue what I thought would be a more meaningful discussion. In spite of such occasional contaminations my experience has been that the advantages of having the mother in the room far outweigh the disadvantages.

Reducing Guilt over Anger at a Parent. The game then continued.

Therapist: Okay, My card says, "You're sitting on the beach and a bottle with a piece of paper washes up on shore. You take the paper out of the bottle. What does it say?

It says here in this bottle, "I have run away from home because my mother thinks it's terrible for a child to be angry at her ever and I have mean parents. They don't know that it's perfectly all right for a child to get angry at a parent once in a while and they think it's terrible so I've run away. Please help me."

Patient: You get a chip.

Therapist: I get a chip for that?

Patient: Yep.

Therapist: What do you think happened to that kid?

Patient: Well, like someone might help him.

Therapist: And what might they do?

Patient: Bring him back.

Therapist: And say what?

Patient: And tell their parents not to be mean and talk to them and maybe get a psychiatrist like you.

Therapist: Yeah, and what would the psychiatrist like me say to the parents?

Patient: Well, talk to them about being mean and something else.

Therapist: And what would he say?

Patient: Oh, I can't tell you everything he'd say!

Therapist: Right, but just what would be one — suppose you were the psychiatrist and let's say I was the guy who was bringing the kid and I would say and have the parents . . . first I would have that boy there . . . we got him back from that desert island and we got the parents and we say, "Sir, could you please say something to these parents to help their situation?" What would you say to them?

Patient: Well, "Why are you always mean? You shouldn't always be mean."

Therapist: Let's say I'm the father and . . .

Patient (interrupts): "You shouldn't always be mean."

Therapist: What's mean? What have I done that's mean Mr. Psychiatrist?

Patient: Well, I found . . . the man found this piece of paper . . .

Therapist (Interrupts): Yeah.

Patient: . . . in the bottle. Read it.

Therapist: Okay, and I'll read it. And it says here that my son is saying that I'm mean and wrong because I think that a child shouldn't be angry at his parents. What do you say about that?

Patient: Well, I think you should . . . (mumbles) . . .

Therapist: You thing what?

Patient: I think you should get a chip for that.

Therapist: But we're playing this game where you are the psychiatrist and I'm the father and I'm saying, "I don't think it's right for a boy to be angry at his father." And what are you saying, Mr. Psychiatrist?

Patient: "It's right for a boy to be angry at their parents once in a while."

Therapist: You're saying that.

Patient: But not all the time, just once in a while.

Therapist: Uh huh. All right. And suppose the father is doing something.

Patient: Doing what?

Therapist: Let's suppose the father is doing something to make the child angry. Is it all right for him to be angry?

Patient: For him?

Therapist: For the child to be angry?

Patient: Yes.

Therapist: Uh huh. What should the child do when the father does something that makes him angry?

Patient: Just say that he's angry and say not to do it.

Therapist: Hh hmm. Tell the father what he's angry about. Right. Okay. Let's go on.

At the beginning of this interchange I was not sure that I was "getting through" to Martin. However, as is clear, by the end he revealed that he understood what I was trying to say regarding anger and its expression.

Chapter Eight
The Board of Objects Game

In The Board of Objects Game, designed with Dr. Nathan I. Kritzberg, a board of sixty-four squares (a standard checker board serves well) or a larger board of one hundred squares is used. In each square is placed a small figurine of the type readily purchased in most stores selling children's games and equipment (Figure 3). The figurines include family members, zoo animals, farm animals, small vehicles (police car, fire engine, ambulance, etc.), members of various occupations (doctor, nurse, policeman, etc.), and a wide assortment of other common objects (baby bottle, knife, gun, lipstick, trophy, lump of brown clay, etc.). A pair of dice is used with one face of each die colored red. Lastly, there is a treasure chest filled with token reward chips.

The game begins with the child's throwing the dice. If a red side lands face up (and this should occur once every three throws of the dice) the child can select any object from the board. If he can say anything at all about the object, he gets *one* reward chip. If he can tell a story about the object, he gets *two* reward chips. The therapist plays similarly and the winner is the one who has accumulated the most chips when the alloted time is over. If a person is "lucky" and both red sides land face up, the player can select two objects and gets double rewards. He may tell one story in which both objects are included or he may tell two separate stories. When commenting on, or telling a story about, an object it is preferable for the player to hold it and sometimes even move it about in accordance with what is going on in the story. The child will often do this spontaneously and the therapist should do so as well in appreciation of the enhanced efficacy of the dramatized communication. The therapist's various gestures, animal sounds, vocal imitations, accents, etc. can further involve the child and enhance his receptivity to the therapeutic messages. After being used, the figurine can either be replaced on the board or placed on the side, depending upon the preference of the players.

Although the figurines are selected so as to elicit fantasies covering a wide range of issues usually encountered in most children's therapy, their exact nature, form, and variety is not crucial. As mentioned, I believe that the pressure of unconscious material to be released in a form specifically meaningful for the child is far greater than the power of the facilitating stimulus to distort the projected material. Accordingly, the therapist need not be too concerned about his selection of objects if he wishes to make up such a game himself. The usual variety of such figurines found in most toy stores will serve well.

Again, the therapist should try to create an atmosphere in which conversations may take place about the comments made or stories told; rather than one in which there is fierce competition for the accumulation of chips. The therapist plays in accordance with the same rules to create stories of his own that are either specifically related to the comments or stories just related by the child or else relevant in other ways to the child's life and his problems.

The game is a very attractive one and it is a rare child who does not respond in the affirmative when shown it and asked: "Would you like to play this game with me?" The child below five or six, who has not yet reached the point where he can meaningfully appreciate the rules and organization of the standard board games, will still usually want to "play." Some will enjoy throwing the dice until they get a red and will then choose an object. Such younger children may not be able to tell well-organized stories but may still provide meaningful, although fragmented, fantasies — especially because there is a reward chip that can be obtained for such revelations. The therapist must try to select from the disorganized fantasies those threads or patterns that are atypical, idiosyncratic, or pathological, and then use these as the focus for his own responding comments. Often such younger children will be content to just play, fantasize, and collect chips without giving the therapist his turn. Generally, in such situations, I allow the child to tell a few "stories" — by which time I have gotten enough material to create one of my own. I then request my right to take my turn to tell stories (a request that is rarely refused) and use the opportunity to relate my responding messages, either in story or nonstory allegory.

When the allotted time is up, the person with the most chips takes a prize from the previously described box of trinkets.

Again, the aforementioned "rules" are those that I have found most useful. However, the therapist may wish to utilize his own variations and I, too, at times have modified the game (as in the aforementioned description of its use with younger children). I have found the game particularly useful with children at the kindergarten to second-grade level. At that age their reading ability is usually not great enough for them to play some of the more sophisticated games I describe in this book. Yet they do appreciate game structure and so generally become absorbed. At about the age of nine or ten, most children consider the game "babyish" and prefer the more advanced games described herein.

Clinical Examples

Regressive Fantasies in a Girl with MBD. Sally was born with multiple congenital anomalies. She had a thyroglossal cyst, bilateral pes planus and genu recurvatum, hypertelorism, bilateral epicanthic folds, bilaterally shortened fifth fingers, a café au lait spot on her right leg, and coordination deficits. In addition, she was hyperactive, distractible, had rage outbursts over minor inconsequential irritations, and could not get along well with peers. In spite of all these manifestations of organic neurological impairment, her IQ on the Stanford-Binet was 127. Furthermore, psychogenic problems were also present. She was obsessed with her shoelaces, continually fearing that they weren't tied tightly enough; and no matter how tight her parents made them she was still dissatisfied. She complained often that her arms were bleeding, that they were dirty, that her back itched, and that her neck was coming off. These complaints, however, did not have a delusional quality and so I did not consider her to be psychotic.

Sally was referred at five and a half for the the treatment of the aforementioned psychological difficulties. During her sessions Sally would often hold a "Bozo" hand puppet, which I had in my office and which was identical to one that she had at home. It often symbolized herself and at times her mother. Many of the things she did in treatment involved the Bozo doll. In the phase of therapy to be described most of our interchanges focused on stories she told and fantasies she revealed while playing the Board of Objects Game. Actually, as can be seen in the transcript of our interchanges, she did not play according to the formal "rules," as is often the case with younger children, especially those with minimal brain dysfunction.

During her eighth session, Sally took a small rabbit figurine from the Board of Objects and placed it inside a hole in the armpit area of the Bozo hand puppet. This little tear provided the puppet with a new orifice. After putting the rabbit in the hole she stated, "The rabbit is inside Bozo's hole. It's warm inside and he's sleeping there." I was unable to elicit further comments by the patient about the rabbit and/or Bozo.

I understood the play to represent Sally's desire to regress to an intrauterine state in response to the frustrations she suffered in her attempts to cope with the world. Accordingly, I asked her if she would like me to tell a story about Bozo and the little rabbit. She readily agreed and gave me the hand puppet and rabbit for use in my story. I related a tale about a little rabbit who was scared to play with other children because sometimes they teased him and sometimes he would fall down and hurt himself. Because of that he got inside the hole of the Bozo doll and slept there. It was warm and comfortable and he was very happy, for a while. Suddenly, however, his sleep was interrupted by strange noises. He put his two ears outside the hole in order to determine more precisely what these noises were. At that point I slowly protruded the rabbit's ears outside the hole in the Bozo puppet. "What can those noises be?" said the rabbit. At this point I verbalized various laughing sounds: "Ha, ha, ha. Hee, hee, hee." I related then that what the rabbit was hearing were the sounds of children playing. I asked her to join in with me in making the sounds and she readily did so. I then introduced the sounds of barking dogs ("Woof, woof, woof") and cats ("meow, meow, meow"). The patient joined me again in imitating these sounds, but this time started to jump and dance around the room as we both imitated the sounds of the laughter and the dogs and the cats. Adding these dramatic elements served to enhance not only the patient's pleasure in the game but, I believe, her receptivity to my messages.

Getting back to the story, I then related how the rabbit became increasingly interested in what these sounds were and finally protruded his head far enough so that he could look and see what was going on. Observing the children at play, he became ever more interested in what was going on. However, each time he was tempted to go out of the hole and join them he because frightened and thought about how he might be teased by them, how he might fall down when playing with them, and how much warmer and safer the hole in the Bozo doll was. Such thoughts would then result in his once again retracting his head into the hole in the Bozo puppet. The patient was intently interested in the ambivalent little rabbit and his deliberations. Finally, some of the children call out to the little rabbit: "Come on out and play here with us, little rabbit. Join us. We're having a great time." These invitations were tantalizing to the rabbit and only increased his amblivalent conflict. Finally, "although his knees were knocking and his teeth were chattering," the rabbit decides to join the children. After an initial period of great tension and anxiety, he gradually becomes more comfortable with them and then joins in the fun. The story ended with both the patient and I rollicking to the sounds of the children's laughter and the animal's noises.

My hope was that my story might contribute to a

lessening of the patient's fears of involving herself with others and her associated tendency to regress. One cannot hope to interrupt or reverse regressive processes without providing pleasureable experiences in the here and now. In my story Sally was provided with encouragement to assume a more mature adaptation, emphasizing the pleasure that one can enjoy at the maturer level.

Teaching Reality. One week later, in her ninth session, this interchange took place.

Therapist: Good morning boys and girls, ladies and gentlemen. Today is Wednesday, the 27th of September, 1972, and I am happy to welcome you all once again to Dr. Gardner's Storytelling Program. I am happy to tell you that Sally is on our program. We're going to play the Board of Objects Game. You want to say hello to everybody?

Patient: Hello.

Therapist: Hi.

Patient: (laughs and picks up Bozo puppet and a toy cow)

Therapist: Okay.

Patient: Once there was a cow who moved Bozo. Get up. Move, move, move, move, move! Get out of my way. (Bozo pushes the cow away)

Therapist: Get out of my way, huh?

Patient: Then Bozo ate the clay. (laughs while putting clay in her mouth)

Therapist: He ate the clay? Ugh! Ugh!

Patient: Ooey, gooey. (laughs while teasingly licking the clay)

Therapist: Ugh! Eating clay, ugh! Disgusting! Ugh!

Patient (continuing to laugh): Why, Bozo — why did you eat the claaaaaaay!?

Therapist: Why did he eat the clay?

Patient (laughs again)

Therapist: Ugh. Are you supposed to do that?

Patient: No.

Therapist: Why not?

Patient: Because . . . (mumbles) . . .

Therapist: Because why?

Patient: Because it's phooey .. . (mumbles) . . .

Therapist: Why is it phooey?

Patient: Because it's . . . (mumbles) . . .

Therapist: Because it's what?

Patient: It's . . . (mumbles) . . .

Therapist: It's what?

Patient: It's dirt.

Therapist: It's dirt! What will happen if you eat dirt?

Patient: You'd get sick.

Therapist: And how would you feel?

Patient: Sick.

Therapist: And what will happen when you get sick?

Patient: You'll throw up.

Therapist: Yeah! Show me how. What will happen. Make believe you're sick.

Patient: (spits downward, all over her dress)

Therapist: Ooh! No, no, don't. Can I (to patient's mother) have a Kleenex please. No — don't. Just make believe. Don't spit that way. (Therapist wipes spit off patient's dress.) You know what will happen? You'll get up in the morning and you'll say, "Ooh, I feel terrible" and you go "eeeech" (long retching sound) and you may even vomit. That's what will happen and you'll — ugh — it will be dirty all over the place. That's what will be.

Patient: And on you and on your dress. And Mommy will put it in the washing machine.

Therapist: Yeah, but Mommy won't feel good. She'll be mad that you vomited all over your dress. So tell me why shouldn't you eat dirty clay?

Patient: Because you'll get . . . (mumbles) . . .

Therapist: You'll get what?

Patient: . . . (mumbles) . . .

Therapist Uh. What's going to happen to you if you eat that?

Patient: You'll get sick.

Therapist: You'll get sick and what will happen to you when you get sick?

Patient: You'll throw up. (now picking up a stale Tootsie Roll used as a game object).

Therapist: Right. I don't think you should eat that. That's a dirty old Tootsie Roll. Ugh! That's a filthy Tootsie Roll.

Patient: (laughs out loud): Remember Johnny . . . (mumbles) . . .

Therapist: Remember what?

Patient's Mother: Johnny vomited.

Therapist: Johnny vomited. Why did he vomit?

Patient: Because he (speaks very low) . . .

Therapist: I can't hear you.

Patient (almost shouting): Because he ate a dirty Tootsie Roll!

Therapist: Because he ate a dirty Tootsie Roll. Right. Right. (Patient takes a lollipop.) Will you throw that stick away in the garbage, in the wastepaper basket?

Patient: Hhmm. (puts lollipop stick in basket).

Therapist: Oh, you want to get another lollipop? Okay. Now what are you going to do?

In this first part of our interchange I focused primarily on reality issues. I tried to teach the patient, through the vehicle of dramatic play, certain principles about the ingestion of inedible substances. As can be seen, such play often involves the therapist's reducing himself to the most primitive levels of behavior. However, children uniformly respond to such antics, and they can be a valuable mode of therapeutic communication. Of course, there is always the danger that things will get a little out of hand and this is what happened here. Sally was so swept up in our antics that she spit all over herself while playing out my messages. In addition, there was a teasing and a tension element in her repeatedly putting the clay in her mouth. She was not completely oblivious to the fact that the clay and the Tootsie Roll were inedibles. Placing them in her mouth allowed her to stimulate an enjoyable game with me. Such pleasurable interchanges not only are ego-enhancing to the patient, but serve to strengthen the relationship with the therapist.

Incorporation of the Therapist's Message. Our interchange then continued as the patient picked up a small toy lion and brought it close to the Bozo hand puppet.

Patient: A lion.

Therapist: Okay.

Patient: Once upon a time there was a lion who went right in here. (puts the lion into the hole in the Bozo hand puppet)

Therapist: He went right in there. Uh huh. What's that that he went into?

Patient: See, in the hole in Bozo.

Therapist: The hole in Bozo. Okay. The lion went into the hole in Bozo. Yeah. And then?

Patient: She heard strange noises.

Therapist: He heard strange noises where? Where did he hear the strange noises? Huh?

Patient: "He, he, ha, ha, woof, woof."

Therapist: Where were those noises.

Patient: Down in the . . . (mumbles) . . .

Therapist: What?

Patient: Outside.

Therapist: Outside.

Patient: From outside.

Therapist: He heard the strange noises outside.

Patient: . . . (mumbles) . . .

Therapist: I can't hear you. What were they saying?

Patient: "And will you come out?"

Therapist: Who said, "Will you come out?"

Patient: The children.

Therapist: The children said to the lion who was in the hole in Bozo, "Will you come out?" Okay. What were the noises they were making? What were the noises? Hmm? What were the noises?

Patient: "He, he, ha, ha, woof, woof."

Therapist: What kinds of noises were those?

Patient: People noises and a doggy noise.

Therapist: Uh huh. Were they good noises or bad noises?

Patient: Good noises.

Therapist: What were they doing when they were saying, "He, he, ha, ha, ho, ho?"

Patient: They were singing.

Therapist: They were singing. Were they having a good time?

Patient: Yes.

Therapist: Okay. And so what did they say to the lion?

Patient: "Lion, will you come out?" "I ... (mumbles) ... come out."

Therapist: He said "I *will*" or "I *won't*"?

Patient: "Then you'll have to go back in that hole."

Therapist: I'm sorry. Did the lion say. "I *will* come out" or "I *won't* come out."

Patient: "I will."

Therapist: "I will. Why did the lion want to come out?

Patient: Because he wanted to.

Therapist: Why did he want to?

Patient: Because he wanted to. (laughs while putting old Tootsie Roll into her mouth)

Therapist: You want to put that in your mouth. It's up to you. That dirty Tootsie Roll.

Patient: Eat it up.

Therapist: So I'm interested in knowing what happens to that lion. Did he come out of the hole in Bozo?

Patient: Yes.

Therapist: And then what happened? What happened then? Huh?

Patient: "He, he."

Therapist: Pardon me.

Patient: "Ha, ha, woof, woof, roar!"

Therapist: What was the lion doing?

Patient: He was roaring.

Therapist: Uh huh. And what else was he doing? Is he there with the children now?

Patient: ... (mumbles) ...

Therapist: Huh? He came out of the hole in Bozo. Is that it?

Patient: Yeah.

Therapist: Uh huh. Where is he happier — outside playing with the children here or inside the hole in Bozo?

Patient: Outside playing with the children.

Therapist: Hhmm. Okay.

The patient's play here is a clear demonstration that my messages from the previous session regarding her regression conflict have been received. After one week she had remembered my story and reenacted it in her play. This time, however, she chose a lion instead of the rabbit. Perhaps this reflects her desire to choose an animal known for its bravery as opposed to the rabbit who generally symbolizes timidity. However, the lion toy happened to be within easy reach, whereas the rabbit was not; and this may also explain the choice of the lion. In either case I do not consider the specific animal utilized as important as the function for which it is being used. The pressure to project outward unconscious fantasies is far greater that the "pull" of any specific external stimulus. Accordingly, the nature of the stimulus is far less important in determining the child's stories than the inner psychic needs which are being represented in such fantasies.

Repeating the story in the way the patient does here is part of the working-through process. Each reiteration allows for a desensitization and an accommodation to the new and anxiety-provoking material. In this way the patient becomes used to alternative modes of adaptation and can more comfortably utilize them.

At one point the patient interrupted the story about the lion and the children and reverted to the Tootsie Roll game, engaged in during the earlier part of the session. I considered this to be a manifestation of the anxiety that was being aroused by the game. She reached for the Tootsie Roll just at the point when the lion was leaving the hole in the Bozo puppet. At such points the therapist may have a dilemma. Recognizing that such a digression serves to alleviate anxiety, he must respect it. If he does not, he may cause the patient increased anxiety and thereby compromise his therapy. However, such respect for the patient's needs might also simultaneously be respect for resistances and other avoidance mechanisms. Accordingly, it behooves him to attempt to discourage them. What I do, in such situations, is to sympathetically and benevolently attempt to bring the patient back to the material from which he is diverting himself. If he once again goes off on the tangential issue, I do not push things. In this case my one attempt to bring her back was successful. I indulged her for a short period in the Tootsie Roll game and then asked her a question about the lion and Bozo. She did not have much trouble getting back to the original game, demonstrating, I believe, that such directing of the fantasied material need not produce intolerable anxiety or need not be antitherapeutic.

During the week following this session the mother described a significant diminution in some of Sally's psychogenic symptoms. Her rage outbursts were far less frequent and she was significantly less concerned with her body preoccupations. In addition , her concern that her shoelaces were not being tied tightly enough had also diminished markedly. I do not consider these changes to be entirely the result of her interchanges with me. She was also on medication (chlorpromazine) and the mother was advised on how to manage her as well.

Reacting to a Congenital Defect. In addition, Sally's thyroglossal cyst had been a source of preoccupation from the very beginning of her treatment. It was mildly inflamed and she would often pick at it. Although not readily apparent to others, Sally considered it to be a most disfiguring defect. I felt that she was focusing many of her inadequacies on this lesion, and I hoped that by making her feel more secure she would be less sensitive to it. The family pediatrician did not believe that she was old enough to have it removed. Because I considered its removal to be of possible psychological benefit to Sally (deep-seated psychodynamic contributions to her preoccupation notwithstanding), I suggested the parents consult a plastic surgeon I knew who was quite sensitive to the psychological effects of cosmetic defects. He disagreed with the family pediatrician and felt there was no contraindication for surgery at that time. He felt that a short hospitalization of two-to-three days would be all that was necessary. The session below, her twelfth, occurred two weeks after the just described sequence and about a week prior to her operation. Just before beginning this story she stated that she wanted to tell a story about "something without a neck." Again, she was holding the Bozo hand puppet as we began.

Therapist: Good morning, boys and girls, ladies and gentlemen. Today is Monday, the 9th of October, 1972, and Sally is here again and she's going to tell us a story. Here she is. Now you said something about a story about something without a neck. Is that right?

Patient: Yes.

Therapist: Let me hear about that.

Patient: I like Bozo with no neck.

Therapist: You want Bozo with no neck?

Patient: Um, but Bozo's chin hides his neck.

Therapist: Bozo's chin hides his neck. Okay. What else?

Patient: That's why.

Therapist: Okay. Let's hear more about Bozo's chin hiding his neck. Let's hear more about that.

Patient: That I pretend I see Bozo's chin hiding his neck. I think he has no neck.

Therapist: Uh huh. Okay. What else can you tell me about that? Tell me more about that.

Patient: No neck — if no neck your head wouldn't stay on.

Therapist: If you had no neck your head wouldn't stay on. So what happens to Bozo now that he has no neck?

Patient: He grows a neck and the chin hides it.

Therapist: Hh hmm. Is his head going to stay on?

Patient: Yes.

Therapist: His head will stay on. Does he want to hide his neck? Does he want to hide his neck?

Patient: No.

Therapist: Hh hmm. Is there something on his neck that he doesn't like?

Patient: Nothing.

Therapist: Nothing. Hh hmm. Should I tell a story about that?

Patient: Whoop.

Therapist: Whoop. You want me to tell a story about Bozo and his neck?

Patient: Uh, no!

Therapist: You *don't* want to hear a story.

Patient: Tell a story about Bozo and Queenie (the name Sally had given to the toy elephant).

Therapist: And Queenie. Okay. I'll tell a story about Bozo and Queenie. Once upon a time — (Patient picks up toy telephone and tries to pull it apart.) — uh — uh — uh — uh — uh — I don't want you to break that telephone.

Patient: (laughs)

Therapist: Do you want to hear about Bozo and Queenie?

Patient: Yes.

Therapist (holding the Bozo puppet and Queenie the elephant): Okay. Now sit down and listen to my story. Okay? Once upon a time Bozo was sitting and his neck — his head was bent down like this — so you could hardly see his face. And Queenie was coming along and she said, "Bozo, why are you bending down that way? I can hardly see your face." She said, "Lift up your head. I want to speak to you." But Bozo just kept his head down like that. And Queenie said — she took her trunk — and said, "Come on, Bozo, lift up your head. Come on." And Bozo would keep his head down like that. And she said, "What's the matter with you, Bozo? Why don't you lift up your head, Bozo? Come on."

She took her long trunk and she went like that and Bozo put his head right down like that. She said, "Are you trying to hide something on your neck or something like that?" And Bozo didn't say anything. And she said, "Come on. Are you trying to hide something on your neck?"

And Bozo said, "Well, yeah. There is something I am hiding."

And Queenie said, "Well, what is it?"

He said, "My neck is very ugly. I don't want anyone to see it."

And Queenie said, "Why is that?"

And Bozo said, "Because I have a little red bump on my neck."

And Queenie said, "Yeah, what about it? I saw that. That isn't so terrible."

And Bozo said, "Oh, everybody will think I'm very bad and ugly."

And Queenie said, "You know that's not so. I've seen that little bump many times. In fact, I hardly notice it."

And Bozo said, "I think I'm the ugliest person in the whole world for having that little bump."

And Queenie said, "No, you're not. You just have that little bump. Look, I'll bet you if you walk around and hold your head up, no one will even notice it and no one will call you ugly."

And Bozo said, "I don't believe you. I believe that all the animals and all the people around are going to call me ugly if they see that little bump on my neck."

So then Queenie said, "Well, let's try." (therapist turns to patient) So what animal did they go over to? (patient doesn't answer) She said, "Let's go over and play with somebody and see if they notice it? Okay. We won't say anything. All right." So who did they go over to?

Patient: The alligator.

Therapist: They went to the alligator. They went over and Queenie and Bozo said, "Alligator (this time Bozo keeps his head up high), would you like to play with us?" And what did the alligator say?

Patient: "Ugly."

Therapist: "Ugly!" Why did the alligator say "ugly?" Why did the alligator say "ugly?"

Patient: Because he . . . (mumbles) . . .

Therapist: Because what? Because why?

Patient: Because he rubbed his neck too much.

Therapist: The alligator rubbed his neck or Bozo did?

Patient: Bozo did.

Therapist: Well, I'll tell you. That's what happened in your story. You know what happened in my story?

Patient: No.

Therapist: The alligator said, "Sure I'd like to play." So they played and they had a lot of fun and they danced and they sang and they did different things.

And then they walked away and Queenie said, "You see, the alligator didn't say anything about your neck. He didn't say anything about your neck." Now what do you think Bozo said then?

Patient: He said, "Ugly."

Therapist: Nope. He said, "Gee whiz. Maybe you're right. Maybe children don't notice that. Maybe animals don't notice it. Maybe they don't think I'm ugly." So then they said, "Let's go back and ask the alligator."

So then Queenie said to the alligator, "Alligator, do you think Bozo is ugly?"

And the alligator said, "I do not."

And then Queenie said, "Even though he has that little red dot on his neck, that little red spot?"

And the alligator said, "So what. Everybody has some little spot somewhere. That doesn't bother me. Bozo is a lot of fun to be with and that's what is important."

And that's the end of the story. And what did Bozo think after that? What did Bozo think after that?

Patient: He looked pretty.

Therapist: He thought he looked pretty. Right. And he realized that one little spot doesn't make you ugly all over. The end. And you know what else also? When Bozo got older they were able to take off the spot. That's what happened after that too. The end. But he had to wait awhile. Okay. That's the end of that story.

I fully recognized that Sally's preoccupation with her thyroglossal cyst could not simply be understood as a reaction to the defect itself. Rather, it symbolized all the defects in her body, both real and fantasized. It was as if she were putting all her deficiencies in one little spot and hoping that by removing it she would rid herself of all her liabilities. In addition, by focusing on its removal she could avoid attending to more serious problems that were far more difficult to alleviate. It could serve as a face-saving excuse for her alienation. It's as if she were saying to herself: "It is not because of my asocial behavior, poor social judgment, temper outbursts, perceptual impairments, etc. that other children will not play with me; rather, it is because of my spot on my neck."

The therapeutic approach to her obsession, therefore, involved directing one's attention to the various contributing factors. One does best to confine oneself to one of these factors at a time, depending upon which element seems most appropriate to focus upon at a given point. One does best to follow the patient's lead in this regard and to direct one's therapeutic communications at the same level as that of the patient. Here there was conscious embarrassment over exposure of the cyst and so I attempted to impart the message that others were not as concerned with the cyst as she was. In addition, I tried to help the patient appreciate that others are primarily concerned with the kind of person she is and how enjoyable her company is, rather than whether or not she has an unimportant defect. Although this interchange directs itself to one of the most superficial levels of the neurotic pattern, it is nevertheless a part of its treatment.

Although I knew that the patient would be undergoing surgical removal of the cyst in about a week, I did not consider the interchange to be irrelevant. My hope was that it would lessen the likelihood that she would use similar maladaptive mechanisms following her operation.

Competition for Mother's Love. The patient then continued.

> *Patient:* Tell a story about this pig! (Patient hands me a pig figurine with sucklings at her breasts.)
> *Therapist:* Okay, you tell a story first.
> *Patient:* And Bozo and Queenie.

Therapist: Okay, about the pig?

Patient: Yes.

Therapist: Should the story have the spot in it — the spot on Bozo's neck?

Patient: No.

Therapist: Oh, you want a different kind of story?

Patient: Yes.

Therapist: Nothing about the . . .

Patient (interrupting): . . . the pigs drinking milk and Bozo wanted that milk and Queenie said, "You can't have it."

Therapist: Okay. The little pigs were getting milk from the mommy pig. Right?

Patient: Yeah.

Therapist: They were drinking the milk from the mommy pig. And Bozo wanted some milk from the mommy pig?

Patient: Yeah.

Therapist: And Queenie said, "You can't have it." Okay, you finish up your story and then I'll tell mine. So what happened in your story?

Patient: The pigs were drinking some milk and Bozo wanted some milk and Queenie said, "You can't have any."

Therapist: Okay. Now what happened after that?

Patient: One pig came one day the daddy pig came.

Therapist: And what did he say? What did he do?

Patient: He saw a nipple there and he put his nose on it.

Therapist: Oh, he saw a nipple there. There was one nipple there that wasn't being used. Huh? Then what happened? What happened after that?

Patient: The pigs were drinking milk. The daddy pig sucked on the nipple.

Therapist: Uh huh. Then what happened? What happened with this pig and the nipple and everything and the daddy? What happened then?

Patient: They lived happily after after. They lived happily after . . .

Therapist (interrupting): . . . happily ever after.
Patient: Yes.
Therapist: Uh huh. What happened to Bozo? Did he get any of the milk? Hhmm?
Patient: No, he doesn't like it.
Therapist: Hh hmm. All right. Now should I tell a story?
Patient: Yes.

I considered Bozo here to represent the patient. Queenie and the pig both represent her mother. The pig is the good mother who gives milk and Queenie is the refusing and rejecting mother who would deprive her of this nutriment which is symbolic of mother's love. The little piglets sucking at the mother's breasts represent the patient's siblings (Sally had two younger siblings). Her father too is seen as a competitor for mother's time and affection. Sally's mother, by no stretch of the imagination, could be considered rejecting. She was most loving and devoted to her children and was deeply concerned with their welfare. Sally, like just about all children, considered any time her mother spent with her siblings and/or her father to be a reflection of her mother's disinterest in her. The story ends with a "sour grapes" theme. Bozo never gets the milk but "doesn't like it" anyway. It's as if the patient were saying: "Who likes mother's milk anyway?" With this rationalization she can lessen the pain of her fantasized rejection. With this understanding of the patient's story, I related mine.

Therapist: Okay. Once upon a time Bozo was walking past and he saw a mommy pig with all of her little babies.
Patient: Yes. (Patient moves out of the field of the television camera.)
Therapist: Do you want to be on television? Then you'd better sit over here. And he said, "Ooh, that looks good. All those little babies there are getting milk from that mommy pig. I wish that I could have some."
And Queenie said, "You can't have some!"

And Bozo said, "Maybe I can. I'll see. And they began to fight. And Bozo said, "I want it."

And Queenie said, "You can't have it."

And Bozo said, "Who are you to tell me? I'm going to ask the pig." So Bozo went over to the pig and he said, "Mrs. Pig, Mrs. Pig, how do you do? My name is Bozo."

And she said, "How do you do, Bozo. Very glad to meet you."

And he said, "Can I please suck some milk from one of your breasts? I'm very thirsty and I love milk." And what do you think Mrs. Pig said?

Patient (shouts): No!

Therapist: No, she didn't say no. She said, "You'll have to wait a little while because the other pigs are now having their milk and that's why you can't have any. But as soon as one of the pigs is finished you can go over and you can have some too." And she said, "However, you're getting bigger and bigger and after a while I won't let you have more milk so much because you're getting so big and milk from the breasts is mainly for little babies. If you want to drink milk you drink it from a glass like big kids."

So anyway Bozo had some of the milk when one of the other little pigs got finished and then after that, when he got a little older, he drank it from a glass. The end. That's the end of that story.

In my story, I emphasize the sharing element. In the resolution of sibling rivalry and/or oedipal problems it is important to help the child appreciate the importance of sharing. The child would like everything and he sees himself as getting nothing. Sharing is the compromise position which is most in tune with the reality of the situation. I also imparted the important message that Sally would have to prepare herself for a gradual diminution in mother's milk — a necessary concomitant of her independent growth and development. In my story the good and bad mothers are not divided between Queenie and the pig. Rather, I present only one mother who is both benevolent and reasonably restricting. In this way I hoped to help Sally gain a more balanced view of her mother. The interchange then continued.

More Reactions to a Congenital Defect. The interchange then continued.

Patient: Queenie, Bozo — Bozo — hold up a mirror for Queenie. (Patient puts toy mirror in front of Queenie's face)

Therapist: Okay. Bozo held up a mirror for Queenie. Okay. Now what? Now what's happening?

Patient (Queenie looks at herself in the mirror and then falls to the table.): Queenie jumped on it like this and then fell off.

Therapist: Uh huh.

Patient: And Bozo laughed. Ha, ha, ha (laughs loudly).

Therapist (joins in): Ha, ha, ha. He laughed. What was so funny?

Patient: Queenie fell down on the mirror.

Therapist: Queenie fell down on the mirror.

Patient: Queenie fell down off the mirror.

Therapist: Okay. What was so funny about that?

Patient: He fell and hurt himself.

Therapist: What was so funny about that?

Patient: He was going to hurt himself.

Therapist: Well, why was that funny that Queenie hurt himself. I don't see why that was so funny. Huh? Why was that so funny?

Patient (laughing): Because he fell off the mirror.

Therapist: What's so funny about that?

Patient (still laughing)

Therapist: What's so funny? What's so funny about Queenie falling off the mirror?

Patient (still laughing): Very funny.

Therapist: What's so funny? Huh?

Patient: He's going to fall and hurt himself.

Therapist: Uh huh. Well, what's so funny about that? Hmm? What's so funny about that?

Patient: He jumped down and he fell off.

> *Therapist:* What's so funny about his falling off the mirror?
> *Patient:* He's going to hurt himself.
> *Therapist:* Okay. Now should I tell a story?
> *Patient:* Yes.
> *Therapist:* About Queenie and the mirror and Bozo?
> *Patient:* Yes.
> *Therapist:* I'll take Bozo. I'll take the mirror. Okay. Give me Queenie.
> *Patient:* Here.
> *Therapist:* Okay.

As soon as the patient put the Queenie doll in front of the mirror she purposely dropped the doll to the table in a most deliberate fashion. There was no question that this was not an accident. I considered the Queenie elephant toy to represent the patient, and its falling from the mirror her feeling that were she to look at herself what she would see would be ugly. The hurt that Queenie experienced on falling to the table was not so much related to the trauma of her fall as much as it was a reaction to her self-confrontation. This displacement of the pain served to lessen Sally's feelings of low self-worth that were being revealed in her play. It is as if she were saying: "I am not hurt by what I see in the mirror but rather by the physical pain I experienced when I fell." In addition, I considered her compulsive laughing about the incident to be a reaction formation to the deep sense of pain that she felt. Lastly, I felt that the self-confrontation was related to the earlier experience in the session when Bozo learned that exposing his neck defect did not result in the alienation he had anticipated. With this understanding of the patient's play, I related my story.

> *Patient:* (giggles)
> *Therapist:* Where are you going? (Patient gets lollipop.) Okay? When you come back here I'll start telling my story. Okay. You got your lollipop? (Patient throws lollipop wrapper on the floor.) Where are you supposed to put that?
> *Patient:* In the garbage!

Therapist: Right. That's where that goes. That paper from the lollipop goes in the garbage. Okay, come on over here now. Okay. Good.

Once upon a time Bozo was walking along (Patient hands the therapist the elephant.) — I'll get Queenie in — don't worry — and he said, "Oh, here's a mirror, a nice mirror." And he picked up the mirror and he said to Queenie, "Hey, Queenie, let's look at ourselves in the mirror, and see what we see." Do you want to hear the rest of this story?

Patient: Yes.

Therapist: Anyway, Queenie looked in the mirror and said — Oh, I'm sorry. — Bozo looked in the mirror and said, "Oh, I have such a nice face. It's very nice. Look at that." And then Bozo said, "I like what I see."

And Queenie said, "But you know, Bozo, you have a little dot on your neck. Do you like that too?"

And Bozo said, "Well, I have that little dot. I have that little dot but I'm still very pretty. Even though I have that little dot I'm still very pretty. One little dot doesn't make you completely ugly all over."

Well, Queenie was very scared to look in the mirror because Queenie had some little things that she didn't like about herself and she was afraid that if she looked in the mirror she would see them and then she would hurt herself. And she'd feel very bad and she'd feel terrible. What were the things — the little part of Queenie — that weren't very good that she was scared to look at?

Patient: The trunk and the ears.

Therapist: What was wrong with her trunk?

Patient: It was going up.

Therapist: And was that the good way to go?

Patient: No.

Therapist: How should it go?

Patient: Down.

Therapist: Okay. Now what about the ears?

Patient: The ears are going out.

Therapist: And how should they go?

Patient: They should go in.

Therapist: Okay. Anyway, so she was kind of scared to look in that mirror, Queenie, because she thought that she would look very ugly because her nose didn't go the same way as some of the other elephants and her ears were a little bit different. So she said to Bozo, "Oh, I don't want to look in that mirror."

And Bozo said, "Why not?"

She said, "Oh, I think I'll feel very bad."

And Bozo said, "Why would you feel bad?"

She said, "Because my nose and ears don't go exactly the way everybody else's go."

And Bozo said, "Yeah, they are a little bit different but that's not so terrible. You'll see. You'll look in the mirror and see that you're very pretty, even though your nose doesn't go exactly the same way and your ears don't go exactly the same way. But every part of you is just like everybody else — every other part of you." So what do you think Queenie did?

Patient: She looked in the mirror.

Therapist: And what did she say when she looked in here? Come on over here and look in the mirror. (I ask the patient to look at Queenie's image in the mirror).

Patient: Ugly!

Therapist: What is she saying? What is she saying as she looks in the mirror?

Patient: What a . . . (mumbles) . . .

Therapist: What?

Patient: What a nice face.

Therapist: Right! She says, "What a nice face. Even though my nose is a little bit different and even though my ears are a little different, the rest of me is just like everybody else. That sure is pretty." And then Queenie felt good and she realized that just because one small part of you isn't working right or not very good or a little different doesn't mean you're all no good. The end.

Anything you want to say about that story? Huh? You want to say anything about that?

Patient: And Queenie — and you know what?

Therapist: What?
Patient: In my story Queenie fell and hurt himself.
Therapist: And in my story?
Patient: No.
Therapist: Uh huh. Right.

In my story I tried to once again impart to the patient my opinion that her defect was not particulary unsightly and that looking at it should not cause self-disgust. In addition, I imparted the message — so important to children with minimal brain dysfunction — that one defect does not make one totally unworthy.

Fear of Body Disfigurement and Deterioration. We then continued playing.

Therapist: Okay. What else should we do now? We have a little more time to tell stories.
Patient: Tell a story about this whale and this skeleton.
Therapist: The whale and the skeleton. You tell a story first and then I'll tell one.
Patient: Um, and Bozo.
Therapist: Okay. You tell one about Bozo, the whale, and the skeleton and then I'll tell one.
Patient: And Queenie.
Therapist. Okay. You tell one first. Make it a short story and then I'll tell one.
Patient: Once upon a time Queenie wished for a skeleton and Bozo said, "You have a skeleton inside you, an animal skeleton."
Therapist: Hh hmm.
Patient: This skeleton will just look like a person skeleton.
Therapist: Hh hmm.
Patient: The whale came and it made the house all wet!
Therapist: The whale came and made the house all wet. How did he do that?
Patient: He swam in the house.
Therapist: Hh hmm. And where did the water come from?

Patient: The pool.

Therapist: I see. Is that the whole story?

Patient: Yes.

Therapist: Uh huh. So the whale came in and made the house all wet. Now what happened with the skeleton here? Bozo told Queenie that she had a skeleton inside of her and this is a skeleton from a person. Right? So what happened with Queenie when Bozo said that? Hhmm? What did Queenie say?

Patient: That just looks like — this is from a person's skeleton.

Therapist: Hh hmm. Did Queenie feel good or bad knowing that he had a skeleton inside of him?

Patient: Good.

Therapist: He felt good. Okay. And what happened to this person that this person became the skeleton?

Patient: The skin fell off.

Therapist: How did the skin fall off?

Patient: It just jumped off.

Therapist: The skin jumped off. How did the person feel about that?

Patient: Bad.

Therapist: Because?

Patient: The skin jumped off.

Therapist: Hh hmm. Can skin jump off people?

Patient: No.

Therapist: Right. Okay I'll tell a short story.

Patient: And here and a lady came. A lady came and she made the house all wet.

Therapist: And she made the house all wet too.

Patient: Yes.

Therapist: I see.

Patient: And Bozo took a mop and mopped it all up.

Therapist: Uh huh. I see.

Patient: And Bozo and Queenie said, "You made the house all wet in the cellar."

Therapist: Uh huh.

Patient's Mother: As far as the skeleton is concerned, she has asked me, "Can my bones bleed?" or "My bones are bleeding." She's very fearful of her body.

Therapist: Hh hmm. Yeah.

Patient: Where do you live?

Therapist: Where do I live? I live in the next town. I live not far from here. Not too far. Okay, should I tell a story? Hhmm?

Patient: Yes.

The patient's productions included many themes, none of which was elaborated upon to the degree that I could be certain what its psychological meaning might be. The theme that appeared to be most worthy of inquiry was the one about the skeleton, suggesting concerns with death and body deterioration. The patient's mother offered some valuable information that convinced me that the skeleton issue was the one to pursue. This is a good example of how the mother's participation can be of assistance to the therapist. Sally's mother's comments confirmed my suppositions that the skeleton theme related to the patient's concern with body disfigurement and deterioration. Accordingly, I told this story.

Therapist: Okay. Once upon a time Queenie was scared that she would turn into a skeleton. You want to come over here. She was scared that after she saw a skeleton she was scared that she would turn into a skeleton, that all her skin would come off, and she would die and become a skeleton. And she said to Bozo, "Am I going to become a skeleton?"

And Bozo said, "No. You're not going to become a skeleton for a long long long time until you're very much older than even Grandma. It's only old people that become skeletons. You're very young, Queenie. You're just a little girl elephant and you're not going to become a skeleton for a long long long time. You've got a whole life to live for many many years." And then Queenie felt better. And that's the end of the story.

Patient: Toys can't die.

Therapist: Right.

Patient: Toys can't turn into a skeleton.

Therapist: Right! Do little girls die? Or just old people?

Patient: Just old people.

Therapist: Right. Once in a while a little girl dies but that doesn't happen often. Mainly it's very old people. Okay. You want to watch some of this now?

Patient: Yes.

Therapist: Let's watch. Okay.

In my story I tried to provide the patient with reassurance that the likelihood of her dying was extremely low. She listened intently and I believe that my message had meaning to her and served to reassure her.

One week later the patient was admitted to the hospital and her thyroglossal cyst was excised. I visited her in the hospital on the day following the operation and there was every indication that she was tolerating the procedure quite well. Although she exhibited a normal degree of irritability and dissatisfaction with the restraints that were placed on her arms so that she could not touch the dressing on her neck, I in no way considered her responses to be pathological. She was discharged from the hospital two days after the operation.

During the two-month period following her discharge I saw Sally eleven times. During this period the frequency of her sessions was reduced from a twice-weekly to a once-weekly basis. By this time she had given up entirely her obsession with her shoelaces not being tied tightly enough. In addition, there was a marked decrease in her hostile outbursts. However, she still exhibited some (as does any child), and at times they were exaggerated (as is often the case with children with minimal brain dysfunction); however, they occurred on the average of only once a day and I did not consider this frequency to warrant treatment for that symptom. Her relationship with peers improved as did her social sensitivity. By the time she was discharged there was a complete absence of somatic complaints.

Her stories during this terminal period were often ones that I would consider normal. They related to holidays, school activities, and stereotyped play. Some stories, however, revealed feelings about her coordination deficits. The children in them would fall down stairs, trip, drop

balls, etc. In my responding stories I stressed the importance of practice in contributing toward the alleviation of
such deficits. In addition, I communicated that these
children improved as time went on.

I considered Sally's improvement to be primarily the
result of the psychotherapeutic approaches which I have
described. In addition, her medication without doubt
contributed. At the time of discharge she was being
maintained on Thorazine Spansules, 75 mg per day, and
arrangements were made for her pediatrician to continue
prescribing her medication.

Asserting Oneself More Effectively with Peers.
Norman, a five-and-a-half-year-old boy, presented with a
history of lag in his developmental milestones and
coordination deficits. He had a tendency to withdraw and to
"tune out," especially when an activity might expose his
deficits. At such times he seemed to be in another world. A
problem that was particularly apparent at the time the
interchange below took place was inhibition of self-
assertion. He could not fight back when teased by other
children and accordingly was being scapegoated.

The patient often spontaneously told stories about the
various figurines on the Board of Objects without formally
playing the game. The cowboy, which he chose to talk about
in the interchange below, had a removable holster belt
attached to which were two holsters with guns inside. In
order to remove the belt, however, one had to pull the top
half of the figurine away from the bottom half, to which it
was attached by a small plug. If the holster belt were so
removed and then the two halves of the body replaced, a
waistline defect was still present where the holster belt had
been. This is the interchange that occurred regarding the
cowboy.

> *Therapist:* Hello, today is Monday, August 28th, 1972,
> and I'm here with Norman and he and I are going to
> play a game with these objects. Norman, can you pick
> one? The Storytelling Game. Okay. What is that?
> *Patient:* A cowboy.

Therapist: Okay, that's a cowboy. What are you going to tell me about the cowboy?

Patient: Cowboys have guns.

Therapist: They have guns. Yeah.

Patient: And they shoot.

Therapist: Yeah. Go ahead.

Patient: Make believe he took his pants off.

Therapist: Okay.

Patient: He took his pants off.

Therapist: Yeah.

Patient: If he take his holsters with it only would that be as far as it would be?

Therapist: If you take his holster off what? I'm not clear what you're saying.

Patient: I think I'll try taking . . .

Therapist: Go ahead. Now what? You took off his holsters. Right?

Patient: Right.

Therapist: Now what did you ask me about that, about taking off his holster? I didn't understand your question. What was your question?

Patient: Is this as far as it goes when you keep the gun on but you take the holsters off?

Therapist: Yep. Right. You mean does the body go together with the feet after you take the holsters away?

Patient: Yeah.

Therapist: No, it doesn't. There's still a space there. What do you think about that?

Patient: Why is there still a space?

Therapist: Because that cowboy was made so he should have guns and when he doesn't have his guns his body and his feet don't go together. That's the way they made him. Do you know why they made him that way?

Patient: Why?

Therapist: What do you think? Why do you think they made him so that the gun should be there? Hh hmm?

Patient: Mmm.

Therapist: Why do you think they made him that way?

Patient: I don't know.

Therapist: Hh hmm?

Patient: I don't know!

Therapist: Does a cowboy need guns?

Patient: Yeah.

Therapist: What does he need them for?

Patient: Shooting.

Therapist: Now do you know why they made him with guns? Why do you think?

Patient: I don't know.

Therapist: What are the guns for?

Patient: Shooting.

Therapist: And why does he do that?

Patient: In case someone starts to bother him.

Therapist: Right, in case someone starts to bother him. Right. So what can he do in case . . .

Patient (interrupting): Some Indians have bow and arrows.

Therapist: Right. Hh hmm. That's right.

Patient: Did you ever see a bow and arrow?

Therapist: Of an Indian? Sure. What would happen to that cowboy if he didn't have his guns?

Patient: I don't know.

Therapist: What would happen now? You say the guns are good because if someone starts to bother him then he could use them. Right?

Patient: Right.

Therapist: Now what would happen to him if he didn't have his guns?

Patient: If he had a bow and arrow (pauses) . . .

Therapist: Yeah and then what?

Patient: If someone comes along . . . (pauses) . . .

Therapist: Yeah.

Patient: . . . and bothers an Eskimo.

Therapist: If someone comes along and bothers an Eskimo? Is that what you said?

Patient: He said, "If you don't go away, I'll kill you with this spear!"

Therapist: All right. Who says that? Who said that?

Patient: The Eskimo.

Therapist: Is the Eskimo the same as the Indian or is he somebody different?

Patient: He's somebody different.

Therapist: Okay. So what good is the spear then? How does the spear help the Eskimo?

Patient: He hunts with the spear.

Therapist: Right. What else does it do for him? How else does it help him?

Patient: I don't know.

Therapist: What did you say before about what the Eskimo does with his spear?

Patient: Hunts.

Therapist: Anything else?

Patient: Yes.

Therapist: What?

Patient: "If you don't go away I'll kill you with this spear."

Therapist: Right. And what is the person trying to do who the Eskimo says that to — the person to whom the Eskimo says, "If you don't go away I'll kill you with this spear"? What is that person trying to do to the Eskimo? Huh?

Patient: Trying to shoot him.

Therapist: All right. Now what about the cowboy and his gun? What is the good of the guns? What would happen to the cowboy if he didn't have his guns?

Patient (accidentally drops the holster belt on the rug and can't find it): The guns disappear into the rug.

Therapist: Oh my, we can't find it.

Patient: I got a G.I. Joe at home.

Therapist: I want to ask you a question that you're not answering.

Patient: But he's a bigger G.I. Joe. These are smaller G.I. Joes.

Therapist: All right. I want to ask you one question now. What happens to the cowboy if he doesn't have his guns?

Patient: If he doesn't have — if he left his guns at his ranch . .

Therapist (interrupting): What would happen to him?

Patient: He would have to go back to his ranch.

Therapist: Why would he have to go back?

Patient: To get his guns.

Therapist: What does he need them for?

Patient: He says, "If you don't go away I'll shoot you."

Therapist: Right, if people bother him. Right? Is that right? Huh? Oh, here's the gun. Is that right that if people bother him he'll have the gun?

Patient: Hh hmm.

Therapist: Now why did they make this cowboy with guns then? Why did they make him with guns?

Patient: And then another boy comes along.

Therapist: Yeah and then.

Patient: "Then if you don't go away I'll jump on you." (hums to self). (puts down the cowboy and picks up an airplane)

Therapist: What happened there?

Patient: New airplane and then he flew . . . (makes airplane sounds) . . .

Therapist: Then what happened?

Patient: And then the propeller breaks off.

Therapist: Then what happens?

Patient: And then the propeller broke my — and then his father . . .

Therapist: His father what?

Patient: Glues it back on.

Therapist: Hh hmm. And then what happens?

Patient: So it can never grow, so it cannot, so it can never, so it can't . . .

Therapist: Can't what?

Patient: So it can never — so the propeller can never come off again.

Therapist: Uh huh. Did he watch it himself to make sure that it didn't come off?

Patient: Yeah.

In this interchange I did not directly tell a story; rather, I tried to introduce my therapeutic communications in the context of the discussion about the cowboy and, subsequently, the Indians and Eskimo. I tried to communicate the importance of weapons in defending oneself. Hopefully, Norman would utilize this information in more effectively asserting himself. And this is what ultimately happened. Sequences such as these were contributory toward the patient's ultimately asserting himself more effectively with peers.

The interchange demonstrates well how many children of this age (including those without brain dysfunction, as well) will introduce new figures into the conversation without informing the listener of their appearance in his mind. This is what happened here with the sudden introduction of the Eskimo about whom I had heard nothing previously. However, the Eskimo and his spear certainly served as well as the Indian with his bow and arrow and the cowboy with his guns to not only manifest the patient's inhibition in expressing hostility but served as well as excellent objects for my own communications.

At the end of the interchange the patient suddenly put down the cowboy and picked up a toy airplane. While flying it in the air he spoke about how the propeller had broken off and then how his father fixed it so it would never come off again. The sequence suggests castration anxiety. One could speculate that the father as the repairer might be a reaction formation to his underlying fantasy that his father was the castrator. One might further speculate that his fear of self-assertion might relate to castration fears. An alternative explanation would be that the father represents the therapist whose story has just served to help him feel more intact; considering the feelings of impotency he felt prior to the interchange. Although I prefer to believe the latter explanation to be more applicable, I cannot deny the possible validity of the former. Accordingly, I chose not to respond specifically to the airplane story because of my uncertainty regarding its meaning. Furthermore, I had already provided the patient with a meaningful therapeutic communication and have found that "overloading" can dilute and undermine previously effective messages.

Chapter Nine
The Bag of Toys Game

The games described in this and the next two chapters are attractive in that they appeal to the child's traditional enjoyment of the grab bag game in which the child closes his eyes and pulls out an unknown object from a bag. In each, *one* reward chip is given for a simple response and/or *two* if the player can tell a story about what has been taken from the bag. The therapist enhances the child's curiosity and enthusiasm by occasionally warning him not to peek and by exhibiting excitement himself when it is his own turn. The reward chips are contained in a treasure chest, which serves to further enhance their value. Again, the winner is the player who has accumulated the most chips at the end of the allotted time and he selects a prize from the same box of prizes (Figure 2) described for previous games.

The Bag of Toys Game (Figure 4) requires a bag clearly labeled BAG OF TOYS containing about forty to fifty figurines of the kind used in The Board of Objects Game (Figure 3). When putting his hand into the bag, the child is warned against peeking ("Keep your eyes closed. Remember, it's against the rules of the game to peek."), and spending time feeling the objects is also discouraged ("No fair feeling. Just pick out one of the objects."). After the object has been selected and used as a focus for comment and/or story, it is laid aside rather than returned to the bag. Again, the child will often add dramatic elements to his story and it behooves the therapist to do so as well.

Clinical Examples

Negative Reinforcement of Antisocial Behavior. Ian, age six and three-quarters, suffered with a significant impulsivity problem. He would lash out at classmates and on a few occasions, try to choke them. On other occasions he would spit at adults. These episodes had occurred on the average of once a month prior to the interchange to be presented.

We were playing The Bag of Toys Game and the patient's sister was also present. As mentioned, I usually bring into the office other family members who may have accompanied the patient, and will have them join in the therapeutic activities, as indicated. With regard to a sibling, if he or she has proved to be an asset then his or her participation is invited; otherwise the sibling must remain quiet or leave the room. Ian's sister had proved herself helpful on a number of occasions and so joined us in our game.

Therapist: And now boys and girls, ladies and gentlemen, we're going to play The Bag of Toys Game, and our guest and his sister (picks up bag) are going to play. Now, just in case you don't remember, it's very important when you play this game not to look. Okay? You've got to keep your eyes closed.

Sister (interrupting): Is this the game we played last time?

Therapist: Yeah, we played this last time. (directs attention to patient) We've played this before, haven't we?

Patient: Yeah. But I thought it was another one.

Therapist: Okay. Now you stick you hand in. No looking — no peeking.

Patient: (removes a plastic baby figurine)

Therapist: Now if you can tell something about that you get one chip. But if you can tell us a story about it then you get two more. Okay?

Patient (as he fingers and twists around baby figurine): I know ... once upon a time there was a little baby who loved to lie in the crib. And one day (places baby figurine on table) his big brother didn't like what he was doing in his crib. It was one of the little baby's toys. So he socked him and he was crying.

Therapist (interrupting): Wait. Excuse me a second. This baby was in his crib and he had a toy of his brother's. It that it?

Patient: No, his.

Therapist: He had one of his *own* toys.
Patient: Yeah.
Therapist: And what did he do with it
Patient: He played with it.
Therapist: Yeah. And then what?
*Patient:*He, um, his brother didn't like what he was doing so his brother socked the little baby.
Therapist: Yeah.
Patient (places baby on table): So the baby started to cry and his mother came up and the baby, and his mother found out.
Therapist: Yeah.
Patient: So he tried to stand up (tries to stand baby figure up on table), but fell down. Tried again but fell down. Tried again and fell down. Tried again and fell down (picks up doll). Why doesn't it stand up? (inspects baby's feet)
Sister: Cold feet. Perhaps he has cold feet. Why don't you just hold him?
Therapist: Yeah. So go ahead. Let's hear the rest of the story.
Patient (tries to get doll figure to stand up): Um.
Therapist: Go ahead.
Patient: His mother found out so the baby pushed the crib into. It was a TV, um, that he was watching.
Therapist: Ian, I don't understand what's happening in that story.
Patient (continuing): And his brother — and his brother was being naughty when he was watching TV. And the baby said, "Waaaa" (makes some sounds).
Therapist: Ian, I can't follow that story at all.
Patient: And the brother was being bad and so the mother found out. "What happened?" asked the mother. Um, am I going to get two chips?
Therapist: You haven't finished the story yet and I have to understand it or else you don't get the chips.
Sister: I don't understand it either.
Therapist: Do you understand it Carol?
Sister: No.

Therapist: No. Carol and I don't understand the story.

Patient: Why do you have to understand?

Sister: I thought he was mumbling a lot.

Therapist: Oh, well, that's the rules of the game. If you wanted to tell a story that no one understood that's okay, but in this game we don't play that way. You don't get chips for that. Just telling a story that can't be understood doesn't get credit in this game.

Patient: All right. I'll make a new story up.

Therapist: Okay. Go ahead.

Patient: Once upon a time there was a little baby and she [sic] was lying in his crib. His mother and father tickled him a lot one day. I don't like that. The end.

Therapist (shaking head): I haven't heard a story yet.

Patient: That's the end of the story. You see this little baby was lying in his crib and, um, his mother and father tickled him a lot.

Therapist: Tickled him a lot. Yes. Okay. That's a good beginning of a story. That's not a whole story.

Patient: One day when he got older, when he learned how to stand up, his brother pushed him down, and the baby way crying. And the baby said, "Um, brother pushed me down." And the mother said "Brother, apologize." "I apologize, little brother." The end.

Therapist: And after he apologized, what happened?

Patient: His mother wasn't mad at him.

Therapist: I see okay.

Sister: Can I go [tell a story]?

Therapist: No. I'll tell you what. The way we play it is he gets (addressing patient as he places two chips in front of him) — you get two chips for that story. Then I go second and then you (pointing to sister) can go, and then I go after you. I go after each kid. That's how the game is played. (reaches into Bag of Toys) I wonder what I am going to get.

Sister: I hope he gets a spider.

Therapist (pulls out a small tiger figurine): Ooh, what's that?

Sister: Oh, it's a tiger. It's so cute.

Therapist (showing tiger figure to patient and sister): It's a cute little tiger. What a cute little baby tiger. It's a cute baby tiger. Once upon a time there was a tiger and he had a baby brother. And one day his baby brother was in a crib — in a tiger's crib — and he went over to that baby brother and hit that baby brother. He went (pretends he's hitting patient, who is listening attentively as is his sister, while imitating an angry tiger's sound) "Grrr . . . Grrr." Just like that. (Patient and sister smile.) And that baby brother started to cry (therapist imitates crying baby), "Oh, oooohhhh." (Therapist crosses arms in front of chest and winces in pain.)

Patient: (laughs gleefully and puts hands on head)

Therapist: The tiger was crying terribly. You see, this tiger, when he would hit his baby brother, he didn't think about whether it would hurt him or not, although people — other tigers would hit him or bite him or hurt him — he didn't think about the fact that when he hit that little baby brother tiger he would hurt that baby brother tiger very bad. (directs attention to patient) Let's make believe you're the baby brother tiger. Okay? And I'm the big tiger. Make believe. I won't really hit you. I'll just make believe I'm hitting you. Okay? Now I'll go (therapist pretends to hit patient) "Rahhhh!"

Patient: (pretends to be crying).

Therapist: What do you do?

Patient: I start to cry.

Therapist: Does it hurt?

Patient (rubbing left arm which therapist had pretended to hit): Yeah.

Therapist: Does it hurt a lot?

Patient: And I start to hit you back. (raises hand as if about to hit therapist back)

Therapist (holds hand up): In my story it doesn't go that way.

Patient: (begins to pretend crying again, shaking head and body up and down)

Therapist: Well, okay, but maybe you'd want to hit me back. Let's say you hit me back.

Patient: (pretends to hit therapist with fist)

Therapist (clutches chest and winces in pain): Ohh, that hurts! Ooooh, oooh.

Patient: (laughs)

Sister (who had seemed momentarily distracted immediately responds to patient): Did you hit him? Did you really hit him?

Therapist: No, we're just making believe. Now what happened then was the baby started to cry — the baby brother. He went, "Whaaaaaaaa. He hit me."

Patient: (puts hands to head and smiles gleefully)

Therapist (still crying): "Oh, he hit me. My brother hit me." And the mother came running in and she saw what had happened. And she said, "Did you hit your baby brother?" Well, he had to admit that the did. He said, "Yeah, I did it, but I'm sorry. I'm very sorry."

And she said, "Go to your room immediately. And you're not coming out for a whole hour and you can't watch any television in there." You see, in my story tigers can watch television.

Sister: Yeah, must be real old . . . (mumbles) . . .

Therapist: Pardon me?

Sister: He must be real live tigers.

Therapist: Yeah, well in my story they do these things. Anyway, the tiger said, "But I said I'm sorry."

And the mother said, "I know you said you said you were sorry, but you hurt your brother and you still must be punished for it."

And he said, "But I thought if you say you're sorry you're not supposed to get punished."

Sister: Yeah, that's in your story (referring to story "Say You're Sorry," written by the therapist).

Therapist (looking at sister): Yeah, you read that story. Right?

Sister: (nods affirvatively.)

Therapist (pointing to patient): Did you read that story?

Patient (answer is almost inaudible): Yeah.

Sister: Yeah, "Say You're Sorry."

Therapist (looking at patient): Did you read that story?

Patient (nods head affirmatively)

Therapist: What was that story about?

Patient: Eric, um . . .

Therapist (interrupting): Eric, that's right. That was the boy's name in the story. Yeah. And what happened there?

Patient: He hit — he tripped the girl in his class.

Therapist: Yeah? Go ahead.

Patient: And he had to go to the principal's office.

Sister: I think that's another one. I thought . . .

Therapist: No, no. (to patient) Go ahead. What about saying you're sorry? Was that in the story?

Patient: Um, yeah. I don't remember.

Patient's Mother (who is sitting out of view of the camera): That's not true. He just told me yesterday, on line at the supermarket, he said, "I'm sorry" to a little girl — "not like the little boy in the story. I'm really sorry."

Therapist: Oh, yeah. But he's a little bit confused about that now. Now let's go back to my story . The mother said, "You still get punished even though you said you're sorry." So what do you think happened then?

Patient: I don't know.

Therapist: He had to go to his room. And she said, "You still get punished. Saying you're sorry doesn't mean you're not going to get punished." What do you think happened then?

Patient (smiling): He went to his room.

Therapist: Yeah, and he was very sad. And he said, "Well, can't you ever say you're sorry? Will I always get punished?"

And the mother said, "Well, if something really

happened and it was an accident and you really didn't do it on purpose and then you say you're sorry then you won't get punished. But I know you purposely hit your brother and you could stop yourself from hitting your brother and that kind of thing you get punished." All right. So he went up to his room and he was very sad. And he started to think about the two different kinds of sorry. Do you know the two different kinds of saying you're sorry?

Patient: Yeah.

Therapist: What are the two different kinds?

Patient: Purposely doing something and accidentally doing something.

Therapist: Right! And when you purposely do something should you get punished?

Patient: Yeah.

Therapist: And what about when you accidentally do it?

Patient: No.

*Therapist:*All right. Now in my story when the tiger hit his baby brother did he purposely do it?

Patient (has fingers in his mouth): Yeah.

Sister (raises hand): Yes.

Therapist: So should he have been punished?

Patient and Sister: Yes!

Therapist: Right? And could he have stopped it if he wanted to ?

Sister: Yes.

Patient (reaching over to grab tiger): Let me . . .

Therapist (pointing to sister while looking at patient): She's answering. I'm talking to you. Could he have stopped it?

Patient: Yeah.

Therapist: Right! Now you (looking at patient) wanted to say something.

Patient: You could tell a better story. He went into his baby brother's room and he kissed his baby brother.

Therapist: Well, that would be another kind of story, but often kids are angry at their baby brothers and they don't feel like kissing them very much, and they may even want to hit them a lot. But most kids know that you shouldn't and that if you do you'll get punished. And most kids, when they get the feeling that they want to hit their baby brothers, they usually stop and they say, "I'd better not do that. It will hurt him." They know that if you hit somebody you will hurt him. And also they'll get punished. They know that too.

Patient: Hmm.

Therapist: What are the two things that kids think of that make them stop trying to hit their baby brothers? What are the two things they think of?

Patient: I don't know.

Therapist: Remember. I just told you.

Patient: Um, I don't remember.

Therapist: It goes through their minds when they're ready to hit their baby brothers and they want to hit them. They think of two things. What do they think of?

Patient: Um, they stop themselves.

Therapist: They stop themselves. That's one. And the other thing is?

Patient: Uh, they get punished.

Therapist: They'll get punished. And the other thing is that they know that it will hurt the baby brother very much when you hit someone. And that's the end of my story. Look, we have to stop today, but we have a little time to watch some of this. Do you want to watch some of this?

Patient: Yeah.

Therapist: Okay, let's watch. Okay, let's say good-bye. So long everyone. Want to say good-bye?

Sister (smiling and waving): Good-bye.

Patient: (looking sad and remains silent)

The sequence does not demonstrate well the value of Ian's sister. At one point, early in the interchange when I asked Ian why the baby figurine kept falling down, she offered the answer, "Cold feet." This was clearly a contaminant. However, at other times she did contribute. For example, when the patient mumbled and I told him that I could not understand what he was saying, she also agreed that she found his comments incomprehensible. Such negative reinforcement of antisocial behavior — when used judiciously and in a benevolent manner — need not be psychologically devastating nor lower significantly the child's self-esteem.

The vignette well demonstrates the importance of structuring the therapeutic interchanges. Especially when a child with minimal brain dysfunction is telling a self-created story, he tends to ramble and if the therapist does not help him confine himself to a particular theme he will get such a barrage of material that it may be difficult for him to decide which are the important themes to serve as foci for his own responding stories or comments. The interchange also demonstrates the use of dramatization, so helpful in the treatment of these children. The written transcription cannot convey fully the various sounds and gestures utilized by the children and the tiger. These attracted the patient's attention and fostered his involvement.

In Ian's story the boy says that he is sorry and is then exonerated. He is not punished for having hit his baby brother because he has said that he was sorry. The patient and his sister had both read my story, "Say You're Sorry" (1972a), but apparently Ian was still unclear about its significance. He would prefer to go along believing that one is not punished for one's transgressions if he merely says that he is sorry. In this way there would be no repercussions for his unacceptable behavior. In my story I tried to "refresh" Ian's memory regarding the proper utilization of the term "I'm sorry." The tiger in my story is still punished by his parents for having hit his baby brother. And the incident served as a point of departure for clarifying the appropriate and inappropriate uses of the term. It is of interest that, although Ian did not recall the proper utilization of the word "sorry" during the early part of the session, his mother offered the information that on the previous day he was well aware of its significance. This is not surprising. Painful new insights are not readily accepted and the patient would usually waver in his conviction regarding them. My purpose here was to engender a little more superego in the hope that it would serve to lessen the patient's impulsivity.

Magic Cure Fantasy. Bernard entered treatment at the age of seven-and-a-half because of significant classroom difficulties. He was disruptive in the classroom fought frequently with his classmates, was not attentive to his studies, and concentrated poorly. Although very bright, he was not doing well academically. At home he was frequently argumentative and often entered into power struggles with his parents. They, on the other hand, were using him as a focus for their own marital conflict.

During his third session the following interchange occured while Bernard and I were playing The Bag of Toys Game.

> *Therapist:* Okay, ladies and gentleman. This is Bernard and the date is April 19, 1974. Okay, you go first. No looking. Close your eyes. You can only open your eyes after you take the thing out of the bag.
>
> *Patient:* (reaches into bag and pulls out a dog figurine)
>
> *Therapist:* What's that?
>
> *Patient:* A dog.
>
> *Therapist:* A dog. Okay. Now if you can say anything at all about that dog you get one chip. But if you want to tell a story about that dog, a completely made-up story, you get two chips.
>
> *Patient:* Once upon a time there was this dog. So this dog went away with his master. He was looking for hunting and they were hunting for ducks.
>
> *Therapist:* Go ahead.
>
> *Patient:* And when they came back he went to sleep.
>
> *Therapist:* Hh hmm.
>
> *Patient:* And after he woke up he got a bone and then he went back to sleep again.
>
> *Therapist:* Excuse me. I'm a little confused. He went hunting with his master for ducks and then he went to

sleep and when he got up there was a bone there for him?

Patient: Yeah.

Therapist: What about the — is that the whole story?

Patient: No.

Therapist: Okay. Go ahead.

Patient: And then he went back to sleep.

Therapist: Hh hmm.

Patient: Then he woke up and he went around with a boy.

Therapist: Hh hmm.

Patient: And he was walking him with the leash.

Therapist: The boy was walking this dog. Yeah. Go ahead.

Patient: And the boy hurt the dog.

Therapist: Go ahead.

Patient: He had to go to the , the — he had to go where? Where's the place that dogs have to go to when they're sick?

Therapist: Oh, a veterinarian?

Patient: Yeah.

Therapist: Well, how did the boy hurt the dog? What happened?

Patient: He was pulling on the leash too hard and his neck started to hurt.

Therapist: Go ahead. And they went to the vet.

Patient: And he fixed his neck up. And it took two days.

Therapist: Uh huh.

Patient: And then he went back and he had a bone, another bone.

Therapist: Uh huh.

Patient: And that's the end.

Therpist: Okay. Good.

Patient: I get two chips.

Therapist: Two chips. Right. Now it's my chance.

Patient: I'm winning.

Therapist: What? You're winning. All right. But I go now. (reaches into Bag of Toys). Whoops. What do I have here? (Picks out a boy figurine). I've got a . . .

Patient (interrupts): It's a boy. Are you going to tell a story?

Therapist: Yeah. Right. I don't have to, but I want to. The same rules hold for me. It's a game. If I can say anything about the boy I get one chip, but if I can tell a story about the boy I get two.

Patient: If it's a tie then you mean we . . .

Therapist (interrupts): Then we both get prizes. Right, if it's a tie. Okay.

The story presents two themes, both of which were relevant to Bernard's difficulties. The dog's main activity appears to be sleeping. Although there is some mention of his going with his master and hunting for ducks, the emphasis is on his sleeping and on his acquiring a bone. The issue of his working for his reward is deemphasized. This quality reflected well Bernard's attitude toward his schoolwork and complying with his parents' requests that he perform chores around the home. He much preferred to shirk responsibilities.

In addition the story exhibits the magic cure fantasy so frequently seen in children during the early phases of treatment. It is especially common among children, like Bernard, who do not wish to apply themselves. The dog is injured, goes to a vet, and is cured in two days. Little is said about any efforts on the dog's part to cooperate or inconvenience himself during the course of his treatment. The way in which the dog got sick is also of psychodynamic interest. We are told that the boy was pulling on the dog's leash too hard and this hurt the dog's neck. I believe that this image symbolized Bernard's relationship with his mother, who was somewhat rigid in her handling of him. Although she nagged, in part, in order to get him to do anything, there was no question that her standards were high and she would have been "on his back" even if he were more receptive to her requests. She would insist, for instance, that he finish every bit of food on his plate and was rigid with regard to his bedtime. It was not surprising then that Bernard exhibited this fantasy. Depicting himself as a dog might also have been a reflection of his feelings of low self-worth.

It was with this understanding of Bernard's story that I told mine.

> *Therapist:* Once upon a time there was a boy and he had a dog and this dog went out with him hunting, but instead of — they were going to go duck hunting — and when they got to the place where they were to hunt ducks, this dog suddenly decided to go to sleep. And the boy said, "Hey, come on. I brought you out here to hunt ducks, to help me hunt ducks. You're not doing anything."
>
> And the dog just ignored him completely and went to sleep. And as the dog was sleeping he was dreaming that when he woke up there would be a big nice juicy bone there as a kind of surprise. And when he woke up, he looked around and he smelled around and there was no bone, and he was kind of disappointed. And the dog said to the boy, "Do you have a bone?"
>
> And the boy said, "I would have given you a very nice juicy bone had you helped me with the hunting for ducks, but you didn't want to do that. Instead you just went to sleep. I'm not going to give you a reward." Do you know what a reward is? What's a reward?
>
> *Patient:* It's something that you do very good on and you get something.
>
> *Therapist:* Right. It's kind of a prize or present for doing something. He said, "I'm not going to give you a bone. You didn't help me hunt ducks. You just went to sleep."
>
> Well, anyway, as they were walking home the leash that the boy had the dog on got caught in a bush. It stretched and it injured the dog's neck. The boy didn't want to injure the dog. It was one of these accidents that sometimes happen. Anyway, they had to go to a vet. The vet said to the boy and the dog, "Now look I'm going to give you some medicine. You have to take this three times a day." And also he said to the dog, "You have to do certain exercises with your neck in order to

help the muscles get better and the tissues get better."

So they took the bottle of pills and when the boy gave the dog the first pill, the dog didn't want to take it. And the boy said, "Listen, if you want to get better, you'd better take these pills."

The dog said, "Nah, I don't have to take those pills.

Patient: Dogs can talk?

Therapist: Well, you know, in my story a dog can talk. It's a make-believe story. And the boy said, "What about those exercises that the doctor said you should do, you know, stretch your neck and move it in different directions so that the muscles will get strong?"

He said, "I don't have to do that."

Well, a week later the dog had not taken any of the medicine and the dog had not done any of the exercises, and they went back to the vet and the vet said, "It doesn't look very good here. It doesn't look very good at all."

And the dog said, "Ah, I don't need that medicine."

And the vet said, "Have you been doing the exercises?"

And the dog said, "Well, I'm kind of busy."

He said, "Well, it's up to you. If you take the medicine and do the exercises your neck will get better. It's not going to get better on its own. It just doesn't happen like that, by sitting there and doing nothing. The only way that neck is going to get better is if you do the exercises and take the medicine." So what do you think happened?

Patient: He took the medicine.

Therapist: Well, he didn't like it. He didn't like it because he had to think about it three times a day, but he realized that the vet was right. And what do you think he did about the exercises?

Patient: He did them.

Therapist: Yeah. He found that the more he did the exercises, the faster his neck got better. And the lesson of that story is — well, actually there are two lessons to that story. One has to do with the duck hunting. What do you think the lesson of that part of the story is?

Patient: That if your neck gets hurt . . .

Therapist (interrupts): No, the duck hunting part. The story has two lessons. What do you think the lesson is about the duck hunting?

Patient: Hmm. I don't know.

Therapist: Well, what did we learn from that about — remember the boy and the dog and the hunting?

Patient: Oh, yeah, I remember.

Therapist: Okay. Go ahead.

Patient: The boy went duck hunting with his dog and the dog didn't want to go duck hunting, and he fell asleep. He wanted a bone, but in the morning when he woke up the dog found that there was no bone.

Therapist: So what did he learn from that?

Patient: He learned that if you do something the other person will get a bone.

Therapist: Put that in other words. I'm not sure I understand you.

Patient: If you help another person with hunting then you will get something.

Therapist: Right! You don't get something for nothing. If you're just going to sleep you're not going to get any of the rewards or prizes or things that come to those who work at it. That's the first lesson. So if you're going duck hunting, and if you're a dog, and you're helping a boy hunt ducks, he's going to be very unhappy with you if you don't work and he won't give you any presents, prizes, or rewards.

The second lesson is that if you are sick, if you have some problem like your neck is injured, you just can't sit around and wait for it to get better; you have to do the things the doctor says if you really want to get better. Usually things don't get better just by doing nothing. You have to do something about them. The end. Okay. I get two chips. Huh?

Patient: (nods affirmatively)

In my responding story I communicated two messages to alter the unrealistic views of the world that Bernard held. I have found that such communications can be quite helpful in reducing such magical views of the world. I did not deal extensively with the issue of Bernard's mother's nagging him, as symbolized by the boy's pulling the dog's leash too hard. In my story the neck is injured by accident. I attempted here to convey to Bernard a feeling of his mother's psychological blindness with regard to this trait. More importantly, however, I was dealing with this directly with her and she was quite capable of reducing some of her pressures on him. Accordingly, I did not introduce anything into the story encouraging Bernard to handle this problem. In addition, it is unwise to try to introduce too many themes into one's story simultaneously. The child can just absorb so much at a time. When I have tried to introduce too many messages into my story, I have found the child to be overwhelmed and then he becomes bored and disinterested as he tunes himself out from the multiple stimuli.

Enhancing Social Sensitivity in a Child with MBD. James entered treatment at the age of ten with many manifestations of neurological impairment. His IQ was around 80 and he suffered with a significant memory deficit. Often he could not remember what had happened one minute previously. Accordingly, he had a severe learning disability. In addition, he was extremely naive socially. A significant impairment in his ability to conceptualize made all but simple communication very difficult. One of the patient's problems related to his insensitivity to the effects of his behavior on others. He was hyperactive, impulsive, and often interrupted those around him. Accordingly, he frequently made a nuisance of himself and did not refrain from such antics even though threatened with punishment. The comments below are mine that I made in association with having selected a gorilla figurine from the Bag of Toys. I am not presenting the patient's previous story because it was unrelated to my comments.

Therapist: Once upon a time there was a gorilla and this gorilla used to make a lot of noise. He used to (makes loud growling noises) gr . . . gr . . . grrrrr . . .

Patient (interrupts in a pleading manner): Please don't do that.

Therapist (makes another growling sound): Grrrr ...

Patient (interrupts): Come on.

Therapist (stops action): What's the matter?

Patient: Ah, don't do that again. The noise bothers kids.

Therapist: People would be sleeping in the middle of the night and he'd be yelling, "Ah ... ahhhh." (makes further loud sounds)

Patient: Sounds like you're gargling.

Therapist: No, that's the kind of noises gorillas make. And people used to say, "Shut up! We're trying to sleep around here!"

Patient (interrupts): They used to say, "Ah, shut up, you big ape!"

Therapist: Right. "Shut up, you big gorilla!" But he ignored them and he still continued to make all those noises. And so finally one day, in the middle of the night while he was sleeping, everybody all around got all kinds of rocks and sticks and they started to make all kinds of noise.

Patient: Why?

Therapist: They wanted to give him a lesson. They wanted to show him how he sounded. They wanted to teach him a lesson about how he was. Do you understand? So all of a sudden, in the middle of the night while he was sleeping, all — there were about twenty five gorillas — stood around where he was sleeping and they all together went, "Ahh ... ooh ... ugh ... slam ... bam (very loudly)." They made all kinds of noises. They were screaming and they were jumping around and dancing.

Patient (interrupts): Sounds like a party.

Therapist: They were really making noises. They were hitting things with sticks and everything. And suddenly the gorilla woke up and he said, "Huh? Hey! Ooh, ooh. What happened? Where am I?"

Patient: Who did that?

Therapist: The gorilla woke up.

Patient: I never heard of a talking gorilla.

Therapist: Well, in my story they talk. This is a make-believe story. And he got up and all the gorillas around were making all these noises. He was really frightened.

And he said, "Why are you doing this to me? Why are you making all that noise?"

And they said, "We want you to see what you do to us. We want you to see what happens when you make all these noises and everything, how much it bothers people."

And after that the gorilla realized how much he was bothering people by all the noise he was making and so after that he stopped making so much noise, and then people were much friendlier to him. The end.

Patient: Boy, you should get thousands!

Therapist: Why is that?

Patient: Because that was such a good story!

The story is typical of the kind I will often tell children with minimal brain dysfunction. It touches on one simple element and is presented without much symbolization or disguise. The story is a good example, as well, of my utilization of various dramatic elements to enhance the efficacy of my message. The written transcript does not communicate fully the extent of my various growling sounds, shrieking voices, and dramatic intonations. In addition, none of the gesturing has been included. The patient was quite swept up in the presentation and his final comments confirm that he was involved. Children with organic problems who are significantly impaired in appreciating social situations need to be frequently helped to see how they affect others. They seem to have a deficiency in being able to project themselves into another person's situation. And it behooves the therapist to try to help them develop this capacity.

Hostility Toward a Rejecting Father. Tom, seven years old, was referred because of significant disinterest in his schoolwork. Although he was very bright, he would spend hours in the classroom dawdling and preoccupying himself with nonacademic activities. Even when given individual attention by both his teacher and special tutors, he would not concentrate and would refuse to apply himself to his tasks.

An older brother, seventeen, had had an organic learning problem and was a significant disappointment to Tom's father. Over the years Tom had observed frequent fighting between his father and older brother and this exposure was, without doubt, contributing to Tom's difficulties. In addition, his father was a somewhat aloof man who could not involve himself meaningfully with his children.

During his second month in treatment, the following interchange occurred while we were playing The Bag of Toys Game.

> *Patient   1 (selects bed object): A bed.*
> *Therapist:* A bed. What are going to say about a bed?
> *Patient:* (mumbles)
> *Therapist:* What's that?
> *Patient:* This bed is plastic.
> *Therapist:* The bed is plastic. Okay, you get one chip for that.
> *Patient:* (mumbles)
> *Therapist:* Pardon me.
> *Patient:* I think we're going to have a tie today.
> *Therapist:* We're going to have a tie? Well, maybe.
> *Patient:* Yeah.
> *Therapist:* Hmmm. Who can tell?
> *Patient:* Once there was a bed and it was a very hard bed and it was very mean.
> *Therapist:* It was very mean?
> *Patient:* Yeah, it was a very mean bed.
> *Therapist:* How was it mean?
> *Patient:* If someone laid on it, it would dump — it would tilt itself — and it would dump everybody off and the lady liked it until one day she died. And that's the end. It's short. It's like yours, a little short one.

Therapist: Uh huh. I see. Let me understand something. This bed was mean and it dumped everybody off it who would want to lie on it. Is that it?

Patient: Yeah.

Therapist: And the lady who owned the bed died?

Patient: No, the bed died.

Therapist: The bed bied.

Patient: Make believe.

Therapist: Yeah. How did the bed die?

Patient: By doing that when everybody, when . . . when . . . when he tilted himself always he was getting weaker and weaker 'till he died.

Therapist: I see. Okay. You get two chips for that story. Now it's my chance.

I considered the bed to represent the patient's father. In his comment about the bed he stated that it was plastic. And this was reminiscent of his father's personality — especially his lack of feeling. But more important, the bed's practice of dumping everyone who tried to use it is a good representation of his father's rejecting attitudes. Those who would try to get close to his father, as symbolized by getting into the bed, would be rejected. Finally the bed dies. This, I believe, represents Tom's hostility toward his father being released in symbolic fashion. The lady, who owned the bed, represents his mother. Although not stated, the story suggests that even she was dumped from the bed and this too is a good representation of the parental relationship.

With this understanding of Tom's story, I related mine.

Therapist: Now it's my chance. All right. Let's see what I have. (reaches into the Bag of Toys and pulls out a table) A table!

Patient: That's a table?

Therapist: Yeah, what do you think it is?

Patient: Yeah, oh yeah. (patient throws bed onto nearby chair)

Therapist: What are you doing? Do you want to keep your things over there?

Patient: Yes.

Therapist: Okay, Now we'll keep things over there. This table. The table didn't like people to sit next to it. I get one chip. Now for my story.

Once upon a time there was a table and this table, when people would put food on it, it would wobble. It would go (imitates by sound wobbly table) . . . let's say this was food here . . . somebody put a plate on it or something (puts reward chip on table to simulate a plate of food). It would go (imitates wobbly sound while shaking table) and it would knock it off. They'd put it back on and (imitates wobbly sound again and puts back chip) it would knock it off. It just didn't like to have food on it. Once in a while it did. Once in a while you'd put food, you'd put a plate on it and it would let the plate stay. But other times it just didn't want the plates and it would go "oooooooohhhhh" and the plates would go off.

So the people in the family decided that the best thing that they could do was to see what the table's mood was. If they saw the table was going to shake they'd put a little something on it. If the table would shake they'd just take it off and then they'd say, "Okay, we'll just use another table. That's all." But if they put something on it and the table let it stay, then they'd all sit around and they would then use it. Now sometimes they would get angry at the table . . .

Patient (interrupts): They should — you know what they should do? Cut it if it shakes all the plates out. Cut it in half.

Therapist: Cut it in half?

Patient: Yeah.

Therapist: Why do that?

Patient: Just do it.

Therapist: Why? Are you saying that — why should they cut it in half if it — you mean when it shook the plate?

Patient: Yeah.

Therapist: Why cut it in half? What would that do?

Patient: They should.

Therapist: But why? What would that accomplish? What would that do if they cut it in half?

Patient: Nothing. It would just, you know, then it would be no good and then they'd be sad about it.

Therapist: It would be no good?

Patient: Yeah, then it wouldn't have — it wouldn't be — then he wouldn't have a lot of fun or anything.

Therapist: Who's that, the table?

Patient: Yeah.

Therapist: Oh, in other words . . .

Patient (interrupts): They would shake it and shake it and everything.

Therapist: You mean they would punish him that way? Is that what you are saying?

Patient: Yeah.

Therapist: I see. Would he still shake things off the table if they cut him in half?

Patient: No.

Therapist: Why not?

Patient: He wouldn't have two legs to do it.

Therapist: I see. Well, now one of the kids in the family thought that would be a good idea to cut the table up in half and to hurt it that way. But one of the teenagers, an older kid, said, "No, that's foolish because that table is still good. Sometimes it stays still and sometimes it lets us put plates on it. We might as well use it when we can and when we can't we'll just use another table and this way we can get some use of the table because it's a very fine table. It's a very good table." So they said it was a good table and there's no reason ruining it or cutting it up. So what do you think finally happened? Hmm?

Patient: Uh, they didn't . . . (pauses) . . .

Therapist: They didn't what?

Patient: They didn't ruin it.

Therapist: They didn't ruin it. What did they do?

Patient: They just left it alone and they wouldn't use it anymore.

Therapist: At all?

Patient: Yeah.

Therapist: Or did they use it when it wasn't rocking around?

Patient: No, they didn't use it at all.

Therapist: No, that's not how my story ends. In my story they use it when it's not rocking around and when it is rocking around they don't use it. That's how my story ends. So I get two chips for that.

Patient: That was a long one.

Therapist: Okay, let's put this table over there. Okay, you go now.

In situations in which a child's mother and/or father have significant inhibitions in involving themselves in a child, one cannot encourage the child's attempting deep involvement with such parents. In fact, it would be cruel to do so because it would only increase the child's frustration and resentment and this could only intensify his difficulties. Accordingly, in such situations, I generally try to help the child see the parent as having deficiencies with regard to providing affection but, in addition, I try to help him recognize that such a parent can still provide him with affection at times. It behooves such a child to have a realistic view of such a parent and to involve himself when such involvement is rewarding and to remove himself and seek gratifications elsewhere when the parent is not inclined to provide it.

In my story I make this recommendation symbolically. The table in my story (like the bed in Tom's story) represents the father. Just as the bed dumps those who would try to sleep in it, my table wobbles and shakes off any food that would be set on it. However, my table is not uniformly rejecting. There are times when it will allow the food to remain. Those who use the table learn to test it out first to see whether the food will be allowed to stay. In this way I encouraged Tom to approach his father and involve himself with him when the latter was receptive and to remove himself when his father was not.

During the telling of my story Tom suggested that the people cut the table in half as a punitive action, as well as a way of preventing it from shaking off the food. Again, he was not only expressing his hostility in an extreme way but also trying to find a method of stopping the rejection. Neither of these represented reasonable adaptations. He cannot kill his father nor can he prevent his father from rejecting him. Accordingly, I rejected these alternatives for incorporation into my story in order to maintain what I considered to be the healthier adaptations.

The transcript does not fully communicate the various movements of the table and plates that were utilized to enhance Tom's interest. Although he stated in the end that it was a long story, he did appear to be significantly involved throughout most of it.

Misguided Attempts to Enhance Self-esteem. A little later, during the same game, Tom drew a camel from the Bag of Toys and related this story.

Patient: Once there was a camel and it was a very small camel and it was the smallest one in the world. So then he stayed like that. Then he growed up and down. Once he was the biggest camel and then he was the smallest. And he was going bump, bump, bump and he didn't like it. He was going like this (patient jumping up and down) bump, bump, bump, bump, bump and he was growing like one, two, three, one, two, three, one, two, three, and he was like eighty feet high for the biggest camel in the world. And then he stayed like that. That's the end.

Therapist: I see. How is it he got smaller? What made him . . .

Patient (interrupts): He got bigger and smaller . . . it was the stuff he eat — he ate.

Therapist: He ate. I see eating can make you bigger, but how can eating make you smaller?

Patient (jumping): He's going bump. He's eating a kind of camel food and he's going bump, bump, bump, bump, bump.

Therapist: Okay, but how does the camel food make you smaller? I can see how it makes you bigger but how smaller?

Patient: It's going because it's the kind of camel food and it goes . . . and it goes bump, bump, bump, bump, bump, bump, bump.

Therapist: Well, you didn't answer my question. How does it make you smaller?

Patient: It's a special kind of camel food.

Therapist: Oh, there's camel food that makes you smaller. I see. Okay. Sit down. Have a seat.

Patient: Two chips.

Therapist (giving patient chips): Two chips. Sit down.

I was not completely sure about the full meaning of this story. Actually, Tom did more jumping around than storytelling in response to his taking the camel from the Bag of Toys. Of course, the camel's being "eighty feet high" is a statement about Tom's desire to be quite large and mighty. And the fact that the camel was also the smallest in the world is a statement about Tom's feelings of inadequacy. There is a magic element in the story, however. These changes in his size all result from the ingestion of food: the food is capable of making him either the biggest camel in the world or the smallest camel in the world. In either case these changes in size do not require any particular effort on Tom's part and it was to this issue that I directed my subsequent story.

Therapist: Okay, now it's my turn. (reaches into the Bag of Toys and pulls out a lion figurine) What have I got here?

Patient: A lion.

Therapist: A lion. Okay. Once upon a time . . . oh, first I get a chip for saying something about the lion. This lion would not eat his food. I get a chip for that. Now I tell a story.

Once upon a time there was a lion and this lion was very small. He was much smaller than the other lions and one day he was crying about that. (imitates crying sounds) "Waaagh, I'm such a small lion and look at all those other lions. They're so big!" And he was really very sad.

And his brother was walking along and his brother said, "What are you crying about?"

He said, "All the lions are much bigger than I am. I wish I was as big as they are."

And the brother said, "Well, it's very obvious why you are not as big as they are," he said, "because you're not eating your food. You're not eating your breakfast. You don't eat your lunch. You hardly eat anything at all. No wonder you're small."

So what did the lion say?

Patient: I don't know. I don't know. I can't remember.

Therapist: The lion said, "Well, I don't like to eat some foods."

And the brother said, "Well, maybe you don't like some food, but it can't be that you don't like all foods. There must be some food you like."

He said, "Oh, I don't know. I just don't like to eat any foods. There are some foods I may like, but I don't like to eat all those different kinds of food."

The brother said, "Well, if you want you can just eat the kinds of food you like. Maybe sometimes you'll have to eat a little food you don't like if you want to grow. But if you want to be as big as the other lions you'd better eat the food you like and maybe once in a while food you don't like."

Well, the lion said, "I don't want to do that. I want to be as big as them and I don't want to eat!"

The brother said, "Sorry, I can't help you. You cannot get bigger if you are not going to eat."

So what's going to happen then?

Patient: He ate and he got much bigger than all the lions because he ate a lot more.

Therapist: Did he eat some foods that he did like?

Patient: Yeah, he ate a lot of foods that he did like and he ate a lot of foods that he *didn't* like.

Therapist: Yeah, well, mainly he ate foods . . .

Patient (interrupts): And he grew much bigger than all the other lions.

Therapist: And he felt kind of silly for not having eaten before because he found out that if he ate then that was the only way he could be as big as the others.

And the lesson of that story is: If you are a lion and you are smaller than other lions the only way you can get to be bigger is to eat. And sometimes you'll have to eat some foods that you don't like, but you can also eat foods that you do like. The end.

In this story I directed myself to Tom's lack of interest in his schoolwork. He had a very low tolerance for frustration and anything uncomfortable. Since schoolwork necessitated a certain amount of toleration for unpleasant drill and self-application, Tom would have little to do with it. He was somewhat hedonistic in response to the deprivation he suffered in his relationship with his father. In his story, however, growth occurred by merely eating. In my story growth (here intellectual growth) requires one's eating, at times, distasteful foods. In other words, I was trying to communicate to Tom that if he wished to do as well in school as others he would have to suffer certain discomforts. Tom did involve himself in the story and, at the end, provided an answer that indicated his appreciation that one has to eat both good foods and, on occasion, distasteful foods if one wishes to grow.

Dealing with Denial. Following this the patient again reached into the bag.

Patient (picks out a baby figurine from the Bag of Toys): Is that a boy or a baby?

Therapist: It's a baby. What is it — a boy or a girl? What do you think?

Patient: A boy, I think.

Therapist: A boy?

Patient: Let's make a boy of him.

Therapist: Okay, make him a boy. What do you want to say about him?

Patient: He has a pin . . . he has a pin on him.

Therapist: He has a pin on him. Okay.

Patient: I guarantee it's going to be a tie.

Therapist: You think so, huh? You guarantee that, huh? Okay. You've got a very good vocabulary, you know that? Do you know what that means? When you say *guarantee* it means you have a good vocabulary.

Patient: What?

Therapist: It means you know a lot of good words. You know a lot of very large words. Most kids your age do not know as many words as you do. It's true. It's too bad, however, that you don't read as well as other kids your age because you know many more words than most kids your age. Okay, go ahead. What are you going to say about the baby? What's the story?

Patient: I told you. It has a pin already. I told you.

Therapist: You get a chip for that. Now tell a story.

Patient: Once there was a baby and it was a boy, and he was a very, very small baby. He was an inch tall.

Therapist: He was an inch tall. That is small, that's for sure.

Patient: Yeah, and he was only as big as your finger. He was Tom Thumb. He was Tom Thumb. And he . . . and he liked it like that.

Therapist: He liked it like that? He liked being that small. So go ahead. You continue telling me the story. So he liked being one inch tall.

Patient: And he liked that until finally he died. And that's the end.

Therapist: He died.

Patient: Yeah, because he was so small.

Therapist: He died because he was so small. Tell me something. Did he really like being one inch tall?

Patient: Yeah.

Therapist: I don't believe it.

Patient: He does a lot of more things.

Therapist: Like what?

Patient: And he had more fun getting up on the toilet . . the big toilet.

Therapist: He had more fun standing up on the big toilet?

Patient: He was doing it with a rope — getting up on it with a rope.

Therapist: All right, that was more fun than just standing up at the toilet?

Patient: With a string. And he had only . . . and he . . . and he didn't even weigh anything. He was so small.

Therapist: Yeah, okay. You get two chips for that. Now it's my chance.

The story is a clear statement of one of Tom's other problems. He used the mechanism of denial to a significant degree. Tom smiled quite frequently and was considered by most who did not know him well to be a happy-go-lucky and friendly child. His smile, however, was a thin veneer to cover up the basic embarrassment he felt over his difference from other children, the pain he felt over his father's rejection, and, I suspect, angry feelings as well.

In this story the one-inch baby represents, of course, Tom. It is a statement of his massive feelings of inadequacy — he's only one inch tall. However, we are told that he liked being one inch tall. When I responded somewhat incredulously that I found it difficult to imagine someone's liking being one inch tall, Tom insisted that was the case. However, the story ends with the baby's dying because he was so small. Here is another statement of Tom's feelings of abandonment and the anticipation of death that could ultimately result from his deprivations.

As I drew Tom out further, he related another example of his denial mechanism. The one-inch baby has fun standing at the big toilet and looking up while others use it. He uses a rope to get up to the toilet. Although other figures are not clearly described in this story, it is reasonable to envision their being there and using it from above. A more dramatic picture of Tom's feelings of inadequacy would be hard to create.

The reader should note that in the early part of the story I was sure to compliment Tom on his using the word *guarantee* — a word that is not frequently used by children of his age. It behooves the therapist to take every opportunity to praise a child when he realistically exhibits behavior worthy of praise. All patients, regardless of their difficulties, benefit from enhancement of their self-esteem. The therapist must take care, however, not to praise without conviction. Such lack of honesty will be appreciated by the patient and this cannot but be antitherapeutic.

This is the interchange we had in response.

Therapist (reaches into the Bag of Toys and pulls out a zebra figurine): Okay, what is this? What's that?

Patient: A zebra.

Therapist: A zebra. Okay. Once upon a time ... oh, first of all the statement about the zebra. The zebra was one inch tall. I get a chip for that.

Patient: I don't think an animal could be that small. Maybe an inch — could be an inch tall.

Therapist: Well, in my story he is. Once upon a time there was a zebra and he was one inch tall. And he really wanted to be big like all the other zebras, but he said, "I like being one inch tall."

And they said, "Come on, you can't like being one inch tall."

He said, "Oh, yes, I love being one inch tall."

You see, this zebra really didn't like being one inch tall. He just used to say that he liked being one inch tall.

Patient: (laughs).

Therapist: He used to say ... he was the kind of a zebra who when things were bad or there was something that he didn't like, instead of saying he didn't like it, he used to smile and laugh and say, "I like it."

Patient (trying to interrupt): That's because you're just going to cry a little more.

Therapist: That's because he would cry a little more.

Patient: He's going to cry ... he's going to cry.

Therapist: Now this zebra used to do that in order not to cry. Is that it? He used to laugh.

Patient (affirmatively): Hh hmm.

Therapist: Well, do you think that was a good idea that when something was bad or bothering him . . .

Patient (interrupts): He would lie about it.

Therapist: How would he lie? Why do you say he would lie?

Patient: (mumbles)

Therapist: What?

Patient: He would say, "I like being one inch tall."

Therapist: Yeah, he'd say. Did he really like being one inch tall?

Patient: No.

Therapist: But he used to say that.

Patient: In my story he liked being one inch tall.

Therapist: Yeah, but in *my* story he really didn't like it. For instance, when he would go to the toilet and all the other zebras would stand at the toilet and they were big enough to go to the toilet and he was only one inch tall, he would look up there and he would say, "Gee, look at those zebras. They can go to the toilet by themselves. I am only one inch tall and I have to stand way down here. I can't even reach up that high." And he used to say, "Ha, ha, ha. Who cares? I like being one inch tall. I can just take a rope and go up to that toilet. It's fun." (patient repeatedly picking his nose and eating the mucus)

And the others said, "It can't be fun. We know inside that you would like to be as big as we are and you can be as big as we are." Excuse me, can I make a suggestion to you, hmm? You were just doing something that most people consider a little impolite. You don't want to talk about it?

Patient (ashamedly removing finger from nose): No.

Therapist: Okay, we won't talk about it, but you know what I am talking about because I don't want to embarrass you if I discuss it.

Patient: No.

Therapist: Okay. Anyway, getting back to the story, so this zebra began to listen to what they were saying and they said, "Listen, if you would only eat like the rest of us and get some more exercise, you'll find you'll be as big as we are. And we think that there's something funny about your laughing about being small because you can't feel very good being only one inch tall."

So what did the zebra say?

Patient: He . . . he is . . . he said he'd quit the lie.

Therapist: He'd quit the . . .

Patient (interrupts): And he said, "I think you're right."

Therapist: He said, "You're right!" That's right! And he started to eat and sure enough he did grow. Now, of course, some of the things that he ate were things that he didn't like too much but he decided to eat them anyway; he felt so good when he grew as big as the other zebras. And that's the end of my story.

There was no question that I was "hitting home" in my discussion of Tom's denial mechanism. As can be seen from the transcript, he actively participated in the discussion and even introduced comments about it himself. In addition, he was also quite tense during the interchange and manifested this by picking his nose and putting the mucus into his mouth. After this had occurred on a few occasions, I decided to bring it to his attention. Recognizing it as a manifestation of his tension made me hesitate. However, I also felt that it behooved me, as his therapist, to confront him in as benevolent a manner as possible with his socially alienating behavior. He immediately became embarrassed and I respected his right not to discuss it — especially in front of a television audience (a videotape was being made of our playing the game).

In addition to dealing with the denial mechanism and its obvious maladaptive function, I also directed my attention to the fact that Tom had within him the power to grow (i.e., learn in the classroom) by doing something himself. In this case it was not only eating but on occasion eating foods that might be somewhat distasteful. Here, I reiterated a message from my previous story.

Chapter Ten
The Bag of Things Game

The Bag of Things Game requires a bag clearly labeled BAG OF THINGS, in which are forty to fifty objects that are far less recognizable than those in the BAG OF TOYS (Figure 4). Whereas in The Bag of Toys Game the objects are readily identified (soldier, car, boy, fire truck, etc.), in The Bag of Things Game objects have been specifically selected because they are not clearly recognizable. Accordingly, the bag contains various kinds of creatures, monsters, wiggly things, a lump of clay, a few blocks, a plastic ring, an odd-looking seashell, some strange-looking robots, and assorted figurines that vaguely resemble people or animals. Because they are not clearly recognizable they tend to be less contaminating of the child's fantasies than toys in The Bag of Toys Game. Often the child tends to anthropomorphize the objects; but their amorphous quality allows their utilization for a wide variety of fantasies. In the course of play, used objects are laid aside and dramatizations are encouraged.

Clinical Examples

"Unconditional Positive Regard." Ronald, age seven, exhibited many social perceptual difficulties as part of his minimal brain dysfunction syndrome. He was of at least average intelligence and did not have significant visual-perceptual or auditory-perceptual problems. However, he did behave differently from other children, mainly because of his impulsivity, angry outbursts, and insensitivity to the nuances of appropriate social interaction.

While playing The Bag of Things Game he drew an object that closely resembled a robot. There was a slot in the back enabling one to use the figurine as a bank. This is the interchange that took place.

Therapist: Just stick your hand in and take whatever one you want. One thing, please.

Patient (taking figurine out of bag): Ooh, what's that?

Therapist: I don't know. What does it look like to you?

Patient: Bank.

Therapist: A bank? I guess it can be used as a bank.

Patient: But how would you get the money out of it?

Therapist: I think it's more than a bank — well, what does it look like?

Patient: A bank because of that (points to a slot in the back).

Therapist: Right. You can put money in it. But what is the bank? I mean there are things like piggy banks. What is that? What kind of a bank is that? This is a treasure chest bank here we're keeping the reward chips in. What kind of a bank would you call that? What does that look like?

Patient: Maybe a robot bank.

Therapist: Now if you want to say something about the robot you get one chip and if you can tell a story about it you get two.

Patient: Once upon a time there was a robot and it had one little baby and everybody loved that little baby. Everybody came to visit him. And they loved that little baby so much. The end.

Therapist: I have a question about that. What was there about that baby that they loved so much?

Patient: Uh, his eyes. They liked to play with that baby.

Therapist: Hh hmm. What else made them like the baby?

Patient: Everything.

Therapist: Is that it?

Patient (whispers): Yeah.

Therapist: Okay. You get two.

The story is typical of those told by many children with minimal brain dysfunction. Having few assets that they consider worthy of gaining them the affection of others, they hope to be loved for innate qualities. In this case the baby is liked because of his eyes. In addition, we are told that people like to play with the baby; but again, no specific ingratiating qualities on the baby's part are described. Lastly, when I specifically asked the patient, "What else made them like the baby?" he replied, "Everything." Again, this is an avoidance answer and does not provide specifics.

With this understanding of Ronald's story, I related mine after choosing a somewhat nebulous little wiggly creature from the bag.

Therapist: Now it's my chance. (holds up figurine) What does this look like?

Patient: I don't know.

Therapist: Okay, let's just call him a baby. Okay?

Patient: Okay.

Therapist: Once upon a time there was this baby and everybody looked at this baby and everybody said, "Ooh, what a cute little baby. Isn't that a nice little cute baby? Ooh, how cute." (pretends he's kissing baby while making kissing sounds) They used to coo with him and they would hold him and hug him. "Ooh, what a cute little baby."

This little baby, as he grew up, he found that people weren't cuddling him so much and weren't saying, "Ooh, what a cute little baby." And he thought that just by sitting there and doing nothing that people would continue to love him. Well, that's how it is with babies. Babies can sit and do nothing and everybody will love them, or most people will love them. But as you get older, if you want to get people to like you, you have to be doing things. You have to be nice to them or make things that they may like or do things for people and you just can't sit there and smile and expect everybody to love you.

But he didn't know this, so when he became five, six, seven years old and he would just sit there and do nothing he found out that people weren't going over and saying, "Ooh, how lovable you are. Ooh, we like you so much." And he got kind of lonely because they weren't loving him like they used to when he was a baby. But then when he started doing things — when he started being nice to people, being friendly, and he started learning a lot of things that made him interesting to talk to — then people started liking him more and he wasn't so lonely.

And do you know what the lesson of that story is?

Patient: No.

Therapist: Try to figure it out. What do you think the lesson is?

Patient: (silent)

Therapist: Well, do people like you for sitting there and doing nothing?

Patient: No.

Therapist: Do they like little babies when they sit there and do nothing?

Patient: Yeah.

Therapist: Yeah, but when you get older what happens?

Patient: They don't like you anymore.

Therapist: Right. And what do you have to do when you are older in order for people to like you?

Patient: Be nice to them, make things that will make a person happy.

Therapist: Right. Right. And that's how you will get friends when you're older. The end. Okay. I get two chips for that. Right?

Patient: Right.

Therapist: Okay. Your chance.

The purpose of my story is obvious. I attempted to help the patient appreciate that one is loved for his assets and qualities which attract people, and that if he is to be liked by others he must apply himself. Children with minimal brain dysfunction must be strong adherents to the work ethic if they are to overcome their deficits. And it is the purpose of the therapist to help bring about such commitment.

Feelings of Impotence Regarding Self-assertion. Betty came to treatment at the age of eight because of shyness, generalized tension, and poor peer relationships. She was quite tight, restricted, and inhibited in expressing emotions. She feared asserting herself and was easily scapegoated. Her parents were highly intellectualized professional people who were similarly fearful of expressing feelings. During her second month of treatment the following interchange took place while playing The Bag of Things Game.

Patient (picking from the bag): I hope I get something good.

Therapist: I hope so too.

Patient (holding up an amorphous creature with a similar smaller creature sitting on its head): What's this?

Therapist: What does it look like to you?

Patient: I don't know what it is.

Therapist: Well, make it into anything you want. People see it differently. Call it whatever you want, what it looks like to you.

Patient: It looks like some kind of monster or something like that.

Therapist: Okay, do you want to call it a monster?

Patient: Okay.

Therapist: Now, if you can say something about that monster you get one chip.

Patient: The monster had a little monster sitting on the top of his head and he was green.

Therapist: Very good. You get one reward chip. Now you can get two more if you can tell a completely made-up story about that monster, one completely made up from your imagination.

Patient: Once upon a time there was this monster. And he had this little monster sitting on the top of his head. And he [the big monster] wanted the little monster to get off because he was heavy and he was bothering him.

Therapist: You mean the little monster was bothering the big monster?

Patient: Yeah.

Therapist: What was the little monster doing?

Patient: He was poking him and he was very heavy.

Therapist: So then what happened.

Patient: So the big monster was walking along one day and the little monster fell off his head, landed on the sidewalk, and he died. The end.

Therapist: Is that the whole story?

Patient: Yes.

Therapist: Okay.

The story is a clear statement of the patient's feeling of impotence regarding effective self-assertion. Just as she cannot effectively defend herself against those who tease her (many of whom were smaller than herself), the monster (who symbolizes Betty) is unable to assert himself and use his own powers to rid himself of the little fellow who is bothering him and is a heavy weight on his head. The problem is solved by the little monster's conveniently falling off and dying. No effort is required of the big monster, no self-assertion, no struggle, no anxiety.

The game continued.

Therapist: Okay. Now it's my turn. I wonder what

I'm going to get. I hope it's something good. Let me see. (Pulls out a red creature with large lobsterlike claws. On its head is a little yellow creature with similar, but much smaller, claws.) Wow, look what I've got. What do you think that is?

Patient: It looks like some kind of a lobster or something like that.

Therapist: Okay. We'll call it a lobster. Once upon a time there was this lobster. And on his head sat this obnoxious little lobster. And the little lobster was always poking the big lobster. And he would take his little claws . . . do you see his little claws here?

Patient: Yes.

Therapist: Well, he'd take his little claws and he'd sometimes pinch the big lobster on the ears. And he'd poke him with his claws too. So what do you think the big lobster did?

Patient: I don't know.

Therapist: Well, try to guess.

Patient: The little lobster fell off?

Therapist: Well, that's how it happened in your story but it didn't happen in mine. First, the big monster kept hoping that the little monster would fall off and hit his head and even die, but as much as he wished that that would happen, it didn't. He wished it very hard. He would go, "Oooh, oooh, I wish so hard that he falls off." But the little lobster just kept sitting there and poking the big lobster, and biting him with his claws.

And sometimes the big lobster used to cry because it hurt him so when he was poked and bitten. And he'd cry, "Oooh, ooh, you're hurting me." But because he didn't *do* anything the little lobster just kept on bothering him and biting him.

Patient: Did he bleed?

Therapist: Yes, a little bit. In fact, it was the day that he began to bleed when the lobster's teenage brother was passing by and he saw what was happening. And he said to the lobster, "Why are you letting him do all those terrible things to you? You have very big claws and you could easily get him off your head. Look how tightly closed you keep your claws." (Therapist now talking to patient and pointing to tightly closed claws.) Do you see how tightly shut he keeps his claws?

Patient: Yes

Therapist: Why do you think his claws are shut so tight?

Patient: Because he's scared?

Therapist: Right! Because he's scared. So what do you think happened then?

Patient: He opened them up?

Therapist: Right! He was very scared to do it and his knees were knocking and his claws were chattering like this (Therapist chatters his teeth.) and he was scared all over. And the teenager said, "Go ahead, snap at him. You'll see how fast he'll jump off your head." So the big lobster snapped, but it was a very soft and low snap, and so nothing happened. "That's no snap," said the teenager. "Do it harder," the teenager said. Well, the big lobster was even more scared, but he did it.

What do you think happened then?

Patient: The little lobster still stayed?

Therapist: No! The little lobster began crying, "Ooooh, oooh, you've hurt me. Look what you've done to me. I'm bleeding. Mommy, mommy, I'm bleeding." And he jumped off the big lobster's back and went crying to his mother.

And the teenager said, "You see. That wasn't so bad. I knew you could do it."

And how do you think the lobster felt then?

Patient: He felt very good.

Therapist: Right! He felt wonderful. And after that, whenever the little lobster wanted to get on his head to poke him, he would just snap his claws and the little fellow would run away. But at other times, when the little lobster wanted to be friendly and play, they had a good time together.

And do you know what the lesson of that story is? What we can learn from that story?

Patient: If someone bothers you, don't let him do it?

Therapist: Right! If someone bothers you, don't let him do it. It may be scary at first, but if you still fight — even though you're scared — you'll get people to stop bothering you. The end.

The message of my story is obvious. The patient's solution to the problem of dealing with those who bothered her was totally maladaptive. Mine served, I believe, to encourage greater self-assertion, and this is what ultimately happened in the patient's treatment. Stories such as this played, I believe, a role in bringing about such changes.

Chapter Eleven
The Bag of Words Game

The Bag of Words Game requires a bag labeled BAG OF WORDS. In it are approximately four hundred words, each of which is printed with thick ink (a "Magic Marker" or "Flair" pen will serve well) on a 2″ x 3″ card (Figure 4). Different colored cards and inks can be used to make the game more attractive. Words have been chosen that are most likely to elicit comments and stories relevant to issues commonly focused on in therapy, e.g., *breast, anger, mother, father, boy, girl, foolish, doctor, love,* and *hate*. A full list of the words I have found most useful is shown in the accompanying table; however, the reader is likely to think of a number of words on his own and may find some of my words less useful than I have found them. In accordance with the aforementioned principle of the pressure of unconscious material being more powerful than the contaminating effect of the eliciting stimulus, the specific choice of words is not vital. Occasional cards provide the child with extra reward chips ("You get two extra reward chips"), and these increase the child's excitement while playing the game. Used cards are laid aside and dramatizations are encouraged.

Table 1

accident	bird	Christmas	dollar
adult	birthday	cigarettes	draw
afraid	birthday party	circus	dream
airplane	black	clay	dumb
allowance	blame	clean	early
alone	blood	climb	egg
ambulance	boast	clothing	enemy
anger	boat	clown	escape
animal	body	club	eyeglasses
annoy	book	cockroach	fail
ant	bottle	compliment	fall
ape	bowel movement	conduct	famous
apple	boy	cookie	fat
ashamed	boy friend	cop	father
automobile	Boy Scout	counselor	fear
ax	brag	cow	feeling
baby	brat	cowboy	fight
baby-sitter	brave	cripple	finger
backside	bread	crook	fire
bad	breast	cruel	fire engine
bad habit	bug	cry	fireman
bad luck	build	crybaby	fish
bad thoughts	bully	cuddle	fix
ball	calf	curse	flour
balloon	cake	dad	food
bang	camera	danger	fool
bare	camp	daughter	foolish
bath	camp director	dentist	forget
bathroom	candy	die	fox
bathtub	car	dinosaur	freak
beat	care	dirty	friend
beautiful	cat	dirty trick	frog
beaver	catch	dirty words	fun
behavior	cheat	discover	funny
belly button	chewing gum	disgusting	game
best	chicken	doctor	garbage
bicycle	child	dog	garbageman
big	children	doll	gift

Table 1 (continued)

girl	invisible	mean	peacock
girl friend	jail	medal	penis
Girl Scout	jerk	medicine	pet
God	job	mess	phony
good	joke	message	pick on
grab	joy	milk	picture
grade	judge	mirror	pig
grandfather	kangaroo	mistake	piggy bank
grandmother	kill	model	pill
grown-up	kind	mom	plan
gun	king	money	play
hamster	kiss	monkey	playground
happy	knife	monster	please
harm	lady	mother	poison
hate	lamb	mouse	poke
healthy	large	mouth	police car
hear	late	mucus	policeman
heaven	laugh	mud	polite
hell	lazy	nag	pony
hen	leave	naked	poor
hide	letter	nasty	praise
hit	lie	naughty	pray
hole	like	new	present
holiday	lion	nice	president
homework	lipstick	nightmare	pretty
honest	little	nipple	prince
hope	lollipop	note	princess
horrible	lonely	nurse	principal
horse	lose	old	prize
hospital	love	operation	proud
house	lucky	ostrich	psychiatrist
hug	mad	owl	psychologist
hungry	make	paint	punish
hurt	make believe	parent	pupil
ice cream	magic	parrot	queen
ill	man	party	quiet
Indian	manners	pass	rat
insult	matches	pay	refrigerator

Table 1 (continued)

respect	sleep	stone	train
reward	slob	story	treat
rich	sloppy	strong	tree
right	sly	student	trick
robber	small	stupid	tricycle
rotten	smart	suck	trip
sad	smell	surprise	truck
scaredy-cat	snail	sword	try
scary	snake	talk	turtle
school	sneak	teacher	ugly
scold	soap	teacher's pet	upset
scoutmaster	soldier	tease	vagina
scream	son	teenager	vomit
secret	song	telephone	water
secret plan	sore loser	television	weak
see	sorry	temper tantrum	weep
selfish	spanking	thank	whip
share	spear	therapist	whisper
sheep	spend	thief	win
shoot	spider	threaten	wish
shout	spit	thumb	wipe
shy	spoil	tickle	wolf
sick	sport	tiger	worm
silly	steal	toilet	worry
sissy	stick	tooth	worst
sister	stingy	touch	young
skunk	stink	toy	zoo

Clinical Examples

An Inappropriate Resolution of the Oedipus Complex. Marc came to treatment at the age of seven because of tics, excessive tension, and agitated behavior in the classroom. His mother, a very buxom woman, was quite seductive with him. Near the end of his first month in treatment the following interchange took place while playing The Bag of Words Game.

> *Patient:* I've got the word *tree.* Once there was a tree and it was a talking palm tree.
>
> *Therapist:* A talking palm tree. Go ahead.
>
> *Patient:* It was so full of coconuts that he couldn't even move or talk. He was too heavy. So one day it decided that it would quit and just try and make all the coconuts come off, but they wouldn't come off. So he looked around until he found somebody with a gun shooting birds, and he asked him if he would . . .
>
> *Therapist* (interrupst): Who is *he* now?
>
> *Patient:* He was just looking — the palm tree was looking around and he just found someone.
>
> *Therapist:* Oh, the palm tree wanted to get his own coconuts off?
>
> *Patient:* Yeah.
>
> *Therapist:* Okay. It was a he palm tree?
>
> *Patient:* Yeah.
>
> *Therapist:* And then he finally found someone with a gun.
>
> *Patient:* Yeah.
>
> *Therapist:* Okay.
>
> *Patient:* Who was shooting birds with a shotgun. But it wasn't easy because he just had to look around because he couldn't move. So he called him and he asked him if he would shoot them off. And he [the man] said, "I won't shoot them off, but I'll pick them off. I love coconuts." The end.
>
> *Therapist:* So what happened?
>
> *Patient:* And the lesson was if you're a palm tree and

you have coconuts on you, you shouldn't just try and take them off, but if you're a palm tree there's nothing you can do.

Therapist: Wait a minute. The lesson is if you're a palm tree, what?

Patient: There's nothing to do except stay where you are just like other trees.

Therapist: And don't do what?

Patient: Don't try and take your coconuts off.

Therapist: Why not?

Patient: Because they're supposed to come off theirselves.

Therapist: I see. So what was the trouble? Did this palm tree get into any kind of trouble by having this man shoot the coconuts off?

Patient: The man said that "I wouldn't, um, I won't shoot them off but I'll pick them off because I love coconuts."

Therapist: So he picked them off.

Patient: Yeah.

Therapist: The man picked off the coconuts. I'm not clear what the lesson is.

Patient: The lesson is that if you are a palm tree you shouldn't want to make your coconuts come off because they'll come off themselves and all that you should do is stay where you are just like other trees.

Therapist: Hh hmm.

Patient: They don't move.

Therapist: Okay. Now it's my chance.

Although Marc represented the tree as male, I considered it to represent his mother. The coconuts, being round and filled with milk, well serve as a breast symbol. They are high up on the tree and inaccessible. The central theme of the story is whether or not the coconuts will be made available to those on the ground. We are told that the tree was so full of coconuts "that he couldn't even move or talk." This, I believe, represented Marc's view of his mother as being quite buxom and that her breasts were the most prominent part of her anatomy. In fact, Marc's mother was well-endowed in this area and was a very seductive woman, as well.

The man with the gun, I believe, represents Marc's father. He has a powerful phallus which somehow enables him to gain access to the coconuts, that is, the mother's breasts. There is some ambivalence on Marc's part regarding whether or not the coconuts should come off the tree. The tree asks the man to take the coconuts off (with the help of his powerful weapon), but the man refuses to shoot them off. Rather, he decides to pick them off stating, "I love coconuts." Although Marc's presentation is somewhat confusing, the main element that comes through is that the tree is advised not to encourage premature removal of the coconuts; rather, it should wait until they come off naturally.

In essence, I considered this story to reflect Marc's wish that his father not have such ready access to his mother's coconuts, that is, her breasts. He would prefer that she withhold them from access to him as long as possible. However, he sees his father as having the wherewithal to get them at his will; but he gets his father to take them by hand, rather than with a gun. Possibly, this represents Marc's fear that his father might destroy the coconuts and then they would be completely unavailable to him. If his father has to get the coconuts he might as well preserve them. However, Marc would much prefer the tree to be less receptive to the father's ready access to them. The story reveals, as well, his appreciation that his mother wishes to provide the father access, and this is symbolized by the tree's wishing that the coconuts would come off. It was with this understanding of Marc's story that I related mine.

> *Therapist:* Okay. Now it's my chance. (picks card from bag) I've got the word *boy*.
> Once upon a time there was a palm tree and this palm tree had many coconuts on it, and there was a boy who lived next door to the property where this palm tree was. He used to look up at that palm tree and he would

say, "Boy, those would be great coconuts to have. That would be terrific if I could have those coconuts. I'd like to get them off that tree. I'd like to split a couple open and eat the coconut and drink the milk that's in the inside and . . ."

Patient: (gestures to speak)

Therapist: Do you want to say something about that?

Patient: I just wanted to say that I hate coconut trees.

Therapist: You hate coconut trees. Anyway . . .

Patient (interrupts): Coconut juice!

Therapist: Anyway, in my story this boy liked coconut juice and he like those coconuts, and he used to eye those coconuts every day. And one day he thought, "Gee, it would be great to get those coconuts." But he knew they belonged to the man next door.

So one day — he knew that if he went on the property there or tried to climb the tree to pull down those coconuts the man would get very angry. So one day he thought he would get a gun, and probably shoot down some of those coconuts. Anyway, as he was taking aim to shoot down a coconut, just at that moment, the owner of the house — the owner of the coconut tree — came out and he saw the boy and he said, "What are you doing, Sonny?"

He said, "Oh . . . I . . . uh." He was really trying to think of some kind of a lie but he really couldn't because it was obvious what he was really doing and he sort of had to confess that he was going to try to shoot down the coconuts.

Patient (interrupts): I know what he could say.

Therapist: What could he have said?

Patient: He could have said that he was trying to shoot down birds.

Therapist: Well, the man could see that he was aiming directly at the coconuts and he wouldn't have gotten away with that story. So he had to kind of confess that he was trying to shoot down the coconuts.

And the man said to him, "I'm very sorry. Those coconuts are mine. I'm not letting you shoot them down. But there are two things that we can do. One, I'll give you one of the coconuts because there are lots of coconuts on my tree. However, my suggestion to you is that you plant your own coconut tree or save up some money and buy some coconuts from a store or buy some coconuts from someone else because I'm not selling any." What do you think the boy did?

Patient: He did what the man told him to.

Therapist: What did he decide to do?

Patient: He decided to save up his money and buy more coconuts or buy it from somebody else.

Therapist: Right. He got a job as a newspaper delivery boy and saved up some money and bought some coconuts. In addition, every once in a while the man let him have some of his coconuts and let him know that those were really his and he couldn't have them, but that he could have a little bit. But the main thing was that the boy learned that he couldn't get them from the man so he had to get them elsewhere.

And the lesson of that story is: If you like coconuts and the coconuts you like are owned by another person, ask him. Perhaps he'll give you some or a little bit. But if he won't give you all, which is usually the case, because nobody is going to give you all the coconuts he owns, then try to get them elsewhere, like earning some money and buying some, or planting your own coconut tree. That's the lesson of that story. Anything you want to say about that story?

Patient: (nods negatively)

Therapist: Did you like that story?

Patient: (nods affirmatively)

Therapist: Good. What was it about the story that you liked?

Patient: Well, the coconuts.

Therapist: What was the main thing about it that you liked?

Patient: When he was trying to shoot down the coconuts.

Therapist: Hh hmm. Okay. When he was trying to get down the coconut. Okay.

In my story I tried to communicate to Marc the fact that his mother's breasts were his father's possession. However, he could have some physical gratifications with her, but only to a limited extent. The father, however, does not react punitively. Rather, he is willing to allow Marc some of these physical gratifications, but encourages him to seek them elsewhere through his own efforts, both in the present and in the future. This is typical of the kinds of story I utilize in helping youngsters resolve oedipal problems.

Feelings of Impotence in Dealing with Danger. The game then continued.

Therapist: Okay. You got the word *fire.* Now you tell a story about the word fire.

Patient: Do you have to?

Therapist: No, but you can get two reward chips if you can.

Patient: Okay. Once there was a boy and he saw a fire so he called the fire department on a fire alarm. So the firemen — it took them a very long time because, um, the town's fire department was off duty so the New York Police Department had to come. I mean the fire department. And . . . (pause) . . .

Therapist: Hh hmm.

Patient: And when they arrived it took about five hours to get the fire out.

Therapist: Hh hmm.

Patient: And the fire truck — one of the fire trucks got stolen by a crook, and the other crook who worked for the crook who stole the fire engine started the other fire engine on fire.

Therapist (interrupts): Excuse me, I'm a little confused here. You say one of the fire engines got stolen; one of the town's fire engines?

Patient: No, the New York.

Therapist: Okay. One of the New York fire engines got stolen. Then what happened?

Patient: When they were there, but they didn't see. And the other guy, the other crook started the other fire engine on fire and that's the only one that they had. So they couldn't put out the fire so . . .

Therapist (interrupts): Okay. So one fire engine was stolen and one was started on fire by the second crook. Is that it?

Patient: So they kept going . . .

Therapist (interrupts): Is that correct?

Patient: Yeah.

Therapist: There were two fire engines.

Patient: So they kept on going to people's houses and borrowing water, but then once when they poured one on, the whole thing exploded and they died, and there was a giant, a gigantic fire.

Therapist: Now this was a giant gigantic fire. When they put water on it, it exploded?

Patient: Well, they just had cups.

Therapist: Oh, the cups didn't work. Is that it?

Patient: Yeah.

Therapist: So they couldn't put out the fire.

Patient: And there's no lesson . . . (mumbles) . . .

Therapist: What?

Patient: I don't — there's no lesson of this fire.

Therapist: But no one could put out the fire. Is that it?

Patient: Yeah.

Therapist: So the whole place exploded?

Patient: Yeah.

Therapist: Uh huh. Well, now you get two chips for the word *fire*.

Although the story is somewhat disorganized, the main theme is clear. There is a large fire and the firemen, for one reason or another, are not capable of putting it out. The local firemen are off duty and the firemen who come from New York City are hindered by the fact that one of their fire trucks was stolen and the other was set on fire by a crook. Accordingly, they futilely try to put out the fire with cups of water. However, the fire becomes larger and explodes.

The essence of this story is that the patient feels totally

impotent in dealing with dangerous situations, and he does not feel that the authorities around him can be relied upon to protect him. One can only speculate regarding the exact significance of the fires. It could, on the one hand, represent sexual passion (and this would be consistent with the themes exhibited in the previous interchange). In this case the story would reflect Marc's feelings that his sexual passions will become overwhelming and ultimately destroy him, and he cannot rely upon authority figures around him to squelch them. On the other hand, the fire might represent anger and/or danger. In this case the story again reveals Marc's feelings that he is helpless to control these elements within himself and that authorities around him are equally impotent.

With this understanding of Marc's story, I told the following in response.

Therapist: Okay. I've gotten the word *house*. Once upon a time there was a boy and he used to be scared that if there was a fire in the house that there would be no way of putting it out, that the fire extinguishers wouldn't put it out, that the fire trucks might not come. He thought that maybe the firemen would be off duty in the town where he lived and he thought that maybe if they called the New York City fire trucks that they wouldn't be able to get there because the crooks might steal the fire truck or set it on fire or something like that.

Anyway, one day there was a fire in his house and he was really scared. He thought for sure that no one would be able to put it out. However, his father came in with a fire extinguisher and (makes squirting sounds) squirted and the fire was put out. It was a fire in a wastepaper basket and the father was able to put out the fire. And the boy realized then that if there's a fire it doesn't mean that it has to go completely out of hand, you know, can't be controlled. And he learned that fires can be controlled and after that he stopped worrying so much about fires not being controlled.

The lesson of that story is: If there's a fire in your

house it doesn't mean that it's going to burn down the whole house. Usually you can do something about it. The end. Okay.

I decided not to follow through with any of the specific alternatives regarding the meaning of the word *fire*. Rather, I took a safer course and focused on the issue of impotence regarding squelching fire. In my story I tried to reassure the patient that the authorities around him can be of help to him in dealing with dangerous situations.

Learning Self-assertion from the "Wise Old Owl." Warren, a ten-year-old boy, entered treatment because of extremely difficult peer relationships. He was fiercely scapegoated and on a number of occasions stood crying in the center of a circle of taunting boys and girls. It appeared that this was the only way he could get attention from his peers.

During his second week of treatment, while playing The Bag of Words Game, this interchange took place.

Therapist: Today is Friday, June 28, 1974, and I am here with Warren playing The Bag of Words Game.

Patient: (reaches in bag and pulls out word)

Therapist: Okay, read the word.

Patient: Zoo.

Therapist: Zoo. Okay.

Patient: There is a Central Park Zoo.

Therapist: Okay, you get a chip for that. Now, if you can make up a story using the word *zoo* you get two more chips.

Patient: One day I went to the zoo and I saw a lion, a tiger, and an alligator. And I had fun and I went to eat and I came back and I had a whole day of fun in the zoo.

Therapist: Well, that's something like really happens. That isn't really a made-up story. I like a story with something unusual or some excitement or something special that happens.

Patient: Sometimes they are.

Therapist: You know, make up a story like we played the other day with The Bag of Things Game. You know, think of the word *zoo* and then make up a story, but something unusual or exciting.

Patient: There are crazy zoos around the country.

Therapist: Go ahead. In what way?

Patient: What?

Therapist: In what way are they crazy?

Patient: Well, like they have like lions — lions in cages.

Therapist: What's crazy about that?

Patient: Well, like the cages are like tunnels, you know, like there are little tunnels. And the animals are squeezed in.

Therapist: Yeah, and what's crazy about that?

Patient: Well, like they should be in a big box.

Therapist: You mean with the bars, rather than tunnels.

Patient: Hhmm.

Therapist: You mean the zoo actually keeps a lion in a tunnel rather than in a cage.

Patient: Jungle Habitat [a local animal park] does.

Therapist: I see. Okay. Go ahead. You mean so they're all closed in?

Patient: Wait.

Therapist: Is that what you're saying?

Patient: (nods affirmatively)

Therapist: Go ahead.

Patient: And sometimes the owner is never there (pauses for a while).

Therapist: Go ahead.

Patient: And they usually only feed the animals breakfast and dinner.

Therapist: Instead of what?

Patient: Instead of they should feed them breakfast, lunch, and dinner, but they only feed them breakfast and dinner. And that's it.

Therapist: Hmm?

Patient: That's it.

Therapist: Okay. Does your story have a lesson or a moral?

Patient: What?
Therapist: Does your story have a lesson or a moral?
Patient: No.
Therapist: Okay. Take two chips. Now I go.

Although the story is relatively sparse, it does contain psychodynamic themes of importance to Warren. The story is, in essence, a complaint about the maltreatment of animals in certain zoos. Instead of being served three meals a day, they are served two. Instead of being kept in cages, they are kept in tunnels. Actually, Jungle Habitat, the place where Warren described animals kept in tunnels, is an expansive park where the animals, although fenced in, have great freedom to roam. The tunnels there are decorative and by no means restrictive — but Warren apparently saw them as being so. The fact that Warren saw these freer animals as being treated worse than those in cages is probably a reflection of his feeling so restricted and coerced by those around him that anything with a restricting potential is seen as being so. Accordingly, Warren probably conceived of the animals' voluntarily walking through the tunnels at Jungle Habitat as being incarcerated.

Although the food deficiency probably represents feelings of deprivation of parental affection, there was little evidence that this was significant. Rather, I felt that it related more to the deprivations Warren suffered in his relationships with his peers. In addition, the parents were not that punitive or malevolent that the cruel incarcerators could reasonably represent them. Rather, I felt that they symbolized again the peers who tormented Warren so mercilessly at times.

The story ends with resignation to the status quo. No complaints are made by the animals who are so maltreated. No action is planned to improve their deplorable situation.

When I selected my next word, I tried to keep these themes in mind when I constructed my story.

Therapist (reaches into bag): Okay, *brag.* Brag, um. The lion was always bragging. I get one for that. (takes reward chip) I get two more if I can tell a story. Okay.

Once upon a time there was a zoo in which the people who took care of the animals in the zoo did not treat the animals very well. For instance, instead of keeping them in open spaces surrounded by fences or in cages at times, they would keep them in tunnels and closed-up places. Instead of feeding them three times a day they would only feed them twice a day.

Now the animals were quite upset about this. Some of the animals were afraid to speak up and to say anything about it. Some of the animals — especially one particular lion was always bragging about how he was going to tell those guys off and he would say, "I'm going to tell those guys what I really think of them not giving us enough food, cramming us up in all this space." He would talk a lot about what he was going to do, but he never did anything.

Now there was one animal, he was an owl, who was very wise. He was a very smart animal. This owl said, "Listen, you guys are just a lot of talk (he was speaking to the lion), and you other guys are pretty scared. You don't say anything. I'm going to speak."

So the owl went to the head of the zoo and told the head of the zoo that he was very upset about the conditions under which the animals lived, and told the zookeeper that if he didn't change things he didn't know what was going to be. The animals might revolt; the animals might start fighting, trying to escape, and there really would be a lot of trouble because if there's anything that zoos fear is animals trying to, you know, go on the rampage, escaping and snarling and scaring people and threatening people. So when the zookeeper heard that, he had a meeting with the other people who ran the zoo and they realized that the animals' complaints were justified, were right, and they changed things. And they knew that if they didn't that they'd be in trouble because these animals would really begin to fight and growl and that there would really be a lot of trouble there.

And everybody was happy that the owl had spoken up and this lion who bragged was also a little ashamed of himself for being a big talker, but without much action or follow-through. The end.

Okay, so I get two for that. (takes reward chips) Okay. What are you looking at your watch for?

Patient: I wanted to see how long you said that and it was five minutes.

Therapist: It was a long story, huh?

Patient: Yeah!

Therapist: Did you like that story? Huh?

Patient: Hh hmm.

Therapist: Okay. Go ahead. You go. No peeking.

In my story the animals do not passively submit to those who deprive and unnecessarily restrict them. They speak up for their rights and threaten to fight for them or to flee en masse from their incarceration. The lion who speaks but does not act is criticized by the wise owl (a common figure in my stories) for his passivity and for being "all talk and no action."

Warren's looking at his watch was a manifestation of the anxiety that my story was causing him. However, he did listen intently — suggesting that my message was still "being heard" in spite of his fear.

The Bag of Toys Game and The Bag of Things Game are very attractive to pre-readers; whereas The Bag of Words Game is designed for the child in the second through fourth grade. However, first-grade children will also enjoy playing The Bag of Words Game with the therapist's assistance when they cannot read the words themselves. I have found that most children consider The Bag of Toys Game and The Bag of Things Game "babyish" by the age of nine or so; however, children will enjoy The Bag of Words Game to about age ten or eleven. Of course, children with severe difficulties may continue to involve themselves meaningfully in these games beyond the ages when others become disinterested.

Chapter Twelve
Scrabble for Juniors

Whereas in the standard game of adult Scrabble* the players form their words with letter tiles on a blank playing board, in the child's version, Scrabble for Juniors,† simple words are already printed on the board and the child attempts to cover the board letters with his own letter chips (Figure 5). In the modification of the Scrabble for Juniors game devised by Dr. Nathan I. Kritzberg and myself, all the letter tiles are first placed face down along the side of the playing board. The patient and the therapist then select seven letter tiles each and place them face up in front. The game proceeds with each player in turn placing two letters over those on the board. The patient is advised to try to so place his letters that he will be working toward the completion of a word. The player who places the last letter necessary to finish a word (this need not be the final letter of the word, it can be anywhere in the word) receives a reward chip. If the player can say anything about the word,

---

* Manufactured by Selchow & Richter Co., Bay Shore, New York.
† *Ibid.*

he gets a second reward chip. And if he can tell an original story about the word, he gets two extra reward chips. (Accordingly, the maximum number of chips obtainable for completing a word is four.)

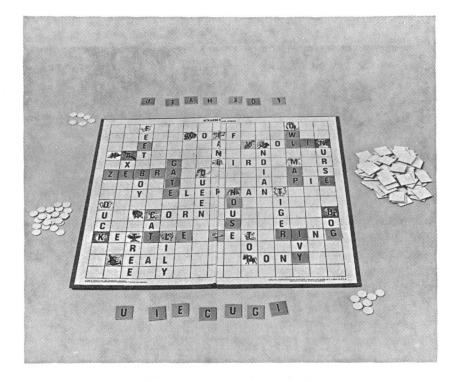

Generally, I try to let the patient be the first to complete a word in order to learn those issues that are uppermost in his mind at that time. This information enables me to relate more meaningful communications when my turn comes to comment on or tell a story about a word that I have completed. Because the players' letter tiles are placed face up, I can see what letters I can place on the board that would make it most likely for the patient to complete his word first. In addition, I may fail to complete a word that I am capable of and "by mistake" use the letter elsewhere. Although I, like most therapists, am a firm believer in being totally honest with my patients, there are times in child therapy when a little duplicity is justified because it serves the purpose of the child's treatment.

Sometimes the child will spot a particular word on the board and try to complete it because he is especially anxious to tell a story about it. In such situations the therapist can be fairly certain that the word has triggered significant associations. More often, however, the child's choice of a word is dependent upon the letters he happens to choose. In addition, most children tend to favor words that are closest to their side of the playing board. In spite of the drawbacks implicit in these determinants of the words chosen, my experience has been that the completed word will generally be used in the service of expressing those issues most pertinent to the child at that time.

Again, the winner is the player who has accumulated the most chips at the end of the allotted time. A slow pace is encouraged so that the words, comments, and stories can serve as a point of departure for discussion. Dramatizations are also encouraged during the course of play. The game is useful from the late first-grade to about the fourth-to-fifth-grade level. Older children find the words too "easy." My attempts to use the standard adult Scrabble game with these older children have not worked out well. They tend to get much too involved in the point values of the various letters and so swept up in the strongly competitive elements in the adult version that comments and storytelling tend to take a secondary role. Accordingly, I do not have adult Scrabble available in the office as one of the games the child can choose to play.

Clinical Examples

"She was loved for her looks." David, aged ten-and-a-half, was of borderline intelligence and exhibited many of the signs and symptoms of the minimal brain dysfunction syndrome. He was hyperactive and distractible and suffered with a significant memory impairment. His social naiveté was extreme and he was functioning in this area at about the five-to-six-year level. This in-

terchange occurred during his fifth month of treatment
while playing the Scrabble for Juniors game.

>*Therapist:* Okay, what word is that that you've just
>completed?
>*Patient: Ring.*
>*Therapist:* That's right. Now you get a chip if you can
>say anything — anything at all — about the word *ring.*
>*Patient:* The man gave the lady a ring.
>*Therapist:* Good, you get one chip. Now, if you can
>make up a story about the word *ring,* you can get two
>more reward chips.
>*Patient:* Once upon a time there was a lady who had a
>very pretty face. A man gave the lady a ring. He wanted
>to marry her. She took the ring and they got married.
>*Therapist:* Is that all? Is there any more to that story?
>*Patient:* No, that's the whole story.
>*Therapist:* Okay.

Although the story is quite meager, it does provide
valuable psychodynamic information. The lady's primary
asset is her "pretty face." No other ingratiating qualities
are described and the man decides that he wished to marry
her only because of her appearance. It was with this
understanding of David's story that I related mine.

>*Therapist:* Okay, now I can get two chips if I can tell a
>story about the word *ring.* Once upon a time there was
>a lady who had a very pretty face. She thought that that
>was all she needed to get a man to marry her. She never
>studied very hard in school and so she didn't learn very
>much. She never learned to play well with friends and
>when she was a child she would often insist that she
>have her own way. She did not like to share her toys
>with other children when she was younger and she was
>kind of lazy.
>When she got older, just because she had a pretty
>face, she thought that everybody would like her and
>that lots of men would want to marry her. One day she
>met a man whom she liked very much and whom she

wished to marry. So she smiled at him and he came over to meet her because she had such a pretty face. However, after speaking to her for a while he realized that there were many things about her that he didn't like. He found out that she was lazy and that she never tried very hard to do anything well. She was kind of selfish and never wanted to share her things with other people.

Although the lady hoped that the man would give her a ring and ask her to marry him, he walked away and didn't spend any more time with her. She felt very sad and almost burst out crying but didn't because there were many other people around. The man met another lady who, although she didn't have such a pretty face, had worked very hard in order to learn how to do many things well. In addition, she was not mean and he shared what she had with others. The man fell in love with her, gave her a ring, and married her. And that's the end of my story.

As is clear, in my story the lady learns that one cannot merely rely upon inborn qualities to attract others. The message that one must work in order to improve oneself is important for all patients in therapy — but especially for those with minimal brain dysfunction. The patient's story reveals that he would want affection without exerting any effort. In my story I attempted to dissuade him from this mode of adaptation.

Overwhelmed by Malevolent Environmental Forces. Timothy entered treatment at the age of nine-and-a-half because of severe behavior problems in school. He was disruptive in the classroom and irritated both his teacher and other children with his antics. A mild organic learning disability was present; however, this was only a small contribution to his academic difficulties. In addition, his parents had been separated but did not get divorced and had been living apart for two years. His father, although consistent in providing for his family's financial needs, was erratic with regard to his visits. When he did come to the home, his relationship with Timothy was poor in that he had little interest in those things that involved Timothy.

After about a year and a half of therapy Timothy exhibited significant improvement in his classroom behavior and, in addition, was able to handle better the angry feelings he felt toward his father. Specifically there was far less displacement of such anger toward classmates and a healthier adjustment to the reality of his relationship with him. It was during this period that the following interchange took place while playing the Scrabble for Juniors game.

> *Therapist:* Okay, you finished the word *seal* for which you get one reward chip. If you can say anything at all about the word *seal* you get a second chip.
>
> *Patient* Once upon a time there was a seal . . .
>
> *Therapist* (interrupts): No, no, no. That's a story. First, just say anything at all about the word *seal* — just a statement about the word *seal*.
>
> *Patient:* The seal is an animal that lives in the cold.
>
> *Therapist:* Okay, you get one for that. Now, you can tell a story about the word *seal*.
>
> *Patient:* Once upon a time there was an Eskimo hunter who was going to catch a seal and there was a couple of the seals. This one seal said, "I'm too smart for that guy." And like he, um, uh — so he put some bait, you know, kind of like fishing, you know, fish and he got the bait and he caught the seal, and the seal was, you know, he killed the seal or put him in a zoo, more or less, put him in the zoo.
>
> And in the zoo he didn't have as much fun. He was in the zoo, you know, bored.
>
> *Therapist:* Hh hmm.
>
> *Patient:* He couldn't catch his own fish and stuff so he was bored. That's where I quit. That's my story.
>
> *Therapist:* That's the whole story. Lesson?
>
> *Patient:* That don't think you're so smart on catching in traps.
>
> *Therapist:* Don't think you're so smart . . . ?

> *Patient:* Don't think — don't be so sure in traps.
> *Therapist:* Can you be a little bit more specific?
> *Patient:* Like, um, don't ... that's what I really mean ... don't, uh ...
> *Therapist:* Don't what?
> *Patient:* Just because you see a little piece of bait lying out you don't just get it.
> *Therapist:* Hh hmm.
> *Patient:* Because it might be led to a trap.
> *Therapist:* Hh hmm. Okay, you take two chips.
> *Patient:* I got two chips already.
> *Therapist:* You got one for completing the word *seal* and saying seals live in the cold. Take two more for the story. Okay.

I considered the seal to represent the patient and the Eskimo trapper those around him whom he considers to be malevolent. There is a healthy element in the story in that the seal's wise-guy attitude is being criticized. However, the seal does get caught and this, I believe, is a statement of the patient's feeling that he is somewhat helpless to protect himself from those who would be malevolent to him. Being put in the zoo symbolizes, I believe, the patient's feeling that he is entrapped by overwhelming forces.

With this understanding of the patient's story, I related mine.

> *Therapist:* Now wait a minute. It's my chance to tell a story now. Okay, you want to wait.
> *Patient* (proceeding with the game): Yeah.
> *Therapist:* Just hold up. Now I tell a story about the word *seal* and I can get two chips for it. Once upon a time ... actually you get one for getting the word, one for saying something about it, and two for the story. Okay?
> *Patient* (nods affirmatively).
> *Therapist:* Now I go. I get two if I can tell a story.

Once upon a time there was a seal and this seal lived up north where it was cold and there were Eskimos who were constantly trying to capture seals. So this seal's mother and father said to him, "Now listen, you know the Eskimos are out to catch us and we have to be very careful. We have to watch out for their traps and watch out for their bait."

Well, this seal was kind of a wise guy and he said, "Ahhh, I don't have to watch out for their bait. I don't have to watch out for their traps. I don't have to watch out. Nothing is going to happen to me."

So whereas the other seals listened very carefully to their teachers and their mothers and fathers regarding the kinds of traps the Eskimos used and the kinds of bait that they used, this seal didn't. And sure enough, one day he got caught in a trap, but fortunately only his fin got caught. He was able to pull himself out of it and he got away. And he had his fin, his little paw — I don't know what they call them — the seals have little flappers. His flapper was . . . (to patient's mother) what do they call it?

Patient's Mother: Flipper.

Therapist: Flipper. His flipper had a little piece of flesh nipped off, but otherwise he was all right. And he came back to his parents and he was bleeding, leaving a kind of trail of blood, but they managed to fix him up.

And for the rest of his life he remembered that little experience and every time he looked at his flipper and saw the scars there it reminded him to be careful. And, of course, after that he learned very much about the kinds of traps that Eskimos have and how to avoid them.

And what do you think the lesson of that story is?

Patient: It's your story, not mine.

Therapist: Okay, the lesson of that story is that often it pays to learn about the things that can be useful to you in life and that can often save you a lot of trouble. The end.

Patient: You can see the scar on his flipper. Nothing was . . . nothing was . . . he didn't have anything cut off.

Therapist: No, no. Just a . . .

Patient (interrupts): . . . scar.

Therapist: A scar and a little piece of tissue was taken out, but the scar filled that up. Okay, I get two chips.

In my story I confirmed the healthy element in Timothy's story by reiterating the inappropriateness of the wise-guy attitude. However, in my story the seal, although scarred, learns that one can avoid certain dangers by considering their possibility in advance. The scar serves as an ever-present reminder of his trauma and helps him remember to avoid difficulties throughout the rest of his life. My main message here, of course, was that one need not be helpless with regard to dangers that may be present; one has within himself the power to avoid them if one wishes to attend to them. I was referring here not only to the patient's classroom difficulties but to his problems with his father as well.

Being Loved for Being Useful. Subsequently, the following interchange took place.

Therapist: Okay, you completed the word *cat*. Wait, you get one chip for the word *cat*.

Patient: A cat is an animal. It's a smaller animal related to the lion.

Therapist: Okay, now you get . . .

Patient (interrupts): Then there's tigers; zee, um, chet . . . cheetahs and jaguars are all cats.

Therapist: All right, now if you can tell a story about the word *cat* you get two more.

Patient: Once upon a time there was a cat and the cat really liked these people, you know. They didn't think — they didn't like him, you know. They . . .

Therapist (interrupts): Wait. The cat liked the people, these people?

Patient: Yeah.

Therapist: Go ahead.

Patient: And it kept on . . . (mumbles) . . .

Therapist: What?

Patient: And the cat didn't like the people . . . the cat liked the people, you know. The people didn't like the cat and the cat's an old bugger.

Therapist: Wait. The cat liked the people, but the people didn't like the cat.

Patient: Yeah.

Therapist: Okay.

Patient: And, um, they'd tell the cat, "Get lost, you old cat." The cat came back the very next day. The cat would not stay away. Hey, that rhymes!

Therapist: Okay, go ahead.

Patient: And they did it again. They kept on doing it and doing it because the cat like was abandoned and he wanted someone to own him, you know, love him.

Therapist: Hh hmm.

Patient: And the cat . . . they'd kick it out and it kept on doing it and this cat came back (sings) the very next day. The cat would not stay away.

Therapist: Okay.

Patient: And, um, so the cat . . . so the cat foretold them, "Don't think that . . ." the cat . . . well, they looked around the place where there were rats, you know, rats and mice.

Therapist: Yeah, I'm not clear. What's that about rats and mice?

Patient: Well, the people lived around a place where there were rats and mice and stuff.

Therapist: Yeah.

Patient: And the cat killed them all, you know.

Therapist Yeah.

Patient: The cat was hanging around and when the cat was hanging around there weren't any mice, so they decided, "Hey, that's cat really helpful. He gets rid of the rodents and stuff." So they got the cat and the moral of the story is like you don't just kick around someone because you don't like them, like they might be very useful and they like you. That's the moral of the story.

Therapist: Hh hmm. Okay. Okay. You get two for that. That was a very good story.

I considered the cat to represent the patient himself and the owner, his father. At first, Timothy is abandoned;

however, when he proves that he has a worthwhile skill he is then reaccepted into the household. The story reveals the patient's lingering feelings of rejection; however, it also reveals his appreciation that one way that one can counteract rejection is to exhibit useful and ingratiating qualities. The fantasy, therefore, is a reflection of a healthy adaptation. However, it does reveal the fact that Timothy has not given up completely his hope to regain his father's affection. With this understanding of the patient's story, I related mine.

Therapist: Okay, now it's time for me to tell my story. Once upon a time there was a cat and he lived with this man and this man decided that he didn't like this cat too much. The cat was all right in some ways, but he decided that he didn't want him. So he told the cat to leave. And the cat went out and he was very unhappy. He said, "Aw, come on, let me come back and live with you."

The man said, "Ah, you're no use."

And the cat said, "I'll show you. I'll show you that I can be useful. You don't like me anymore and you won't let me live with you anymore. Okay, we'll see."

Anyway, the cat went to a nearby house and there were some people there who were really having a lot of trouble with mice and rats and things like that. And he said to them, "You know, I can be very helpful to you in killing off these mice and rats."

And they said, "You can? Would you come to live with us?"

And he said, "You people look like you'll appreciate me." So he went to live with these other people and he was very useful, and they gave him a good home, they gave him good food, and they gave him a good place to sleep.

And then the other man that he had left realized that he had made a mistake in sending this cat off, but it was too late. The cat had already lived with these other people, but he saw his first owner once in a while. He would see the old owner once in a while and the old owner realized that he had made a big mistake in sending this cat off, but it was too late. The cat had another home. And the cat realized a very important lesson, which was what?

Patient: It's your story!

Therapist: Okay, the lesson is that if someone doesn't like you or, you know, may like you very little, it doesn't mean that no one else in the whole world will like you. There are always other people in the world who can appreciate the good things in you. The end.

Anything you want to say about that story?

Patient: (nods negatively)

Therapist: Okay.

Whereas in Timothy's story, his father's appreciation of him and reconciliation with his father are accomplished, in my story there is no reconciliation. To foster such reconciliation would have been unrealistic because of the long period of time that the patient had been separated from his father and the fact that there was absolutely no reason to believe that the father was going to return to the home. However, I did emphasize the ingratiating qualities that the patient possessed so as to reinforce this element from his story.

More significantly, however, in my story the cat finds love and affection in another home but still maintains some relationship with the previous owner. My attempt here was to help Timothy appreciate that others can show him affection in compensation for the deprivations he suffers in his relationship with his father. This need not mean, however, that he has to break completely his relationship with his father; rather, he can maintain gratifying relationships with a number of individuals.

The Innocent Bystander Who Always Gets Picked Upon. Leonard entered treatment at the age of eight because of extensive provocative behavior. He had a reputation as a troublemaker throughout his neighborhood

— so much so that parents prohibited their children from playing with him. He teased, poked, and hit other children and interfered with their play. At home he often thwarted his parents (especially his mother), and there were frequent power struggles over eating, dressing, etc. Leonard was basically angry at his parents for their feuding — especially when his discipline was used as the focus for their fighting. Much of his provocative behavior was consciously controllable; yet he invariably denied his initiation of and participation in his difficulties and always attributed his troubles to others.

While playing Scrabble for Juniors, the following interchange took place.

> *Therapist:* Leonard has completed the word *gate* for which he gets one reward chip. Now if you can say anything at all about the word *gate* . . .
>
> *Patient* (interrupts): . . . (mumbles) . . .
>
> *Therapist:* What?
>
> *Patient:* Sentence?
>
> *Therapist:* A sentence, right. You get a second one. Anything at all.
>
> *Patient:* We got a new gate in our backyard.
>
> *Therapist:* Who got a new gate?
>
> *Patient:* I did.
>
> *Therapist:* Okay, take a second chip. Now if you can tell a made-up story, completely made up from your own imagination, you can get two more chips — about the word *gate*.
>
> *Patient:* Uh, all right, about a gate. Once we got a gate because dogs is bothering me and we had to get a gate because the dogs were bothering us a long time. And we — and we used our gate — when we used it so dogs didn't bother us. So last time when I came home from school a dog bit me on my side. So when he bit me I had to go get a tetanus shot. I got a tetanus shot. The doctor gave me a make-believe, um, let's see — gave me a shot
> . . .
>
> *Therapist:* Well, go ahead. Is this a make-believe story?

Patient: Yeah.

Therapist: All right, then what?

Patient: The part of the dog — the part of the gate part isn't — is a make-believe story.

Therapist: Is a make-believe story.

Patient: The part of the tetanus shot isn't.

Therapist: All right, so the make-believe part is about a gate in order to protect yourself from dogs.

Patient: Yes.

Therapist: Okay, now what happens after that? Continue with that part.

Patient: Well, when he gave me — I was so happy I went out of that doctor's office before . . .

Therapist (interrupts): Wait a minute, was that the real part?

Patient: Yeah.

Therapist: I'm a little confused between the real part and the make-believe part of this story.

Patient: The gate part is the make-believe story and the part I'm telling now is make-believe.

Therapist: Is make-believe too?

Patient: Yeah.

Therapist: Okay, so how do you — all right, so even though there was a gate when you came home the dog still bit you.

Patient: Yes, because when I came out to play.

Therapist: When you came out to play, all right. Then you got a tetanus shot. Then what happened?

Patient: Then we went home, but before I — before I got a chance to clean my side [from the bite] I was playing outside. I was so happy.

Therapist: You were happy because?

Patient: Because I got one of those shots.

Therapist: Okay, is that the end of the story?

Patient: Yes.

Therapist: And the lesson of that story?

Patient: No lesson.

Therapist: No lesson. Okay, you get two chips for that. All right, now it's my chance to tell a story.

Patient (handling his chips): Look at all these chips.
Therapist: All right, now I can get two chips if I can tell a story.
Patient: Wait, I have to put more letters . . .
Therapist (interrupts): After my story. It's my chance now to tell a story. Okay?
Patient: (nods affirmatively)

The story reflects well Leonard's attitude toward the world. He, an innocent party, is bitten by a dog. The gate is built to protect him from malicious dogs who bite without provocation. In addition, he is quickly and almost magically cured of the infection that might result from the bite. This, I believed, was a reflection of Leonard's wish that there be no significant repercussions from his antisocial behavior — regardless of who initiates it. With this understanding of the patient's story, I responded.

Therapist: Now if I can tell a story about the word *gate*, I can get two reward chips. Okay. Here I go.
Once upon a time there was a boy and the dogs in the neighborhood didn't like him and the reason they didn't like him was that when he would go out into the street he would do things, like he would pull the dogs' tails or he would poke them with sticks.
Anyway, he went to his father and he said, "Would you please build a gate in order to protect me from all those dogs who are constantly trying to bite me and pick on me and things like that?"
And his father said, "I'm not going to build a gate because you'd go outside that gate and you'd still bother the dogs. If I know you, you'd bother the dogs and jump over that gate and then they wouldn't be able to get back at you or they might even jump over the gate too. See, the problem is not going to be solved by a gate. The problem is going to be solved by your stopping with this stuff, with pulling dogs' tails and poking them with sticks."
Well, the boy was very mad at his father because his father wouldn't get a gate, so he went out one day and

he was poking a dog and the dog bit him. Then he had to go to a doctor and then he had to get a tetanus shot. And he was very unhappy about that. He came home crying, "I want you to get a gate!"

And the father said, "I'm still not going to get a gate. I hope you've learned a lesson with this bite and I hope you're not going to poke those dogs. If you poke those dogs and you pull their tails, then they are going to bite you and that's all there is to it." So what do you think happened?

Patient: Um, he didn't poke the dogs anymore.

Therapist: Well, what happened was that it took him a long time to learn that lesson. He still was angry at his father for not getting the gate, but gradually he realized that his father was right, that the gate wasn't going to solve any problems. That wasn't the answer, because once he went outside the gate he'd still be in the same situation with the dogs. So he gradually stopped poking those dogs and then they gradually stopped biting him. In fact, what happened was that when they became friendly with him as he gradually stopped poking the dogs and pulling their tails, and then he never spoke about a gate again. The end.

Okay, I get two chips for that.

My story appeals to one aspect of Leonard's difficulties, namely, his denial of his own participation in bringing about his troubles in his relationships with his peers. The story directs itself to this aspect of his problems; it does not focus on the underlying sources of his anger. There was little that Leonard could do directly about his parents' conflicts (I was working with them on this) and so it would have been difficult to create a story that involved him in such efforts. In addition, Leonard's story did not, I believe, touch as directly on that problem as it did on his seeing himself as helpless to protect himself from malicious peers. I appealed to self-recognition of his contribution and conscious control of his acting-out. Hopefully he, like the boy in the story, would then enjoy a better relationship with those around him. There would then be less anger to act out and the vicious cycle would be interrupted.

The Wish That There Be No Repercussions in Response to One's Provocations. A subsequent interchange during the same game occurred.

> *Therapist:* Leonard has finished the word *tiger* for which he gets a red chip. Now if you can say anything at all about the word *tiger* you get a second red chip.
>
> *Patient:* There was a tiger in the zoo.
>
> *Therapist:* Okay. Take another one. Now if you can tell a made-up story about the word *tiger* you get another one.
>
> *Patient:* There was a tiger in the zoo and the boy wanted to go to the zoo and his father said, "No, I have to go to work."
>
> So he never went to the zoo before and he wanted to go badly. So his father . . . (mumbles) . . .
>
> *Therapist* (interrupts): His father what?
>
> *Patient:* He asked his father . . .
>
> *Therapist:* Yeah.
>
> *Patient:* . . . when he didn't have any work, "Daddy, can I go to the zoo? Can I go to the zoo?"
>
> "No, because I have to help your sister."
>
> So, after two years, he asked his father again, "Daddy, could I go to the zoo?" and his mother said, "Yes, you can today — just today!" So when he went he saw a big tiger and so he put his finger in and it took it off.
>
> *Therapist* (interrupts): He put his finger in what?
>
> *Patient:* In the tiger's cage and the tiger bit it and his finger came off. So he was crying, crying. And so the tiger had to go back to the jungle. So he couldn't go to the zoo anymore — the little boy — because he was in trouble and he got his finger bitten.
>
> *Therapist:* Hh hmm. Is that the story?
>
> *Patient:* Yeah.
>
> *Therapist:* Okay, you take two more chips. Now it's my chance.

The first part of the story makes direct reference to Leonard's feelings of neglect. His father is too busy with his sister (who, I believe, symbolizes here Leonard's mother) to spend much time with him. I considered this to reflect Leonard's view that his mother and father were so busy fighting that they had little time to spend with him — a view that was not particularly distorted.

The rest of the story again reveals Leonard's feeling that he suffers from the malice of others and in no way participates in the interpersonal difficulties that befall him. The boy innocently puts his finger into the tiger's cage and the animal bites it off. Although there are probably deep oedipal-castration elements in this fantasy, it also relates to the aforementioned provocation problem as well. Sticking his finger in the tiger's cage symbolizes well the kind of provocative act that Leonard relished. But the story reveals Leonard's appreciation that there may be repercussions — that the provoked may retaliate. Leonard would prefer that he be allowed to indulge himself in his irritating ways (that is, his outlets for pent-up hostility) and that those who would dare retaliate be punished themselves as a deterrent to interference with his antics. The tiger's being sent back into the jungle serves as a warning that all those who strike back at Leonard will be exiled; only those who passively endure his provocations will be tolerated.

It was with this understanding of Leonard's story that I related mine.

Therapist: Once upon a time there was a boy and this boy asked his father to take him to the zoo. And the boy was kind of mad at his father because the father said, "Well, look, I have to share my time. You have a sister, you have a brother, and I'll spend part of the time with them and part of the time with you."

But this boy wanted to have all the time with his father and the father said, "Nope," he said, "I don't spend all my time with you. I share my time." He said, "I give you your share of the time and I give your brother his share, and I give your sister her share."

Well, the boy didn't like that too much because he wanted all the father's time, but he realized that there was nothing he could do about it. So when his time to be alone with the father came, the father said, "Well, where do you want to go?"

And he said, "Well, I want to go to the zoo."

So they went to the zoo and the first cage they came to was the lion's cage and the father said, "Could you please read the sign that is right outside the lion's cage?"

Patient: (interrupts by mumbling)

Therapist: Pardon me?

Patient: Tiger.

Therapist: The lion, oh, I'm sorry. I said lion, I meant tiger. It was a tiger's cage. Excuse me, you're right. Anyway, the father said, "Could you please read the sign outside this tiger's cage?"

And the sign said, "*DO NOT* (the boy read it) *FEED THE TIGER. DO NOT PUT YOUR HAND INTO THE TIGER'S CAGE.*" That's what the boy read.

Well, this kid was kind of a wise guy and he didn't like to listen to signs or rules and things like that, so as soon as his father went to buy some peanuts, this boy immediately went over to that cage and he thought he would have a funny game. He thought it would be a lot of fun to stick his hand in quickly and poke the tiger, you know, and then pull his hand out like that (demonstrates motion) — just poke it and then pull his hand out. So he poked that tiger and the tiger twisted around, "rrrrrrr" (imitates tiger's roar), and snapped. When the tiger snapped he bit a little part of the boy's finger. The boy said, "Awhhhhhh (imitates crying), that tiger bit my finger!"

Patient (laughs out loud): He was a baby.

Therapist: He was crying; he was crying and everybody came running. The zookeeper came running and the father came running and the boy said, "You should send that tiger back to the jungle."

And the zookeeper said, "Look." He said, "I happened to be walking toward this tiger's cage and I saw exactly what happened." He said, "You saw that sign. You're old enough to read. You read that sign and you put your finger in that tiger's cage. That's why it was bitten off."

Anyway, this boy was very mad and he said to his father, "You make them send that tiger back to the jungle."

And the father said, "No, the man's right." He said, "There was a sign there. We both read it together and the sign said, "DO NOT PUT YOUR HAND INTO THE TIGER'S CAGE." There was a warning." The father said, "You have yourself to blame."

Anyway, they took the boy to the doctor. There was a doctor near the zoo. The doctor put medicine on the boy's finger. He needed a couple of stitches. He stitched it up and he had to give the boy a tetanus shot.

Patient (interrupts): Why?

Therapist: Why? Because when you're bitten by an animal you need a tetanus shot.

Patient: Oh, because the tiger is . . . (mumbles) . . .

Therapist: Because the tiger is what?

Patient: Is the tiger related to a dog?

Therapist: Related? No, tetanus is a kind of infection you can get from many kinds of cuts and especially if it's around animals, or farms, or things like that.

Anyway, that boy was really angry that they wouldn't get rid of the tiger, but do you think that he learned any lessons that day?

Patient: (nods affirmatively)

Therapist: What did he learn, what lesson?

Patient: Uh, don't put your fingers in when you see a sign.

Therapist: Right, right! Follow the rules. Follow the signs and if you don't, often you'll have some trouble. The end.

Because I considered the first part of Leonard's story to relate to the deprivations he felt over his parents' fighting, I directed myself to that issue in the first part of my story as well. In essence, I communicate that although there may be times when he cannot have parental affection, there are other times when it will be available (which was indeed the case). Although Leonard has to settle for less than he would want, he need not be completely deprived.

Most of my story relates to Leonard's antisocial behavior. My main messages were that one must assume responsibility for one's acts, that there are repercussions, and that those who would retaliate cannot be so quickly dispensed with. Leonard's involvement while I related my tale convinced me that my message was "heard" and his formulating the lesson confirmed this.

Feelings of Impotence. Cary entered treatment at the age of ten because of a number of difficulties — mainly interpersonal. He refused to fight back when teased or picked upon and so was easily scapegoated, even by younger children. The only way he was able to attract friends was to beg them to come to his house where his parents had always made sure there was a plethora of toys and attractive games. He was very fearful of new situations and would often be unable to fall asleep for two or three nights prior to an anticipated event.

During his third session we played Scrabble for Juniors.

> *Therapist:* Now Cary has finished the word *lily* for which he gets a chip. Now, wait a minute, hold it; don't go on yet. If you can say anything at all about the word *lily*, you get a second chip — anything at all.
> *Patient:* What do you mean?
> *Therapist:* Just say anything at all about a lily, any sentence which includes the word *lily*.
> *Patient:* A lily grows on a pond.
> *Therapist:* A lily grows on a pond. Okay, so you get a second chip. Now, if you can make up a story about the word *lily*, any story at all, but it must be completely made up from your own imagination, then you get two more.

Patient: Once a frog sat on a lily in the swamp and then the frog jumped off onto another lily.

Therapist: All right, that's a good beginning of a story, but that's not a whole story. A story has a beginning, a middle, and an end.

Patient: Hhmmm. I can't think of one.

Therapist: Well, try. See, If I can tell a story about a lily I can get two as well, although you end up with four, I can end up with two. So, you know, the person who has the most chips wins, so if I can tell and story about a lily I can get two and then we'd be even.

Patient: What I said was a beginning. Right?

Therapist: Okay, well, say it again. The frog jumped . . .

Patient: A frog jumped on a lily in the swamp and then it jumped off to another lily.

Therapist: Okay.

Patient: And then — and then the lily started floating down the pond.

Therapist: Okay.

Patient: Then there was this waterfall and the lily fell right into the waterfall.

Therapist: The lily fell into the waterfall?

Pwtient: Hh hmm.

Therapist: And the frog was on it?

Patient: (nods affirmatively)

Therapist: Then what happens?

Patient: The frog died.

Therapist: Okay, you get two for that. Now . . .

Patient (interrupts): I still have one more letter to go.

Therapist: Okay, yeah, but now it's my chance to tell a story. You put it down later. I can get two for telling a story about a lily.

I considered the frog to symbolize Cary. His being on a lily pad is a reflection of Cary's feeling that his situation is an unstable one and that he could easily "sink." Worse, he could meet his doom and be helpless to prevent his demise. Floating down the river and being killed by being thrown over the waterfall is a poignant statement of his feelings of impotence with regard to the destructive forces of the world.

It was with this understanding of Cary's story that I related mine.

> *Therapist:* Once there was a frog and he jumped on a lily pad and he noticed that the water was kind of moving, that it wasn't just a stagnant pond. The water was kind of moving and he saw that the water was moving kind of rapidly. It became more and more rapid and then he heard some noise and it sounded like a waterfall, and he realized that the lily was moving toward a waterfall. So he leaped off onto another pad and then leaped to another one, and leaped from pad to pad until finally he got to shore. He went along the shore and there he saw that there really was a waterfall and he was glad that he had looked around and was careful and had avoided the catastrophe of going over the waterfall.

> And the lesson of that story is: Look around you and listen. It may help you avoid trouble.

In my story I tried to impress upon Cary the fact that he has the capability to protect himself against the dangers of the world; that if he uses his senses and utilizes foresight he can prevent many of the calamities that may befall him. Cary was clearly not trying very hard to deal with his difficulties and my hope was that my story might contribute to his taking a more active role in solving his problems.

"If you have good luck your problems will take care of themselves." The game continued.

> *Therapist:* You got the word *seal.* You get one chip for the word *seal* and another one if you can tell something about the word *seal.*
> *Patient:* I once saw a seal.
> *Therapist:* Okay. Two more for a story.
> *Patient:* There were two seals swimming in the

Atlantic Ocean and they were swimming really far out
and they would have fun. They were playing around
and one time the seal — there was this big fish and the
seal saw it and started to swim away and the big fish
saw it and went and tried to eat it.

Therapist: Tried to eat one of the seals? Yeah, go
ahead.

Patient: And then they went over a rock and then the
fish hit a rock and the seal got away.

Therapist: Wait a minute, now. There were two seals.
Right?

Patient: Right.

Therapist: And were any of them hurt by the big fish
or what?

Patient: No, the big fish was hurt.

Therapist: Oh, the big fish hit a rock and that's why
the seals got away?

Patient: Right.

Therapist: And they weren't hurt at all?

Patient: Right.

Therapist: I see. Okay. Now it's time for me. Did you
take your two chips?

Patient: No.

Therapist: Take two chips for that.

In this story the seals, who represent Cary, are
confronted with a big fish who tries to eat them. The latter
represents, I believe, Cary's tormenting peers and all
others who may be hostile to him. The problem of their
attacking him is readily solved without any effort on Cary's
part. The pursuing fish conveniently hits a rock and the
seals get away. The story reflects Cary's wish that his
problems will be neatly solved by external events favorable
to him, with no effort on his part necessary to bring about
the desired changes in his situation.

With this understanding of Cary's story, I responded.

Therapist: Once upon a time there were two seals.
They were out in the ocean there swimming and all of a
sudden this big fish came along and the fish started to

attack them. Now that was kind of foolish of that fish because these were two seals against one fish, and they were very good friends and they started to fight this big fish. And the first seal was really happy that he had such a good friend because this good friend helped him fight the big fish. In addition, all of a sudden they saw a rock near the shore and they took this rock and they threw it right at the big fish — they threw it right at the big fish. And this hit the big fish right on the head and that big fish then swam away and they got rid of that guy, and they were glad that they had fought him.

One of the fish would have hoped that the big fish might swim into a rock or something like that and in this way they would be able to avoid a fight, but the second one said, "Listen, that's not going to happen. Those big fish don't swim into rocks. He has eyes and he has fins and that's not going to happen to him. If we want to get rid of him we've got to hide and throw some rocks at him." And that's exactly what happened.

And the lesson of that story is: If you are a seal and if a big fish is trying to bite you, there are two things you can do, among other things. You can have a friend and the two of you can fight the big fish or you can do some things, like throw rocks at that fish. But don't just sit back and hope that the big fish will swim into a rock and hurt himself and then go away. Things like that just don't happen. The end.

Okay, I get two chips for that.

In my story I attempted to impress upon Cary the fact that his somewhat magical solution to his problem of being scapegoated was unrealistic. The seal who hopes that the fish will hit a rock and thereby cease his pursuit is dissuaded from this passive and dangerous way of handling the situation. Rather the seals fight, and are successful in driving away their tormentor. In addition, they make use of the strength they have in numbers. In this way I hoped to provide Cary with the motivation to make friends, in part, that they might serve as his allies against those who bullied him.

Chapter Thirteen
The Alphabet Soup Game

The Campbell's Alphabet Soup Game* is packaged in a container that closely resembles a very large can of Campbell's tomato soup (figure 6). The container is quite attractive and therefore readily appeals to the child who is looking over the toy shelves for a game to play. The equipment consists of a plastic bowl filled with plastic letters and two spoons. The modification that I have found most useful therapeutically is for both the patient and therapist to each scoop a spoonful of letters from the bowl and form a word with them. The patient (whom I generally allow to go first) gets a reward chip for having been able to form a word. If he can say anything at all about the word, he gets a second reward chip. And if he can tell a story about

---

* Manufactured by Multiple Toymakers, a division of Minor Industries, 200 Fifth Avenue, New York, New York 10010.

At the time of this writing the author has learned that Minor Industries is no longer manufacturing the game. The interested reader, however, should be able to put together a reasonable facsimile himself. All that is necessary are two spoons, a soup bowl, 1″ plastic letters available in most toy stores, and a treasure chest of reward chips.

the word, he gets two extra reward chips. I then similarly respond to my word. The game can then proceed in a number of ways. One variation is for the players to attempt to form other words from the same batch of letters in order to obtain more reward chips. When the player is no longer able to, he can take a second scoop by "paying" two chips to the bank. These can be added to the original group of letters (the preferable alternative because there are then more letters with which to form words), or serve as a replacement for them. Sometimes trading letters with one another adds to the enjoyment of the game. Or the two players can decide to trade their whole batch of letters with one another to see if they can form other words, not previously used. Whatever the variations utilized (and I am sure the reader can devise his own) the basic principle holds that a player gets one reward chip for the word, a second for a comment, and two more for a story. Again, the winner is

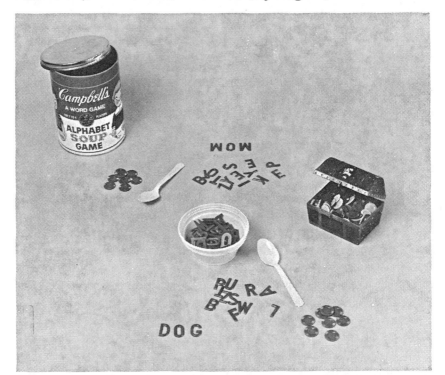

the player who has received the most reward chips at the end of the allotted time. He, of course, receives one of the *Valuable Prizes* from the previously described box of prizes.

Clinical Examples

Reconciliation Fantasies in a Child of Divorce. Paul entered treatment at the age of seven because of disruptive behavior in the classroom, sloppy attitudes toward his schoolwork, isolation from other children, and difficulty falling asleep at night. His parents had separated about six months previously and they were still deeply involved in litigation over financial settlements and visitation. Paul was extremely bright and although his school performance was poor, he could read quite well, even though he was in the middle of the first grade.

During his second month of treatment the following interchange took place while playing The Alphabet Soup Game.

> *Therapist:* All right. Our guest has completed the word *ring* for which he gets a coin from the treasure chest. All right, do you want to say anything about the word *ring*? If you do, you can get one more.
>
> *Patient:* Well, once a boy gave a girl a ring.
>
> *Therapist:* Okay, that gets a chip.
>
> *Patient:* One of those kinds of rings that you wear on your finger.
>
> *Therapist:* Right. Okay, now do you want to tell a story? You can get two more.
>
> *Patient:* Yeah.
>
> *Therapist:* Okay.
>
> *Patient:* Well, once upon a time there was a little girl and she had a boyfriend and later they got — in a few years they got married and the boy gave — well, they got engaged. The boy gave the girl a ring and the girl gave the boy a ring, and then they got married and they lived happily.

Therapist: That's the whole story? That's a very short story. Hh hmm. Okay. Do you want to add a little bit more. I don't know how much of a story that is, if it should really deserve two chips credit. That isn't very much of a story. See if you can add a little bit more to it.

Patient: Well, after they were married they had a nice time, but then once they went down to an old, old . . . (mumbles) . . .

Therapist: They went to where?

Patient: An old, old river.

Therapist: They went to an old river?

Patient: Yeah, on sightseeing — on a sightseeing trip, rather. I said it too slow.

Therapist: Old river on a sightseeing trip, yes.

Patient: And then when they got there, there was a pretty little bridge, and the girl fell in. It was a deep — she didn't know how to swim. The man knew how to swim very well. The man jumped right in after her. (makes splashing sound)

Therapist: Hh hmm.

Patient: And then the man grabbed her up on her back — grabbed her up on his back rather, and then he swammed ashore. And then in that river they took a little walk down by some rocks, and then they had a boat ride in that river. And then they went home and they lived happily.

Therapist: Hh hmm.

Patient: Until their days were over.

Therapist: Until their days were over.

Patient: Yes.

Therapist: Hh hmm. Sounds like an ending of a story I know.

Patient: What?

Therapist: They lived happily to the end of their days?

Patient: Yes.

Therapist: Now what story was that? Oh, they lived together to the end of their days.

Patient: Yes.

Therapist: Yes, what story is that?

Patient: Oh, like in the "Princess and the Three Tasks." [referring to a story in one of the author's children's books (1974a)].

Therapist: Right. Did you notice in my stories they never end with "they lived happily ever after"? Did you know that?

Patient: They always?

Therapist: None of my stories have that ending?

Patient: Never?

Therapist: Never! Not in my stories. Other stories have it, but none of my stories have that ending, "They lived happliy ever after."

Patient: Oh.

Therapist: Do you know why?

Patient: Why?

Therapist: Because no one lives happily ever after.

Patient: How do you know?

Therapist: Because everybody's life is a mixture of happy things and unhappy things. Nobody is happy all the time.

Patient: Yeah. I know.

Therapist: So that's why I don't end a story with "they lived happily ever after" because my stories are, real-world stories. Right?

Patient: Yup.

Therapist: So that doesn't happen in my stories. Okay, so you get two chips for that story. What colors do you want? Take your own colors.

Patient (chooses yellow chips): Yellow.

In the story, as originally presented, a boy and girl meet, the boy gives the girl a ring, "and then they get married and they lived happily." That was the whole story. I considered it to reflect the patient's desire that his parents' marriage would not have ended in separation; rather, that they continue to live happily. However, in order to elicit more information in the hope that it could either confirm or refute my initial supposition, I encouraged Paul to elaborate on the story. Such encouragement was helped by my wondering out loud whether or not such a short story really deserved two chips.

With this encouragement he described how the girl fell in a river while they were in a boat on a sightseeing trip. The man rescues her and then they both go home and live happily. I considered this elaboration to confirm my initial supposition. In reality it was Paul's mother who had left his father, and in this story it is the girl who leaves the boy by falling out of the boat in which they are both traveling. The boy's rescuing the girl symbolized Paul's desire that his parents become reconciled.

The patient's ending of his story with "they lived happily until their days were over" is similar to the type of closing statement I make in my fairy tales for children (1974a). The   stories do not end with "and they lived happily ever after." Rather, they end with such statements as "and they lived together until the end of their days." I used this as a point of departure for a discussion in which I communicated the message: "Everybody's life is a mixture of happy things and unhappy things. Nobody is happy all the time." Such appreciation can help lessen the burden of the child of divorce and, in addition, provide him with realistic expectations about the future. Hopefully, such an attitude might lessen the likelihood of his becoming divorced in the future.

A few minutes later I completed the word *Dad* and the following interchange took place.

> *Therapist:* My word is *Dad* and for the word *Dad* I get one chip. If I can say something about the word *Dad* I get two chips. Okay?
> *Patient* (interrupts): Dr. Gardner.
> *Therapist:* Yes.
> *Patient:* Is your TV on?
> *Therapist:* Oh, yeah, yeah, It's taking our picture. Okay, for my first chip I'll say "Dads are not perfect. They're a mixture of good and bad."
> *Patient:* Right.

Therapist: Right. Okay, that's a second chip, Now if I can tell a story including the word *Dad* I get a third chip. All right?

Patient: Mmmm.

Therapist: Once upon a time there was a boy. Let's make it a girl.

Patient: Okay.

And this girl had a Mom and a Dad and they were happy for a while and they enjoyed being with one another. But one day the Mom said that she did not want to live with the Dad anymore.

Patient: Oh?

Therapist: And she just wanted to separate and this made the boy feel very sad and he wanted . . .

Patient (interrupts): . . . the girl, you mean.

Therapist: The girl, excuse me. I'm very sorry. This made the girl feel very sad and made her want to get her mother and father together again. And she said to the father, "Go after her! Get her back! Bring her back!"

And the Dad said to her, "Nope. We've had a lot of trouble in our marriage and maybe it's better we split."

She said, "Well, get her back for me. I want the two of you to stay together."

And the Dad said, "I know it hurts you very much and it hurts me very much that we're not going to all live together as one family, but I'm so miserable and she's so miserable that it's probably better that we not remain married."

And he kept trying to get his father to get his mother back — to go after her — but the Dad just refused and the Mom refused. And so after a while, what do you think happened?

Patient: So they got a divorce.

Therapist: Right. Now while the boy was very sad . . .

Patient (interrupts): The girl.

Therapist: Excuse me, I'm sorry. While the girl was very sad she stopped doing her schoolwork and she stopped playing with her friends and that was really unfortunate because then she added to her problems. If she had done her schoolwork and played more with her friends, she would have felt better about the fact that her mother and father were getting separated. But she gradually realized that she couldn't get them back together and she also realized that not playing with her friends and fouling up in school were just making her problems worse because then she was even sadder.

Patient: That's kind of in one of your books.

Therapist: In one of my books like that?

Patient: Yeah.

Therapist: I don't — what . . .

Patient (interrupts): Something like that in one of your books.

Therapist: Yeah, which book was that?

Patient: The Boys and Girls Book about Divorce. [1970a, 1970b]

Therapist: Hh hmm. And what do I say in there that's like that?

Patient: You should play more with friends . . .

Therapist (interrupts): Hh hmm. When what?

Patient: They're having a divorce.

Therapist: Right. What do you think of that advice?

Patient: It's pretty good.

Therapist: Good. Have you tried it out?

Patient: Well, I do feel better about it.

Therapist: Hh hmm. What was the main thing that made you feel better about it?

Patient: Oh, well, it really helped me a lot.

Therapist: How did it help you? In what way?

Patient: Well, in your books and the way you tell people — the way you give advice — and so forth.

Therapist: Yes, what advice? You see I give a lot of advice in those books. Which advice was most helpful to you?

Patient: Well, I couldn't say which. It was all very good advice.

Therapist: Hh hmm. I see. Nothing — no special bit of advice?

Patient: No, everything was very special.

Therapist: Hh hmm. Okay. Now let's — we have to stop this game now. Let's count up and see who wins.

I first used my opportunity to make a simple statement about the word *Dad* by commenting on the fact that Dads are a mixture of both assets and liabilities. This is important to communicate to all children; however, children of divorce — exposed as they often are to extreme parental derogation of one another — need to have this point especially emphasized.

In my story, when the Mom and Dad get divorced, they do not reconcile. The child's repeated requests that they do so are to no avail. However, rather than leave her frustrated and unhappy I suggest that she compensate for her loss by involving herself with others. The patient immediately recognized the advice as being similar to that which is found in my *The Boys and Girls Book about Divorce.*

Partial Alleviation of Oedipal Problems. Larry entered treatment at the age of seven-and-a-half because of compulsive touching of walls and furniture. He was a very tense boy and intermittently exhibited tics of the neck and shoulders. On occasion his tics took the form of yawning and throat-clearing sounds. However, the verbal tics were not that prominent that one could justifiably consider him to have a Gille de la Tourette's syndrome. Excessive masturbation was also described by the parents. At the end of the initial interview, while I was standing and talking with the parents and Larry, he began to caress his mother's breasts. She continued to talk to me as if nothing were happening. When I brought this to the family's attention the father stated that he had not noticed that anything was happening and the mother said that Larry caressed her breasts on occasion but that she did nothing in response.

In my subsequent evaluation I found the father to be a man who compulsively spoke about sexual matters — especially in a humorous way. The mother was coquettish and undressed frequently in front of Larry. On one occasion, early in treatment, Larry wrote the following note to his mother: 'Fuck shiter old god damn mommy. Happiness is watching mommy pull her god dam fuckin pants down."

I considered Larry's tensions to be related to pent-up sexual excitation which could not be released directly. As expected, many of his stories revealed sexual and oedipal themes. My responding communications attempted to help him resolve his oedipal conflicts. During the second month of treatment the following interchange took place while playing The Alphabet Soup Game.

> *Therapist:* What word do you have?
>
> *Patient:* Jug.
>
> *Therapist:* Okay. Now you get one chip for completing the word *jug*. Now if you can say something about *jug* you can get another chip, and if you can tell a story about *jug* you can get two more chips.
>
> *Patient:* Don't you get — um, oh yeah.
>
> *Therapist:* Go ahead.
>
> *Patient:* Okay. I'm going to tell a story and . . .
>
> *Therpist* (interrupts): . . . and say something. Go ahead.
>
> *Patient:* Okay. A jug could hold flowers.
>
> *Therapist:* Okay, that gets another chip. A jug could hold flowers. All right. Now a story can get you two more chips.
>
> *Patient:* Okay. Once there was a girl and she was picking flowers. She was cutting off flowers on one of her trees and . . . (pauses) . . .
>
> *Therapist:* Yeah. Go ahead. And . . .
>
> *Patient:* And she was putting it in her mother's jug. So . . . (pauses) . . .
>
> *Therapist:* Go ahead.
>
> *Patient:* And so when she was putting it in she brought the jug over so she could put in all the flowers that she got and it broke because she dropped it.
>
> *Therapist:* What broke?
>
> *Patient:* The jug.

Therapist: Okay. She dropped the jug, yeah, as she was putting the flowers in?

Patient: Yeah.

Therapist: Yeah. Go head. You don't have to wait for me. Go ahead. You tell your story.

Patient: And . . . (pauses) . . . she — so she — so she stopped to think and her friend and her friend's mother were going out to the flower shop and she — and that was the same flower shop where her mother bought the jug so the girl asked her friend's mother if she could go. And she said, "Why?" And she told her the story and then she went to buy her a new one. And so when they got back her mother was just coming back and then she put the same kind of flowers — she just — since she broke that one she cleaned it out and then the flowers that she picked out of the dirt she put in so that . . .

Therapist (interrupts): Oh, did they bring her another jug — this friend and the mother?

Patient: Yeah, but she went.

Therapist: She went with them. And she got another jug.

Patient: Yeah.

Therapist: Go ahead. And then what happened?

Patient: That's the end.

Therapist: And she put the flowers in?

Patient: Yeah.

Therapist: Okay. And the lesson of that story? What do we learn from that story?

Patient: That you should tell your mother if you do something or something bad happens. Or you shouldn't take a jug or a vase and, um, and bring it in the front but in the back you could just take another vase or make your own. You don't have to take your mother's vase or jug.

Therapist: You don't have to take your mother's vase or jug or, or —

Patient: jug.

Therapist: — or jug. You can get another one. Is that it? I'm not clear what that last part is.

Patient: You can make one of your own or you can buy one, or if you have your own you should use your own.
Therapist: Hh hmm.
Patient: You shouldn't use your mother's.
Therapist: Hh hmm. You should use your own.
Patient: Yeah.
Therapist: Okay. Very good.

I understood the jug to represent Larry's mother's vagina. The flowers, which were taken from a tree, in this case I felt were phallic symbols. Although flowers are traditionally a female symbol, in this situation I felt they more likely represented male genitalia in that they were inserted into a jug. In addition, their being taken off a tree suggests that Larry is acquiring his father's genitalia for his own purposes.

Although Larry represented himself as a girl in this story, I did not consider him to have a sexual orientation problem. A child will often represent himself as a person of the opposite sex to disguise the figure and prevent realization that he is talking about himself. As the girl consummates the sexual act, that is, as she inserts the flowers into the jug, it drops and breaks. I felt that this represented Larry's basic feeling that his mother's genitalia were "too hot to handle." By dropping the jug he avoids getting "burned," that is, suffering various anticipated repercussions for his "transgression." In addition, the jug's dropping represents his ambivalence about consummating the sexual act. Dropping the jug prevents the flowers from remaining in it.

He then acquires a jug on his own. I considered this to be a healthy step in the alleviation of his oedipal problems. By getting his own jug he gives up the quest for his mother's. I believe that this story revealed, in symbolic form, an appreciation of messages that I had communicated in previous sessions in which I advised Larry to consider alternative sources of gratification, both in the present and in the future. This, of course, is an intrinsic part of helping a child resolve his oedipal difficulties.

With this understanding of the child's story, I attempted to form a word from my own letters that would enable me to respond appropriately. This is the interchange that followed.

Therapist: Now it's my chance. Okay?

Patient: (nods affirmatively)

Therapist: Now I've got the word *box.* (spells) b-o-x. Now I get a chip for the word *box.* All right?

Patient: (nods affirmatively)

Therapist: And, let's see now, if I can tell something about the word *box* I can get a second chip. I'll say that a box — there are some boxes that are very pretty, very fine boxes. So I get a chip for that. Okay?

Patient: (nods affirmatively)

Therapist: Now if I can tell a story about the word *box* I get a third one. Right?

Patient: (trying to form new word with his letters)

Therapist: Listen, do you want to hear my story or do you want to try to make your word now? What do you want to do?

Patient: Hear your story.

Therapist: Okay, then leave this and then you'll try to make another word from your letters after I finish. Okay?

Patient (nods affirmatively).

Therapist: Okay. Once there was a girl and she wanted to take some flowers off a tree and her mother had a very beautiful box — and this box had been given to the mother by the father — and the father told the girl that she could look at the box once in a while and she could use it once in a while, but that she couldn't have it for herself. It wasn't hers, that it was the mother's. It was a very fine, beautiful box.

Now one day the girl wanted to put the flowers in that box — the flowers that she had picked — and she was kind of scared about that. She was afraid that if she put the flowers in that box, that her father would really get very very angry at her and he might beat her, hit her, or punish her very severely. And so as she was putting the flowers in the box — and her hands were shaking — in fact, it was so much so that she almost dropped it, her hands were shaking so.

Her father came in and he said, "What are you doing?"

And she said, "I'm oh, I'm just using this box for some flowers." She had to tell him what she was doing. It was clear what she was doing.

And the father said, "You know what I told you about that box. That's not your box. That box belongs to your mother. You can use it a little while, but if you want to really keep those flowers, you'd better get your own. And you can use that box for a while to keep those flowers in, but I want you to go to a store with your own allowance and buy your own box and then you can transfer the flowers to that box from the one I gave your mother."

The girl wasn't too happy about it because she thought the box was quite beautiful and she said, "Gee, I wish I had a box like that someday."

And the father said, "Well, someday you may. There's no reason why you shouldn't and when you're older you may get one like that. At any rate now you can't have it. You can only use it a little bit once in a while."

And so she put her flowers in the box and then she went to the store. She took some of her allowance and some money she had saved and bought herself a box, and then put the flowers in that.

And do you know what the lesson of that story is?

Patient: (nods affirmatively)

Therapist: What is the lesson?

Patient: If somebody has something and you want it, you can't have it.

Therapist: Or they may let you use it a little bit, but you can go out and get your own. Do you know what the other thing is called when you get your own?

Patient: No.

Therapist: It's called a substitute. Do you know what the word *substitute* means? What does *substitute* mean?

Patient: Well, is it the kind of person who like when the teacher is absent a substitute comes in?

Therapist: Right! You get a substitute teacher. Right. Okay. So I get two chips for that one. Right?

Patient: Right.

Therapist: Okay.

Patient: I get 50¢ allowance.

Therapist: Who gets 50¢?

Patient: Me, and my brother.

Therapist: Yeah. What do you spend it on?

Patient: . . . (mumbles) . . .

Therapist: What?

Patient: I save it.

Therapist: Uh huh. Are you saving up for something?

Patient: Yes.

Therapist: What?

Patient: At Woolworth's they have a motor that I want to get.

Therapist: Hhmmm. Good. Okay. Let's turn this off.

In my story the box is very much the mother's. However, the girl (again representing Larry) was permitted to use it once in a while, that is, share mother's affection with father. I emphasized the fact in my story that the box is the mother's and that it was given to her by the father. In my story I introduced the element of Larry's fear of paternal retaliation if he were to take his mother's box and use it for himself. Although this issue did not come up specifically in Larry's story about the jug, I knew it to be one of his problems and a significant element in his tension. Because his story contained what I considered to be part of a healthy resolution of the oedipal conflict (namely, acquiring a substitute gratification), I decided to focus on what I considered a still-to-be-resolved element in Larry's oedipal difficulties.

In my story the father does not react punitively to Larry's "transgression." He does allow him to use the box once in a while. He encourages Larry, however, to purchase his own box with money saved from his own allowance. Here, I introduced the notion that Larry will have to apply himself if he wishes to get the same kinds of gratification from a woman that his father enjoys.

In helping a child resolve oedipal difficulties I try to help him appreciate that his mother's affection must be shared with the father. He can get some physcial contact with his mother but cannot enjoy the intense degree of intimacy that his father does. The younger the child, the less likely he is to appreciate that such intimacy involves sexual intercourse. However, the young child is generally not particularly interested in that kind of experience; rather; he is more interested in generalized physical contact, sole possession, and occasional physical pleasure.

Dealing with Oedipal Difficulties. We continued to play the game and it was now Larry's chance to form a word.

> *Therapist:* Okay. Now what word did you get?
> *Patient: Gun.*
> *Therapist:* Okay. You get a chip for the word *gun.* Now you can get a second one if you can tell a story with the word *gun.*
> *Patient:* Okay.
> *Therapist:* Or you can say something about the word *gun.* Do you want to say something about . . .
> *Patient   1 (interrupts): You need a license to have a gun.*
> *Therapist:* Okay. You need a license to have a gun. That gets a chip. Now a story.
> *Patient:* Um. Once there was a man who had a gun and he found a spaceship — part of a — when he was in the ocean on a boat by himself 'cause he was fifteen years old. So . . .
> *Therapist* (interrupts): Did you say he was on a spaceship or he found a spaceship?

Patient: He found part of a spaceship in the ocean when he was on a boat because he's old enough to have his own boat.

Therapist: He found a spaceship in the ocean?

Patient: Part of it.

Therapist: It was floating in the ocean or it was underneath the ocean?

Patient: Floating.

Therapist: Okay.

Patient: Do you know, when a rocket blasts off if it has three stages the stages fall off them?

Therapist: Oh, so he found one of the stages.

Patient: You don't have a capsule, just a stage.

Therapist: Okay. So he found one of the stages floating in the ocean. Go ahead. Then what?

Patient: And he wanted it so he had a rope. So he took the rope and he tied it onto the boat and he tied it on to that part and he got on and he took the motor off of his motorboat and put it on the rocket ship, the stage of the rocket ship.

Therapist: Oh, he took the motor off his boat and he put it on the rocket ship.

Patient: Yeah.

Therapist: Okay.

Patient: So that would move and pull the boat. So when he was moving along he found he went deep, deep, deep into the ocean, all the way in. Out there there were sharks and whales and it was very rough. It was so rough that he fell off the rocket ship. So there was a shark in the water coming toward him; so there was only one thing that he could do. There was an island and the only problem was that it was full of snakes. So the rocket ship went down. So quickly he took the motor off and put it back on his boat. He started it up and he went past it, but he just got a little bite in his foot, and he went back home and he didn't want to go back in the ocean again. That's the end.

Therapist: Okay. And the lesson of that story?

Patient: If you have your own boat or if you're in the

ocean and see something that you want, like something big, you can't have it unless it's like a toy gun or something. You can't take something big.

Therapist: Oh, you can have a toy gun, but you can't take a big rocket stage. Is that it?

Patient: Yeah.

Therapist: Because? Hhmm? Because?

Patient: Because it's too big and anyway there's nothing more you could do with it and there's no room for it.

Therapist: Uh huh. Okay. Very good. You get two chips for that. Okay. Let's turn the tape recorder off while I try to get a word, and then I'll tell a story about my word.

Patient: Turn it off.

In this story we again see strong oedipal themes. The patient wishes to hook his boat up to a rocket ship stage that is floating in the ocean and to be pulled around by it. He would take the motor off his own boat and attach it to the rocket ship stage. I believe that the rocket ship capsule probably represents Larry's father and that the stage that fell off it, Larry's mother. In essence, he has his father discard his mother and she is then available to him as she floats in the ocean. Larry's motor, as a symbol of his genitalia, is hooked up to his mother. However, it is she who pulls him around, and this, I believe, symbolizes his dependency rather than his sexual ties to her. However, the father once again appears — this time as a school of sharks and whales. He immediately "fell off the rocket ship" and tries to find safety on a nearby island. However, "the only problem was that it [the island] was full of snakes." Again, the punitive retaliating paternal figure appears to be ubiquitous. Accordingly, he flees from the scene suffering only a "little bite" in his foot. The story ends with his not returning to the ocean again.

This story is a dramatic statement of Larry's oedipal fears. The retaliating father is ever-present. However, his "bark seems worse than his bite" in that Larry suffers only a "little bite" in his foot. I believe that this represented an appreciation of my message given in the previous story that father will not be as punitive as Larry anticipates. In addition, in the "lesson" Larry sets his sights on smaller prey, namely, a toy gun — in other words, something closer to Larry's size and his ability to handle. One could argue that the rocket ship stage represents Larry's father's penis and that the story reveals Larry's desire to acquire his father's penis and his fear that such acquisition will be met by powerful and dangerous retaliation. This interpretation does not preclude my original. Rather, it is probable that both are operating simultaneously here. And, they are not inconsistent with one another in that they both serve the purpose of Larry's desire for a more intimate involvement with his mother. In short, if the rocket ship represents Larry's mother, the story reveals his attempt to "hook on" to her. If the rocket ship represents Larry's father's penis, the story reveals Larry's desire to acquire this large penis for the purposes of becoming more attractive to his mother so that he can "latch on" to her.

It was with this understanding of Larry's story that I responded as follows.

> *Therapist:* Now I've got the word *pet.* Okay?
> *Patient:* (nods affirmatively)
> *Therapist:* Now I get a chip for the word *pet.* I can get a second chip if I can tell a story about pets. Okay? Or a second chip if I can say something about pets. People like their pets and sometimes they don't want to share their pets, or they don't want to share their pets all the time. And now if I can tell a story about the word *pet,* I'll get two more chips.
>
> Once upon a time there was a man and he had a boat and he was riding his boat in the ocean — it was a motorboat — and he saw a stage of a rocket that was floating in the ocean. And he said, "Boy, it would be great to have that rocket. I'd like to put my motor on it and really have that great rocket and then I could really zoom around the ocean here, zoom around the water, zoom around the island, and everything else.

Well, he didn't know that the sharks who lived in that water and the snakes who lived on the islands had kind of adopted that stage — that rocket stage — as a pet. They liked it and they would swim around it. They would play in it and they would go inside it. The sharks would swim through it; the snakes would swim through it. And when this man put his motor on that stage, they got very upset and they said to him, "Listen, that's ours, that rocket stage. You can't have it. We'll let you play in it a little while, but you're going to have to get your own."

Well, he said, "No, I want it all my own."

And they said, "Listen, you can't have it all your own. It's ours. You can play with it a little bit." And he realized that the sharks meant business and the sharks and snakes were really kind of powerful.

But he said, "Well, what can I do?"

And they said, "Well, look at this ocean — we're near Cape Canaveral here and they fire off these rockets every once in a while and there are other stages here which fall into the ocean. This isn't the only stage that drops into the ocean. Now we suggest you go over there and find out when they're going to shoot off the next rocket and then you just take your boat out into the ocean along the path of the rocket, and I'm sure you'll be able to get a stage."

So what do you think happened?

Patient: He got one.

Therapist: He got one! How did he get it?

Patient: He found out when the next rocket was going off and then one that fell.

Therapist: Right! That's exactly what happened.

Patient: Are you finished?

Therapist: Did you think I was finished?

Patient: Yeah.

Therapist: Yeah, I was finished, but I was just trying to talk about the lesson of it. That's what I was trying to do. What do you think the lesson of that story is?

Patient: Same as mine.

Therapist: What's the lesson?

Patient: In my story it was that if you want something, you can't have it if it's too big or something, like if it's very big and you just want it, like the rocket stages there's no use for it. You take it out of the water or something and there's no place to keep it.

Therapist: Hh hmm.

Patient: Or back in the water if you have a dock.

Therapist: Hh hmm. Well, in my story what does the man do when he finds out that the sharks and the snakes won't let him have that rocket, except that they'll let him play with it for a little while?

Patient: He has to get his own.

Therapist: Right, so that if you want a rocket stage and it's already adopted as a pet by sharks and snakes, then go and get another one. There are usually others around. The end.

Okay. Now I get two chips for that story. Look, I'll tell you. Would you like to watch some of this now?

Patient: Yeah.

Therapist: Okay, let's watch some of it now.

Patient (counting the reward chips): It's even.

Therapist: It's even. Right. So we both get prizes.

In my story the sharks and snakes do permit Larry to spend some time with their rocket ship stage. However, they are firm in not permitting him full ownership of it. However, they suggest that he acquire his own and inform him that there are many other rocket ship stages that fall into the waters because they are quite close to Cape Canaveral.

The poststory discussion revealed that Larry did appreciate my message. On the clinical level Larry did subsequently enjoy an alleviation of his tics and touching compulsion. I believe that interchanges such as those presented here played a significant role in the alleviation of his difficulties.

Concluding Comments

I have found the therapeutic approaches and games described in this book to be valuable additions to the therapist's armamentarium. They are particularly useful in the treatment of children who cannot or will not verbalize about their difficulties — especially when the discussion attempts to take a psychoanalytic bent. Furthermore, they are useful in the therapy of children who are reluctant to freely express their play fantasies or provide self-created stories. My experience has been that the large majority of such children will provide otherwise unobtainable, or difficultly obtainable, material when involved in such activities. In addition, children who *are* capable of freer revelation, both at the primary and secondary process level, will often enjoy involving themselves in these games and thereby will be provided with an additional therapeutic experience. Each child's therapy should be tailored to his particular needs. Accordingly, there should be great variation among patients in the degree to which any of these games are utilized. Also, the methods of play lend themselves to great variation. I have presented here those that I have found most useful. The reader, however, would do well to vary the games in accordance with his own style and the inclinations and preferences of the patients with whom he works. Lastly, I wish to emphasize that none of the methods described in this book are therapies per se; rather they are therapeutic techniques which should be used along with other methods as only a part of the therapeutic approach.

The whole philosophy of the methods I describe here are well epitomized by Jack Point, the jester in Gilbert and Sullivan's operetta *Yeoman of the Guard*, who advises his student Wilfred:

When they're offered to the world in merry guise,
Unpleasant truths are swallowed with a will —
For he who'd make his fellow, fellow, fellow creatures wise
Should always gild the philosophic pill!

References

Aichhorn, A. (1925), *Wayward Youth.* New York: The World Publishing Co., 1954.

Alexander, F., French, T., et al. (1946), The principle of corrective emotional experience. In *Psychoanalytic Therapy: Principles and Application*, pp. 66-70. New York: The Ronald Press.

Alexander, F. (1950), Analysis of the therapeutic factors in psychoanalytic treatment. *Psychoanalytic Quarterly*, 19:482-500.

Baldock, E. C. (1974), *The therapeutic relationship and its ramifications in child psychotherapy.* San Jose, California: The Family Service Association of Santa Clara County Monograph.

Becker, R. D. (1972), Therapeutic approaches to psychopathological reactions to hospitalization. *International Journal of Child Psychotherapy*, 1(2):65-97.

Ellis,A. (1963), *Reason and Emotion in Psychotherapy.* New York: Lyle Stuart.

Freud, A. (1965), *Normality and Pathology in Childhood.* New York: International Universities Press.

Freud, S. and Breuer, J. (1895), *Studies on Hysteria.* New York: Basic Books, Inc., 1957.

Freud, S. (1909), A phobia in a five-year-old boy. In *Collected Papers*, Vol. 3, pp. 149-209. New York: Basic Books, Inc., 1959.

Gardner, R. A. (1968a), The mutual storytelling technique: use in alleviating childhood oedipal problems. *Contemporary Psychoanalysis*, 4:161-177.

——(1968b), Book Review: Ginott, H. G. (1965), *Between Parent and Child.* New York: The Macmillan Co. Reviewed in *Psychology Today*, 1(12):15-17.

——(1969a), Mutual storytelling as a technique in child psychotherapy and psychoanalysis. In *Science and Psychoanalysis*, ed. J. Masserman vol. XIV, pp. 123-135. New York: Grune and Stratton.

——(1969b), Guilt, Job, and J. B. *Medical Opinion and Review*, 5(2):146-155.

——(1969c), The game of checkers as a diagnostic and therapeutic tool in child psychotherapy. *Acta Paedopsychiatrica*, 36(5):142-152.

——(1969d), The guilt reaction of parents of children with severe physical disease. *American Journal of Psychiatry*, 126:636-644.

——(1970a), *The Boys and Girls Book about Divorce*. New York: Jason Aronson, Inc.

——(1970b), *The Boys and Girls Book about Divorce*. New York: Bantam Books, 1971.

——(1970c), The use of guilt as a defense against anxiety. *The Psychoanalytic Review*, 57:124-136.

——(1970d), The mutual storytelling technique: use in the treatment of a child with post-traumatic neurosis. *American Journal of Psychotherapy*, 24:419-439.

——(1970e), Die Technik des wechselseitigen Geschichtenerzählens bei der Behandlung eines Kindes mit psychogenem Husten. In *Fortschritte der Psychoanalyse, Internationales Jahrbuch zur Weiterentwicklung der Psychoanalyse*, ed. C. J. Hogrefe, vol. 4, pp. 159-173. Göttingen: Verlag für Psychologie.

——(1970f), Techniques of child psychotherapy (12 one-hour tapes). Leonia, New Jersey: Behavioral Sciences Tape Library.

(1971a), *Therapeutic Communication with Children: The Mutual Storytelling Technique*. New York: Jason Aronson, Inc.

——(1971b), The private practice of child psychiatry. In *Career Directions: Careers in Child Psychiatry*, ed. J. Schimel, 2(2):35-42. Hanover, New Jersey: Sandoz Pharmaceuticals.

——(1971c), On using anger. *Harper's Bazaar*, July, pp. 63-73.

——(1971d), Mutual storytelling: a technique in child psychotherapy. *Acta Paedopsychiatrica*, 38(9):253-262.

——(1972a), *Dr. Gardner's Stories about the Real World*. Englewood Cliffs, New Jersey: Prentice-Hall, Inc.

——(1972b), The mutual storytelling technique in the treatment of anger inhibition problems. *International Journal of Child Psychotherapy*, 1(1):34-64.

——(1972c), "Once upon a time there was a doorknob and everybody used to make him all dirty with their fingerprints...." *Psychology Today*, 5(10):67-92.

——(1972d), On D. W. Winnicott and some as yet undefined qualities of the child therapist. *International Journal of Child Psychotherapy*, 1(2):7-12.

——(1972e), Little Hans — the most famous boy in the child psychotherapy literature. *International Journal of Child Psychotherapy*, 1(4):24-50.

——(1973a), *Understanding Children*. New York: Jason Aronson, Inc.

——(1973b), Psychotherapy of the psychogenic problems secondary to minimal brain dysfunction. *International Journal of Child Psychotherapy*, 2(2):224-256.

——(1973c), The role of seduction in child psychotherapy. *International Journal of Child Psychotherapy*, 2(2):135-137.

——(1973d), The Talking, Feeling, and Doing Game (therapeutic board game for children). Cresskill, New Jersey: Creative Therapeutics.

——(1973e), The Mutual Storytelling Technique (12 one-hour tapes). New York: Jason Aronson, Inc.

——(1973f), Book Reviews: Winnicott, D. W. (1971), *Playing and Reality*. New York: Basic Books, Inc., and Winnicott, D. W. (1971), *Therapeutic Consultations in Child Psychiatry*. New York: Basic Books, Inc. Reviewed in *Contemporary Psychoanalysis*, 9(3):392-400.

——(1974a), *Dr. Gardner's Fairy Tales for Today's Children*. Englewood Cliffs, New Jersey: Prentice-Hall, Inc.

——(1974b), The mutual storytelling technique in the treatment of psychogenic problems secondary to minimal brain dysfunction. *Journal of Learning Disabilities*, 7:135-143.

——(1974c), The psychotherapy of minimal brain dysfunction. In *Current Psychiatric Therapies*, ed. J. Masserman, vol. XIV, pp. 15-21. New York: Grune and Stratton.

——(1974d), La technique de la narration mutuelle d'historettes *Médecine et Hygiène* (Geneva), 32:1180-1181.

Johnson, A. (1949), Sanctions for superego lacunae of adolescents. In *Searchlights on Delinquency*, ed. K. R. Eissler, pp. 225-245. New York: International Universities Press.

——(1959), Juvenile delinquency. In *American Handbook of Psychiatry*, ed. S. Arieti, Vol. 1, pp. 840-865. New York: Basic Books, Inc.

Khan, M. M. R. (1972), On D. W. Winnicott. *International Journal of Child Psychotherapy*, 1(2):13-18.

Klein, M. (1932), *The Psychoanalysis of Children*. New York: Grove Press, Inc., 1960.

Moskowitz, J. A. (1973), The sorcerer's apprentice, or the use of magic in child psychotherapy. *International Journal of Child Psychotherapy*, 2 (2): 138-162.

Mullahy, P. (1970), *Psychoanalysis and Interpersonal Psychiatry*. New York: Jason Aronson, Inc.

Schooley, Christopher C. (1974), Communicating with hospitalized children: the mutual storytelling technique. *Journal of Pastoral Care*, 23(2):102-111.

Stone, I. (1971), *The Passions of the Mind*. New York: Signet (The New American Library, Inc.).

Sullivan, H. S. (1953), *The Interpersonal Theory of Psychiatry*. New York: W. W. Norton and Co.

Index